Dart Cookbook

Over 110 incredibly effective, useful, and hands-on recipes
to design Dart web client and server applications

Ivo Balbaert

BIRMINGHAM - MUMBAI

Dart Cookbook

First published: October 2014

Production reference: 1171014

Published by Packt Publishing Ltd.
Livery Place
35 Livery Street
Birmingham B3 2PB, UK.

ISBN 978-1-78398-962-1

www.packtpub.com

Credits

Author
Ivo Balbaert

Reviewers
Sergey Akopkokhyants
Claudio d'Angelis
Joris Hermans

Acquisition Editor
Sam Wood

Content Development Editor
Azharuddin Sheikh

Technical Editor
Anand Singh

Copy Editors
Sarang Chari
Adithi Shetty

Project Coordinator
Kinjal Bari

Proofreaders
Simran Bhogal
Maria Gould
Ameesha Green

Indexer
Monica Ajmera Mehta

Production Coordinator
Alwin Roy

Cover Work
Alwin Roy

About the Author

Ivo Balbaert is currently a lecturer in (Web) Programming and Databases at CVO Antwerpen (www.cvoantwerpen.be), a community college in Belgium. He received a PhD in Applied Physics from the University of Antwerp in 1986. He worked for 20 years in the software industry as a developer and consultant for several companies, and for 10 years as a project manager at the Antwerp University Hospital. In 2000, he switched to partly teaching and partly developing software (KHM Mechelen, CVO Antwerp).

Ivo also wrote an introductory book in Dutch about developing in Ruby and Rails called *Programmeren met Ruby en Rails, Van Duuren Media, 2009*. In 2012, he authored a book on the Go programming language called *The Way To Go, iUniverse*. Last year, in collaboration with Dzenan Ridzanovic, he also wrote *Learning Dart, Packt Publishing*.

I would like to thank my wife, Christiane, for her support and patience during the development of this book.

About the Reviewers

Sergey Akopkokhyants is a software architect with more than 20 years of professional experience in designing and developing client- and server-side applications. He is also a certified Java developer and project manager. He has general knowledge of many tools, languages, and platforms. For the last 5 years, he has been responsible for customizing and producing web-oriented applications for wholesale business management solutions projects; he has been doing this for several worldwide mobile communication companies. Sergey's responsibilities include architecture design and guidance of client software development using Flex, ActionScript, HTML, JavaScript, and client-server integration with Java. He is also the founder of and an active contributor to several open source projects on GitHub, including the Dart Web Toolkit (DWT) and Angular Dart UI. He is passionate about web design and development and likes sharing his expertise with others, helping them to increase their skills and productivity. Also, he was one of the reviewers of *Learning Dart, Packt Publishing*.

Claudio d'Angelis is an Italian programmer with 10 years of experience in document digitization, web development, and Linux administration. As an early adopter of Dart, he continues to contribute to the community. His contributions include writing articles, open source projects, speaking at conferences, and presenting episodes on Google Developers Live.

Joris Hermans is a web developer enthusiast who works for Truvo, an online directory company. He is also the proud owner of lots of Dart packages, a real-time dart framework named force, a search engine named Bounty Hunter, a persistent abstraction layer named cargo, a dependency injection for Dart called wired, and so on. He also likes to speak about the Web and Dart, so it is possible that you will meet him at a conference.

www.PacktPub.com

Support files, eBooks, discount offers, and more

You might want to visit www.PacktPub.com for support files and downloads related to your book.

Did you know that Packt offers eBook versions of every book published, with PDF and ePub files available? You can upgrade to the eBook version at www.PacktPub.com and as a print book customer, you are entitled to a discount on the eBook copy. Get in touch with us at service@packtpub.com for more details.

At www.PacktPub.com, you can also read a collection of free technical articles, sign up for a range of free newsletters and receive exclusive discounts and offers on Packt books and eBooks.

http://PacktLib.PacktPub.com

Do you need instant solutions to your IT questions? PacktLib is Packt's online digital book library. Here, you can access, read and search across Packt's entire library of books.

Why Subscribe?

- ▶ Fully searchable across every book published by Packt
- ▶ Copy and paste, print and bookmark content
- ▶ On demand and accessible via web browser

Free Access for Packt account holders

If you have an account with Packt at www.PacktPub.com, you can use this to access PacktLib today and view nine entirely free books. Simply use your login credentials for immediate access.

Table of Contents

Preface

Dart is the new open source programming language for the Web, developed by Google with a steadily growing popularity; it is a single language for both the client and server, which is appropriate for a full range of devices on the Web—including phones, tablets, laptops, and servers. It encompasses the lessons of the last two decades of web programming. This book provides you with a broad range of step-by-step recipes that will increase your expertise in writing all kinds of Dart applications, including web apps, scripts, and server-side apps. It can be used as a companion to *Learning Dart, Dzenan Ridzanovic and Ivo Balbaert, Packt Publishing*.

What this book covers

Chapter 1, Working with Dart Tools, talks about increasing your mastery of the Dart tools and platform. We discuss some of the more advanced and hidden features of the Dart Editor, such as configuration, compilation to JavaScript, and the pub package manager. When relevant, we also take a look at how to perform tasks with command-line tools.

Chapter 2, Structuring, Testing, and Deploying an Application, focuses mainly on all the different tasks in the life cycle of your project that make it more professional, helping you save a lot of time during the maintenance phase. This includes structuring the project and installing a logging tool in it and then testing, documenting, profiling, and publishing it.

Chapter 3, Working with Data Types, is about working with the different data types Dart has to offer. We will talk about the basic data types as well as strings, random numbers, complex numbers, dates and times, enums, and lists. Along the way, we will cover many tricks that will help you out in specific circumstances.

Chapter 4, Object Orientation, delves deeper into the object-oriented nature of Dart to find some new techniques and insights that will help us to be more productive in building our apps.

Chapter 5, Handling Web Applications, covers a wide range of web-related topics dealing with safety, browser storage, caching, event handling, WebGL, and of course, Dart working together with JavaScript.

Chapter 6, Working with Files and Streams, shows you how to work with files in different circumstances, both in synchronous and asynchronous ways. We will delve into the code to download a file both on a web and server clients, with blobs as a special case. We also discuss how transforming a stream works.

Chapter 7, Working with Web Servers, looks at how you can write full-fledged and performant web servers in Dart, more specifically how to receive data on the server, how to serve files, and how to deploy a web service. Sockets and their secure variants, as well as web sockets, are also discussed.

Chapter 8, Working with Futures, Tasks, and Isolates, concentrates on the asynchronous tools in Dart to write elegant code in future and combine their possibilities with the execution of tasks and isolates to enhance the concurrency of our apps.

Chapter 9, Working with Databases, explains how to store data in databases, on the client or server or both. On the client side, we look at IndexedDB and the Lawndart data manager. Then, we investigate how to store data on the server in SQL as well as NoSQL database systems.

Chapter 10, Polymer Dart Recipes, shows how to use Polymer to modularize the way a web client interface is built by using web components that encapsulate structure, style, and behavior. The structure and style come from a combination of HTML5 and CSS with special extensions that enable two-way data binding. Behavior is described by code contained in a class that hooks up with the component.

Chapter 11, Working with Angular Dart, covers how Angular makes it possible to write web-based apps with Model-View-Controller (MVC) capabilities in order to make both development and testing easier. The templating system is discussed along with controllers, components, views, formatters, and services.

What you need for this book

To work with this book's code, you need the Dart SDK and Dart Editor, which you can download from www.dartlang.org. Simply unzip the downloaded file and you are good to go. Because Dart Editor is based on Eclipse, you also need a Java Runtime (http://www.oracle.com/technetwork/java/javase/downloads/jre8-downloads-2133155.html). Choose the appropriate version for your system (32-bit or 64-bit); after the download, double-click on the .exe file to install it.

Who this book is for

If you want to become a better Dart developer and get insights and tips on how to put that knowledge into practice, then this book is for you. Because Dart runs on both clients and servers, web, mobile, and server-side developers alike can benefit from these recipes. The book assumes you know the basics of Dart and have some Dart code. You should also have a basic knowledge of HTML and how web applications with browser clients and servers work.

Conventions

In this book, you will find a number of styles of text that distinguish between different kinds of information. Here are some examples of these styles, and an explanation of their meaning.

Code words in text, database table names, folder names, filenames, file extensions, pathnames, dummy URLs, user input, and Twitter handles are shown as follows: "In the checked mode, types are checked by calling assertions of the form `assert (var1 is T)`, to control that `var1` is of type `T`".

A block of code is set as follows:

```
main() {
  // running an external program process without interaction:
Process.run('notepad', ['tst.txt']).then((ProcessResultrs){
print(rs.exitCode);
print(rs.stdout);
print(rs.stderr);
  });
}
```

When we wish to draw your attention to a particular part of a code block, the relevant lines or items are set in bold:

```
main() {
  // running an external program process without interaction:
Process.run('notepad', ['tst.txt']).then((ProcessResultrs){
print(rs.exitCode);
print(rs.stdout);
print(rs.stderr);
  });
}
```

Any command-line input or output is written as follows:

```
# cp /usr/src/asterisk-addons/configs/cdr_mysql.conf.sample
    /etc/asterisk/cdr_mysql.conf
```

New terms and **important words** are shown in bold. Words that you see on the screen, in menus or dialog boxes for example, appear in the text like this: "First try this; right-click on your project and select **Close Folder**."

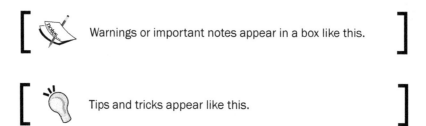

Warnings or important notes appear in a box like this.

Tips and tricks appear like this.

Reader feedback

Feedback from our readers is always welcome. Let us know what you think about this book—what you liked or may have disliked. Reader feedback is important for us to develop titles that you really get the most out of.

To send us general feedback, simply send an e-mail to feedback@packtpub.com, and mention the book title via the subject of your message.

If there is a topic that you have expertise in and you are interested in either writing or contributing to a book, see our author guide on www.packtpub.com/authors.

Customer support

Now that you are the proud owner of a Packt book, we have a number of things to help you to get the most from your purchase.

Downloading the example code

You can download the example code files for all Packt books you have purchased from your account at http://www.packtpub.com. If you purchased this book elsewhere, you can visit http://www.packtpub.com/support and register to have the files e-mailed directly to you.

Errata

Although we have taken every care to ensure the accuracy of our content, mistakes do happen. If you find a mistake in one of our books—maybe a mistake in the text or the code—we would be grateful if you would report this to us. By doing so, you can save other readers from frustration and help us improve subsequent versions of this book. If you find any errata, please report them by visiting http://www.packtpub.com/submit-errata, selecting your book, clicking on the **errata submission form** link, and entering the details of your errata. Once your errata are verified, your submission will be accepted and the errata will be uploaded on our website, or added to any list of existing errata, under the Errata section of that title. Any existing errata can be viewed by selecting your title from http://www.packtpub.com/support.

Piracy

Piracy of copyright material on the Internet is an ongoing problem across all media. At Packt, we take the protection of our copyright and licenses very seriously. If you come across any illegal copies of our works, in any form, on the Internet, please provide us with the location address or website name immediately so that we can pursue a remedy.

Please contact us at copyright@packtpub.com with a link to the suspected pirated material.

We appreciate your help in protecting our authors, and our ability to bring you valuable content.

Questions

You can contact us at questions@packtpub.com if you are having a problem with any aspect of the book, and we will do our best to address it.

Working with Dart Tools

In this chapter, we will cover the following recipes:

- ▶ Configuring the Dart environment
- ▶ Setting up the checked and production modes
- ▶ Rapid Dart Editor troubleshooting
- ▶ Hosting your own private pub mirror
- ▶ Using Sublime Text 2 as an IDE
- ▶ Compiling your app to JavaScript
- ▶ Debugging your app in JavaScript for Chrome
- ▶ Using the command-line tools
- ▶ Solving problems when pub get fails
- ▶ Shrinking the size of your app
- ▶ Making a system call
- ▶ Using snapshotting
- ▶ Getting information from the operating system

Introduction

This chapter is about increasing our mastery of the Dart platform. Dart is Google's new language for the modern web, web clients, as well as server applications. Compared to JavaScript, Dart is a higher-level language so it will yield better productivity. Moreover, it delivers increased performance. To tame all that power, we need a good working environment, which is precisely what Dart Editor provides. Dart Editor is quite a comprehensive environment in its own right and it is worthwhile to know the more advanced and hidden features it exposes. Some functionalities are only available in the command-line tools, so we must discuss these as well.

Configuring the Dart environment

This recipe will help customize the Dart environment according to our requirements. Here, we configure the following:

- ▸ Defining a DART_SDK environment variable
- ▸ Making dart-sdk\bin available for the execution of the Dart command-line tools

Getting ready

We assume that you have a working Dart environment installed on your machine. If not, go to https://www.dartlang.org/tools/download.html and choose **Option 1** for your platform, which is the complete bundle. Downloading and uncompressing it will produce a folder named dart, which will contain everything you need. Put this in a directory of your choice. This could be anything, but for convenience keep it short, such as d:\dart on Windows or ~/dart on Linux. On OS X, you can just drop the directory in the App folder.

How to do it...

1. Create a DART_SDK environment variable that contains the path to the dart-sdk folder. On Windows, create and set DART_SDK to d:\dart\dart-sdk or <your-dart-sdk-path>\dart-sdk when using a dart from another folder (if you need more information on how to do this, refer to http://www.c-sharpcorner.com/UploadFile/6cde20/use-of-environment-variable-in-windows-8/). On Linux, add this to your configuration file .bashrc and/or .profile using the export DART_SDK=~/dart/dart-sdk code. On OS X, export DART_SDK=/Applications/dart/dart-sdk or in general export DART_SDK=/path/to/dart-sdk.

2. The installation directory has a subfolder dart-sdk\bin, which contains the command-line tools. Add this subfolder to the path of your environment. On Windows, add %DART_SDK%\bin instead to the front of the path (system environment) variable and click on **OK**. On Linux or OS X, add export PATH=$PATH:$DART_SDK/bin to your configuration file.

3. Reset your environment configuration file or reboot your machine afterwards for the changes to take effect.

How it works...

Setting the DART_SDK environment variable, for example, enables plugins such as dart-maven to search for the Dart SDK (dart-maven is a plugin that provides integration for Google Dart into a maven-build process). If the OS of your machine knows the path where the Dart tools reside, you can start any of them (such as the Dart VM or dartanalyzer) anywhere in a terminal or command-line session.

Test the environment variable by typing dart in a terminal and press *Enter*. You should see the following help text:

Usage: dart [<vm-flags>] <dart-script-file> [<dart-options>]

Executes the Dart script passed as <dart-script-file>

Setting up the checked and production modes

When developing or maintaining, an app's execution speed is not so important, but information about the program's execution is. On the other hand, when the app is put in a customer environment to run, the requirements are nearly the opposite; speed is of utmost importance, and the less information the program reveals about itself, the better. That's why when an app runs in the Dart **Virtual Machine** (**VM**), it can do so in two runtime modes:

► **The Checked mode**: This is also known as the debug mode. The checked mode is used during development and gives you warnings and errors of possible bugs in the code.

► **The Production mode**: This is also known as the release mode. You deploy an app in the production mode when you want it to run as fast as possible, unhindered by code checks.

Getting ready

Open your app in Dart Editor and select the startup web page or Dart script, usually web\index.html.

How to do it...

1. When working in Dart Editor, the checked mode is the default mode. If you want the production mode, open the **Run** menu and select **Manage Launches** (*Ctrl + Shift + M*). The **Manage Launches** window appears, as shown in the following screenshot:

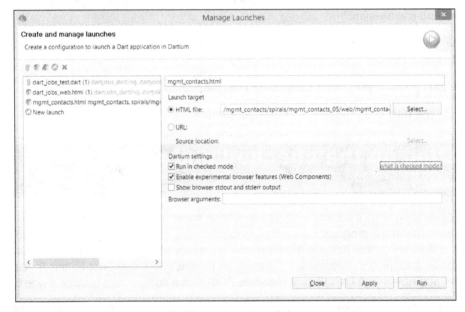

The Manage Launches window

2. Under **Dartium settings**, you will see the checkbox **Run in checked mode**. (If you have selected a Dart script, it will be under the header **VM settings**.) Uncheck this to run the script in the production mode. Next, click on **Apply** and then on **Close**, or on **Run** immediately. This setting will remain in place until you change it again.

Scripts that are started on the command line (or in a batch file) with the `dart` command run in the Dart VM and thus in the production mode. If you want to run the Dart VM in the checked mode, you have to explicitly state that with the following command:

```
dart -c script.dart or: dart --checked script.dart
```

You can start Dartium (this is Chromium with the Dart VM) directly by launching the Chrome executable from `dart\chromium`; by default, it runs Dart Editor in the production mode. If you would like to start Dartium in the checked mode, you can do this as follows:

  ▶ On Windows, in the `dart\chromium` folder, click on the `chrome` file

  ▶ On Linux, in the `~/dart/chromium` folder, open the `./chrome` file

  ▶ On OS X, open the `DART_FLAGS` folder and then open `path/Chromium.app`

Verify this setting by going to the following address in the Chrome browser that you just started `chromium://version`.

When a web app runs in the Dart VM in Chrome, it will run in the production mode, by default.

How it works...

In the checked mode, types are checked by calling assertions of the form `assert (var1 is T)` to make sure that `var1` is of type `T`. This happens whenever you perform assignments, pass parameters to a function, or return results from a function.

However, Dart is a dynamic language where types are optional. That's why the VM must, in the production mode, execute your code as if the `type` annotations (such as `int n`) do not exist; they are effectively thrown away. So at runtime, the following statement `int x = 1` is equivalent to `var x = 1`.

A binding `x` is created but the `type` annotation is not used.

 Avoiding type checks makes the production mode a lot faster. Also, the VM uses the `type` inference to produce faster code; it observes the type of the value (here, 1) assigned to `x` and optimizes accordingly.

There's more...

With the checked mode, Dart helps you catch type errors during development. This is in contrast to the other dynamic languages, such as Python, Ruby, and JavaScript, where these are only caught during testing, or much worse, they provoke runtime exceptions. You can easily check whether your Dart app runs in the checked mode or not by calling the function `isCheckedMode()` from `main()` (see the script `test_checked_mode\bin\test_checked_mode.dart` in the `Chapter 1` folder of the code bundle), as shown in the following code:

```
main() {
  isCheckedMode();
  // your code starts here
}

void isCheckedMode() {
    try {
        int n = '';
        throw new Exception("Checked Mode is disabled!");
    } on TypeError {
```

```
        print("Checked Mode is enabled!");
    }
}
```

The exception message will be shown in the browser console. Be sure to remove this call or comment it out before deploying it to the production mode; we don't want an exception at runtime!

See also

▶ The *Compiling your app to JavaScript* recipe of this chapter for how to enable the checked mode in the JavaScript version of the app

▶ The *Using the command-line tools* recipe of this chapter for other options

Rapid Dart Editor troubleshooting

Dart Editor is based upon the Eclipse Integrated Development Environment (IDE), so it needs the Java VM to run. Sometimes, problems can arise because of this; if this is the case, be sure to consult the Dart Editor Troubleshooting page on the Dart website at https://www.dartlang.org/tools/editor/troubleshoot.html.

Getting ready

Some of the JVM settings used by Dart Editor are stored in the DartEditor.ini file in the dart installation directory. This typically contains the following settings (on a Windows system):

```
-data
@user.home\DartEditor
-vmargs
-d64
-Dosgi.requiredJavaVersion=1.6
-Dfile.encoding=UTF-8
-XX:MaxPermSize=128m
-Xms256m
-Xmx2000m
```

The line beneath -data will read @user.home/.dartEditor on a Linux system.

How to do it...

If you notice strange or unwanted behavior in the editor, deleting the settings folder pointed to by -data and its subfolders can restore things to normal. This folder can be found at different locations depending on the OS; the locations are as follows:

▶ On a Windows system, C:\Users\{your username}\DartEditor

▶ On a Linux system, $HOME/.dartEditor

▶ On an OS X system, $HOME/Library/Application Support/DartEditor

Deleting the settings folder doesn't harm your system because a new settings folder is created as soon as you reopen Dart Editor. You will have to reload your projects though. If you want to save the old settings, you can rename the folder instead of just deleting it; this way, you can revert to the old settings if you ever want to.

How it works...

The settings for data points to the DartEditor folder are in the users home directory, which contains various settings (the metadata) for the editor. Clearing all the settings removes the metadata the editor uses.

There's more...

The **-d64** or **-d32** value specifies the bit width necessary for the JVM. You can check these settings for your installation by issuing the command java -version in a terminal session, whose output will be as follows:

java version "1.7.0_51"

Java(TM) SE Runtime Environment (build 1.7.0_51-b13)

Java HotSpot(TM) 64-Bit Server VM (build 24.51-b03, mixed mode)

If this does not correspond with the -d setting, make sure that your downloaded Dart Editor and the installed JVM have the same bit width, by downloading a JVM for your bit width.

If you work with many Dart projects and/or large files, the memory consumption of the JVM will grow accordingly and your editor will become very slow and unresponsive.

Working within a 32-bit environment will pretty much limit you to 1GB memory consumption, so if you see this behavior, it is recommended to switch to a 64-bit system (Dart Editor and JVM). You can then also set the value of the −Xmx parameter (which is by default set to 2000m = 2 GB) to a higher setting, according to the amount of memory you have installed. This will visibly improve the loading and working speed of your editor!

If your JVM is not installed in the default location, you can add the following line to the .ini file in the line before -vmargs:

```
-vm
  /full/path/to/java
```

If you face a problem, it might be solved by upgrading Dart SDK and the Dart Editor to the latest version. In the Dart Editor menu, select **Help** and then **About Dart Editor**. If a new version is available, this will automatically download, and when done, click on **Apply the update**.

Hosting your own private pub mirror

Another possibility for when the pub repository is not reachable (because you have no Internet access or work behind a very strict firewall) is to host your own private pub mirror.

How to do it...

Follow these steps to host your own private pub mirror:

1. You need a server that speaks to the pub's HTTP API. Documentation on that standalone API does not yet exist, but the main pub server running at pub. dartlang.org is open source with its code living at https://github.com/ dart-lang/pub-dartlang. To run the server locally, go through these steps:

    1. Install the App Engine SDK for Python.

    2. Verify that its path is in $PATH.

    3. Install the pip installation file, beautifulsoup4, and pycrypto webtest packages.

    4. From the top-level directory, run this command to start the pub server dev_appserver.py app.

    5. Verify that it works in your browser with http://localhost:8080/.

2. You need to set a `PUB_HOSTED_URL` environment variable to point to the URL of your mirror server, so that the pub will look there to download the hosted dependencies, for example, `PUB_HOSTED_URL = http://me:mypassword@127.0.0.1:8042`.

3. Manually upload the packages you need to your server, visit `http://localhost:8080/admin` (sign in as an administrator), go to the **Private Key** tab, and enter any string into the private key field.

How it works...

The server from `https://pub.dartlang.org/` is written in Python and is made to run on Google App Engine, but it can be run from an Intranet as well.

Using Sublime Text 2 as an IDE

Dart Editor is a great environment, but Sublime Text also has many functionalities and can be used with many other languages, making it the preferred editor for many developers.

Getting ready

You can download Sublime Text free of cost for evaluation, however, for continued use, a license must be purchased from `http://www.sublimetext.com/`.

Tim Armstrong from Google developed a Dart plugin for Sublime Text, which can be downloaded from GitHub at `https://github.com/dart-lang/dart-sublime-bundle`, or you can find it in the code download with this book. The easiest way to get started is to install the Package Control plugin first by following the instructions at `https://sublime.wbond.net/installation#st2`.

How to do it...

In Sublime Text, press *Ctrl + Shift + P* (Windows or Linux) or *Cmd + Shift + P* (OS X; this goes for all the following commands), click on **Install Package** to choose that option, and then click and choose **Dart** to install the plugin. Any Dart file you then open shows the highlighted syntax, matching brackets, and so on.

Also, click on **Menu Preferences**, **Settings**, and then on **User** and add the path to your dart-sdk as the first line in this JSON file:

```
{
"dartsdk_path": "path\to\dart-sdk",
...
}
```

If you want to manually install this plugin, copy the contents of the `dart-sublime-bundle-master` folder to a new directory named `Dart` in the `Sublime packages` directory. This directory has different locations on different OS. They are as follows:

 ▸ On Windows, this will likely be found at `C:\Users\{your username}\AppData\Roaming\Sublime Text 2\Packages`

 ▸ On Linux, this will likely be found at `$HOME/Sublime Text 2/Pristine Packages`

 ▸ On OSX, this will likely be found at `~/Library/Application Support/Sublime Text 2/Packages`

How it works...

The plugin has a number of code snippets to facilitate working with Dart, for example, typing `lib` expands the library statement. Other snippets include `imp` for import, `class` for a class template, `method` for a method template, and `main` for a `main()` function. Typing a snippet in the pop-up window after pressing *Ctrl + SHIFT + P* lets you see a list of all the snippets. Use *Ctrl + /* to (un)comment the selected code text.

The plugin has also made a build system for you. *Ctrl + B* will invoke the dartanalyzer and then compile the Dart code to JavaScript with the dart2js compiler, as shown in the following screenshot. Editing and saving a `pubspec.yaml` file will automatically invoke the `pub get` command.

Working in Sublime Text 2

See also

▸ Refer to the *Configuring the Dart environment* recipe for the path to the Dart SDK

Compiling your app to JavaScript

Deploying a Dart app in a browser means running it in a JavaScript engine, so the Dart code has to first be compiled to JavaScript. This is done through the `dart2js` tool, which is itself written in Dart and lives in the `bin` subfolder of `dart-sdk`. The tool is also nicely integrated in Dart Editor.

How to do it...

▸ Right-click on `.html` or the `.dart` file and select **Run as JavaScript**.

▸ Alternatively, you can right-click on the `pubspec.yaml` file and select **Pub Build** (generates JS) from the context menu. You can also click on the **Tools** menu while selecting the same file, and then on **Pub Build**.

How it works...

The first option invokes the `pub serve` command to start a local web server invoking dart2js along its way in the checked mode. However, the compiled `.dart.js` file is served from the memory by the internal development web server on `http://127.0.0.1:4031`. This is only good for development testing.

In the second option, the generated files are written to disk in a subfolder `build/web` of your app. In this way, you can copy this folder to a production web server and deploy your web app to run in all the modern web browsers (you only need to deploy the `.js` file, not the `.precompiled.js` file or the `.map` file). However, **Pub Build** in Dart Editor enables the checked mode by default; use the `pub build` command from a console for the production mode.

There's more...

The `dart2js` file can also be run from the command line, which is the preferred way to build non-web apps.

The command to compile the dart script to an output file `prorabbits.js` using `-o <file>` or `-out <file>` is `dart2js -o prorabbits.js prorabbits.dart`.

If you want to enable the checked mode in the JavaScript version, use the `-c` or `- checked` option such as `dart2js -c -o prorabbits.js prorabbits.dart`. The command `dart2js -vh` gives a detailed overview of all the options.

The `pub build` command, issued on a command line in the folder where `pubspec.yaml` is located, will do the same as in option 2 previously, but also apply the JavaScript shrinking step; the following is an example output for app `test_pub`:

f:\code\test_pub>pub build

Loading source assets... (0.7s)

Building test_pub... (0.3s)

[Info from Dart2JS]:

Compiling test_pub|web/test.dart...

[Info from Dart2JS]:	**Took**
0:00:01.770028 to compile test_pub|web/test.dart.	**Built 165**
files to "build"	

You can minify both the JavaScript version and the Dart version of your app.

Producing more readable JavaScript code

To produce more readable JavaScript code (instead of the minified version of the production mode, refer to the *Shrinking the size of your app* recipe), use the command `pub build --mode=debug`, which is the default command in Dart Editor.

Alternatively, you can add the following transformers section to your app's `pubspec.yaml` file:

```
name: test_pub
description: testing pub

transformers:
- $dart2js:
  minify: false
  checked: true

dependencies:
  js: any

dev_dependencies:
  unittest: any
```

For more information, refer to `https://www.dartlang.org/tools/pub/dart2js-transformer.html`.

Producing a single Dart file

The `dart2js` tool can also be used as Dart to Dart to create a single `.dart` file that contains everything you need for the app with this command:

```
dart2js --output-type=dart --minify -oapp.complete.dart app.dart
```

This takes the Dart app, tree shakes it, minifies it, and generates a single `.dart` file to deploy. The advantage is that it pulls in dependencies like third-party libraries and tree shakes it to eliminate the unused parts.

See also

You may be interested in the following recipes in this chapter:

- *Using the command-line tools*
- *Shrinking the size of your app*
- *Debugging your app in JavaScript for Chrome*

Debugging your app in JavaScript for Chrome

In this recipe, we will examine how to debug your app in the Chrome browser.

How to do it...

1. From the menu in the upper right-hand corner, select **Tools** and then **Developer Tools**.

2. Verify via **Settings** (which is the wheel icon in the upper right corner of the **Developer Tools** section) that the **Enable JavaScript source maps** option is turned on. Make sure that debugging is enabled, either on all the exceptions or only on uncaught exceptions.

3. Choose **Sources** in the **Developer Tools** menu, then press *Ctrl + O* to open a file browser and select the Dart script you wish to debug.

 Clicking on the left margin before a line of code places a breakpoint, which is indicated by a fat blue arrow.

4. Now reload the application and you will see that the execution stops at the breakpoint. On the right, you have a debug menu, which allows you to inspect scope variables, watch the call stack, and even create watch expressions, as shown in the following screenshot:

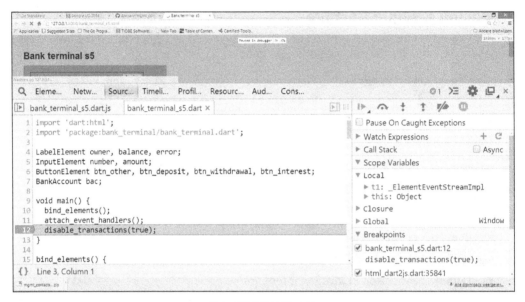

Debugging JS in Chrome

How it works...

Chrome uses the source map file `<file>.js.map` generated while compiling the JavaScript code to map the Dart code to the JavaScript code in order to be able to debug it.

There's more...

In this recipe, we will examine how to debug your app in the Firefox browser.

Debugging your app in JavaScript for Firefox

In Firefox, the source maps feature is not yet implemented. Use *Shift + F2* to get the developer toolbar and the command line. In the top menu, you will see **Debugger**. Place a breakpoint and reload the file. Code execution then stops and you can inspect the value of the variables, as shown in the following screenshot:

Debugging JS in Firefox

Using the command-line tools

Some things can be done more easily on the command-line, or are simply not (yet) included in Dart Editor. These tools are found in `dart-sdk/bin`. They consist of the following:

- `dart`: The standalone Dart VM to run Dart command-line apps, such as server-side scripts and server apps

- `dartanalyzer`: This is used to check code statically

- `pub`: This is the package and repository manager

- `dartfmt`: This is the code formatting tool

- `docgen`: This is the documentation generator tool

How to do it...

1. For every tool, it might be useful to know or check its version. This is done with the `--version` option such as `dart --version` with a typical output of **Dart VM version: 1.3.0 (Tue Apr 08   09:06:23 2014) on   "windows_ia32"**.

2. The `dart -v -h` option lists and discusses all the possible options of the VM. Many tools also take the `--package_root=<path>` or `-p=<path>` option to indicate where the packages used in the imports reside on the filesystem.

3. dartanalyzer is written in Java and works in Dart Editor whenever a project is imported or Dart code is changed; it is started `dartanalyzer prorabbits.dart` with output:

   Analyzing prorabbits.dart...

   No issues found   (or possibly errors and hints to improve the code)

4. The previous output verifies that the code conforms to the language specification `https://www.dartlang.org/docs/spec/`, pub functionality is built into Dart Editor, but the tool can also be used from the command line (refer to test_pub). To fetch packages (for example, for the test_pub app), use the following command in the folder where `pubspec.yaml` lives, `pub get`, with a typical output as follows:

   ```
   Resolving dependencies... (6.6s)
   Got dependencies!
   ```

5. A packages folder is created with symlinks to the central `package` cache on your machine. The latest versions are downloaded and the package versions are registered in the `pubspec.lock` file, so that your app can only use these versions.

6. If you want to get a newer version of a package, use the `pub upgrade` command. You can use the `-v` and `-- trace` options to produce a detailed output to verify its workings.

 Always do a pub upgrade if the project you start working on already contains versions of packages!

7. The `dartfmt` tool is also a built in Dart Editor. Right-click on any Dart file and choose **Format** from the context menu. This applies transformations to the code so that it conforms to the Dart Style Guide, which can be seen at `https://www.dartlang.org/articles/style-guide/`.You can also use it from the command line, but then the default operation mode is cleaning up whitespace. Use the `-t` option to apply code transforms such as `dartfmt -t -w bank_terminal.dart`.

See also

- ▸ Solving problems when `pub get` fails
- ▸ Compiling your app to JavaScript (for `pub build`)
- ▸ Documenting your code from *Chapter 2, Structuring, testing, and deploying an application*
- ▸ Publishing your app to a pub (for pub publishing)
- ▸ Using snapshotting to start an app in Dart VM
- ▸ For additional information, refer to `https://www.dartlang.org/tools/`

Solving problems when pub get fails

The pub package manager is a complex tool with many functionalities, so it is not surprising that occasionally something goes wrong. The `pub get` command downloads all the libraries needed by your app, as specified in the `pubspec.yaml` file. Running `pub get` behind a proxy or firewall used to be a problem, but it was solved in the majority of cases. If this still haunts you, look at the corresponding section at `https://www.dartlang.org/tools/editor/troubleshoot.html`.

Getting ready

This recipe is especially useful when you encounter the following error in your Dart console while trying to open a project in Dart Editor during the pub get phase:

```
Pub install fails with 'Deletion failed'
```

How to do it...

First try this; right-click on your project and select **Close Folder**. Then, restart the editor and open your project again. In many cases, your project will load fine. If this does not work, try the `pub gun` command:

1. Delete the pub cache folder from `C:\Users\{your username}\AppData\Roaming\Pub`.
2. Delete all the `packages` folders in your project (also in subfolders).
3. Delete the `pubspec.lock` file in your project.
4. Run `pub get` again from a command line or select **Tools** in the Dart Editor menu, and then select **Pub Get**.

How it works...

The `Pub\Cache` subfolder contains all the packages that have been downloaded in your Dart environment. Your project contains symlinks to the projects in this cache, which sometimes go wrong, mostly on Windows. The `pubspeck.lock` file keeps the downloaded projects constrained to certain versions; removing this constraint can also be helpful.

There's more...

Temporarily disabling the virus checker on your system can also help `pub get` to succeed when it fails with the virus checker on.

The following script by Richard Schmidt that downloads packages from the pub repository and unpacks it into your Dart cache may also prove to be helpful for this error, which can be found at `https://github.com/hangstrap/downloadFromPub`. Use it as `dart downloadFromPub.dart package m.n.l`.

Here, `package` is the package you want to install and `m.n.l` is the version number such as 0.8.1. You will need to build this like any other dart package, and if during this process the `pub get` command fails, you will have to download the package and unpack it manually; however, from then on, you should be able to use this script to work around this issue.

When `pub get` fails in Dart Editor, try the following on the command line to get more information on the possible reasons for the `pub --trace 'upgrade'` failure.

There is now also a way to condense these four steps into one command in a terminal as follows:

```
pub cache repair
```

Shrinking the size of your app

On the web, the size of the JavaScript version of your app matters. For this reason, `dart2js` is optimized to produce the smallest possible JavaScript files.

How to do it...

When you're ready to deploy, minify the size of the generated JavaScript with `-m` or `--minify`, as shown in the following command:

```
dart2js -m -o prorabbits.js prorabbits.dart
```

Using `pub build` on the command line minifies JavaScript by default because this command is meant for deployment.

How it works...

The `dart2js` file utilizes a tree-shaking feature; only code that is necessary during execution is retained, that is, functions, classes, and libraries that are not called are excluded from the produced `.js` file. The minification process further reduces the size by replacing the names of variables, functions, and so on with shorter names and moving code around to use a few lines.

There's more...

Be careful when you use reflection.

More Information Section 1

Using reflection in the Dart code prevents tree shaking. So only import the `dart:mirrors` library when you really have to. In this case, include an `@MirrorsUsed` annotation, as shown in the following code:

```
library mylib;

@MirrorsUsed(targets: 'mylib')
import 'dart:mirrors';
```

In the previous code, all the names and entities (classes, functions, and so on) inside of `mylib` will be retained in the generated code to use reflection. So create a separate library to hold the class that is using mirrors.

 Make sure your deployment web server uses `gzipping` to perform real-time HTTP compression.

See also

▸ You might want to consult the *Using Reflection* recipe in *Chapter 4, Object Orientation*.

Making a system call

A fairly common use case is that you need to call another program from your Dart app, or an operating system command. For this, the abstract class `Process` in the `dart:io` package is created.

How to do it...

Use the `run` method to begin an external program as shown in the following code snippet, where we start Notepad on a Windows system, which shows the question to open a new file `tst.txt` (refer to `make_system_call\bin\ make_system_call.dart`):

```
import 'dart:io';

main() {
  // running an external program process without interaction:
  Process.run('notepad', ['tst.txt']).then((ProcessResult rs){
    print(rs.exitCode);
    print(rs.stdout);
    print(rs.stderr);
  });
}
```

If the process is an OS command, use the `runInShell` argument, as shown in the following code:

```
Process.run('dir',[], runInShell:true).then((ProcessResult rs)
{ … }
```

How it works...

The `Run` command returns a Future of type `ProcessResult`, which you can interrogate for its exit code or any messages. The exit code is OS-specific, but usually a negative value indicates an execution problem.

Use the `start` method if your Dart code has to interact with the process by writing to its `stdin` stream or listening to its `stdout` stream.

 Both methods work asynchronously; they don't block the main app. If your code has to wait for the process, use `runSync`.

Using snapshotting

One of the advantages of running a Dart app on its own VM is that we can apply snapshotting, thereby reducing the startup time compared to JavaScript. A snapshot is a file with an image of your app in the byte form, containing all the Dart objects as they appear in the heap memory.

How to do it...

To generate a script snapshot file called `prorabbits` from the Dart script `prorabbits.dart`, issue the following command:

```
dart --snapshot=prorabbits prorabbits.dart
```

Then, start the app with `dart prorabbits args`, where `args` stands for optional arguments needed by the script.

How it works...

A script snapshot is the byte representation of the app's objects in the memory (more precisely in the heap of the started isolate) after it is loaded, but before it starts executing. This enables a much faster startup because the work of tokenizing and parsing the app's code was already done in the snapshot.

There's more...

This recipe is intended for server apps or command-line apps. A browser with a built-in Dart VM can snapshot your web app automatically and store that in the browser cache; the next time the app is requested, it starts up way faster from its snapshot. Because a snapshot is in fact a serialized form of an object(s), this is also the way the Dart VM uses to pass objects between isolates. The folder `dart/dart-sdk/bin/snapshots` contains snapshots of the main Dart tools.

See also

▶ Occasionally, your app needs access to the operating system, for example, to get the value of an environment variable to know where you are in the filesystem, or to get the number of processors when working with isolates. Refer to the *Using isolates in the Dart VM* and *Using isolates in web apps* recipes, in *Chapter 8, Working with Futures, Tasks, and Isolates*, for more information on working with isolates.

Getting information from the operating system

In this recipe, you will see how to interact with the underlying operating system on which your app runs by making system calls and getting information from the system.

Getting ready

The `Platform` class provides you with information about the OS and the computer the app is executing on. It lives in `dart:io`, so we need to import this library.

How to do it...

The following script shows the use of some interesting options (refer to the code files `tools\code\platform\bin\platform.dart` of this chapter):

```dart
import 'dart:io';

Map env = Platform.environment;

void main() {
  print('We run from this VM: ${Platform.executable}');
// getting the OS and Dart version:
  print('Our OS is: ${Platform.operatingSystem}');
  print('We are running Dart version: ${Platform.version}');
  if (!Platform.isLinux) {
    print('We are not running on Linux here!');
  }
  // getting the number of processors:
  int noProcs = Platform.numberOfProcessors;
  print('no of processors: $noProcs');
  // getting the value of environment variables from the Map env:
  print('OS = ${env["OS"]}');
  print('HOMEDRIVE = ${env["HOMEDRIVE"]}');
  print('USERNAME = ${env["USERNAME"]}');
  print('PATH = ${env["PATH"]}');
  // getting the path to the executing Dart script:
  var path = Platform.script.path;
  print('We execute at $path');
  // on this OS we use this path separator:
  print('path separator: ${Platform.pathSeparator}');
}
```

When run, the above code gives the following output:

```
Our OS is: windows
We are running Dart version: 1.3.3 (Wed Apr 16 12:40:55 2014) on
"windows_ia32"
We are not running on Linux here!
```

```
no of processors: 8
OS = Windows_NT
HOMEDRIVE = C:
USERNAME = CVO
PATH = C:\mongodb\bin;C:\MinGW\bin;...
We execute at /F:/Dartiverse/platform/bin/platform.dart
path separator: \
```

How it works...

Most of the options are straightforward. You can get the running VM from `Platform. executable`. You can get the OS from `Platform.operatingSystem`; this can also be tested on a Boolean property such as `Platform.isLinux`. The Dart version can be tested with the `Platform.version` property. The `Platform.environment` option returns a nice map structure for the environment variables of your system, so you can access their values by name, for example, for a variable `envVar`, use `var envVar = Platform. environment["envVar"]`.

To get the path of the executing Dart script, you can use the path property of `Platform. script` because the latter returns the absolute URI of the script. When building file paths in your app, you need to know how the components in a path are separated; `Platform. pathSeparator` gives you this information.

There's more...

Don't confuse this class with `Platform` from `dart:html`, which returns information about the browser platform.

2
Structuring, Testing, and Deploying an Application

In this chapter, we will cover the following topics:

- ▸ Exiting from an app
- ▸ Parsing command-line arguments
- ▸ Structuring an application
- ▸ Using a library from within your app
- ▸ Microtesting your code with assert
- ▸ Unit testing a Polymer web app
- ▸ Adding logging to your app
- ▸ Documenting your app
- ▸ Profiling and benchmarking your app
- ▸ Publishing and deploying your app
- ▸ Using different settings in the checked and production modes

Introduction

In this chapter, we focus mainly on all the different tasks in the lifecycle of your project that make it more professional, and will save much more time in the maintenance phase. This includes structuring the project, installing a logging tool in it, testing, documenting, profiling, and publishing it. However, first we see how we can end an app, and how a server app can take command-line arguments.

Exiting from an app

A Dart program starts its execution from the `main()` function in one thread (or isolate) in the Dart VM. The Dart VM by design always starts up single threaded. The program can end in three different ways:

> It can end in a normal way by executing the last statement from `main()` and returning the exit code with the value 0, which means success

> It can terminate abnormally with a runtime exception, returning exit code different from 0, such as 255 in the case of an unhandled exception

> It can wait in an event loop for user interaction (such as in the browser or a web server waiting for requests), and then terminate when the browser is closed or another app is started in the same browser tab

However, how can we exit the app from the code itself? This can be useful, for example, in a server-side VM app with some Futures that may or may not return.

How to do it...

The first possibility is to use the `exit(int code)` top-level function from `dart:io`, as in `exit_app.dart`, to stop the app from an endless loop or at a certain condition, and return the exit code:

```
import 'dart:io';

void main() {
  var message = "Dart is fun!";
  int i = 0;
  while (true) {
    print(message);
    i++;
    if (i == 10) {
      print("That's enough!");
```

```
    exit(10);
  }
 }
}
```

You can also set the exit code value with the property `exitCode`, as shown in the following code:

```
exitCode = 10;
// ... other code can be executed
exit(exitCode);
```

How it works...

The exit (code) function will terminate the running Dart VM process and return the integer code as the exit value to the parent process or OS environment, indicating the success, failure, or other exit state of the program. You can choose the value of the code; there is a convention to use 0 for success, 1 for warnings, and 2 for errors. Another convention is zero for success, non-zero for failure, and a program returning a warning for a successful exit because it naturally reached its end. A concrete example is the dartanalyzer program, which returns 0 if the code generates warnings.

Setting the exit code is preferred because the program can still run to its natural completion, or some cleanup or finalizing code (such as closing a file or database connection) can be run before `exit (exitCode)` ends the app. It is also good practice to start `main()` with `exitCode = 0`, presuming success as the normal ending state.

 What exit codes mean is platform-specific; you will not run into cross-platform issues if you use exit codes in the range of 0–127.

Parsing command-line arguments

A server app that runs a batch job often takes parameter values from the command line. How can we get these values in our program?

How to do it...

The obvious way to parse command-line arguments is as follows (see `command_line_arguments.dart`):

```
void main(List<String> args) {
  print("script arguments:");
```

```
    for(String arg in args)
        print(arg);
}
```

Now, the command `dart command_line_arguments.dart param1 param2 param3` gives you the following output:

script arguments:

param1

param2

param3

However, you can also test this from within Dart Editor, open the menu **Run**, and select **Manage Launches** (*Ctrl + Shift + M*). Fill in the parameters in the **Script arguments** window:

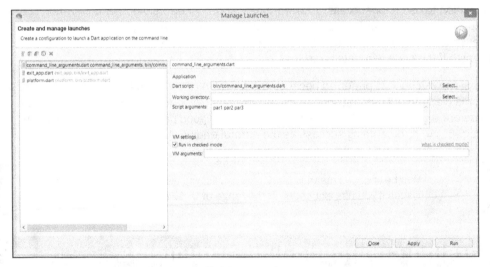

Script arguments

What if your parameters are in the `key:value` form, as shown in the following code?

```
    par1:value1 par2:value2 par3:value3
```

In this case, use the following code snippet:

```
for(String arg in args) {
    List<String> par = arg.split(':');
    var key = par[0];
    var value = par[1];
    print('Key is: $key - Value is: $value');
}
```

The previous code snippet gives you the following output:

Key is: par1 - Value is: value1

Key is: par2 - Value is: value2

Key is: par3 - Value is: value3

The `split` method returned `List<String>` with a key and value for each parameter. A more sophisticated way to parse the parameters can be done as follows:

```
final parser = new ArgParser();
argResults = parser.parse(args);
List<String> pars = argResults.rest;
print(pars); // [par1:value1, par2:value2, par3:value3]
```

Again, use `split` to get the keys and values.

How it works...

The `main()` function can take an optional argument `List<String>` args to get parameters from the command line. It only takes a split of the parameter strings to get the keys and values.

The second option uses the `args` package from the pub repository, authored by the Dart team. Include `args:any` in the dependencies section of the `pubspec.yaml` file. Then, you can use the package by including `import 'package:args/args.dart';` at the top of the script. The `args` package can be applied both in client and server apps. It can be used more specifically for the parsing of GNU and POSIX style options and is documented at `https://api.dartlang.org/apidocs/channels/stable/dartdoc-viewer/args/args`.

See also

▶ Refer to the *Searching in files* recipe in *Chapter 6, Working with Files and Streams*, for an example of how to use the args package with a flag

Structuring an application

All Dart projects that are meant to be used in a production environment should follow best software engineering practices and hence, must contain a particular structure of folders. A well-structured project breathes professionalism and gives developers a sense of recognition; it is much easier to find your way in a standardized structure. Moreover, it is also necessary if you want to use a bunch of application-specific libraries in your app, as we will see in the next recipe.

Getting ready

An app that is meant to run on its own, either as a command-line application or a web application, is an application package; it needs a `main()` entry point. A library package will be used as a dependency in other apps. All Dart projects depend on the configuration file `pubspec.yaml`, which describes the app and its dependencies, together with the `pubspec.lock` file. This dictates which libraries will be contained in the top-level `packages` folder. This file and the `packages` folder are generated by the pub tool (more specifically, the `pub get` and `pub upgrade` commands) and should not be edited.

How to do it...

If you develop an application in Dart Editor when starting up a new project, you will need to choose a project template to begin with, as shown in the following table:

Project type	Template	Project folder
Client or server app to be run standalone	Command line	`bin`
Web or Polymer app	Web application or web application using Polymer, or project	`web`
Chrome app	Chrome-packaged application	`web`
Library	Package	`lib`

The `bin` folder contains a startup script with a `main()` function. It can also contain shell scripts, for example, a script to start a server. In the `web` folder, you will typically have `index.html` and a `main.dart` file, or in general, the `app.html` and `app.dart` files. Other resource files such as CSS, JavaScript files, and images can be contained in their own folders `css`, `js`, and `images`. A Polymer project will typically contain a `web\component` subfolder. Don't place any scripts with `main()` in a `lib` folder.

Then, you will want to enhance the structure of the project as follows:

Folder	Project type	Files
at top-level	All	README.md, LICENSE, CHANGELOG, and AUTHORS files
doc	All	getting_started.md, todo.txt
example	All	Example scripts showing how to use the app
lib	Web	Folders for src, view, and model
src	Server	Folders for src and model
test	All	Unit test scripts

How it works...

The templates from Dart Editor provide you with a basic structure, but usually you'll want to add some folders as specified previously to provide a recognizable and professional structure where you can easily find what you want to look at, for example, which tests are included with the project. As we will see in the next recipe, in order to use application libraries, they have to be placed in the lib folder.

There's more...

The README file (readme.md, which is in the markdown syntax; refer to http://en.wikipedia.org/wiki/Markdown) and the CHANGELOG file are shown in the pub repository on the page of your package, so their content is important.

Optional folders are as follows:

▶ mock: This contains classes to simulate certain behaviors of your app in testing environments, for example, a text file instead of a real database

▶ tool: This contains tooling scripts needed in the project such as a build script, test runners, and so on

▶ benchmark: When the performance is critical, this folder can contain examples to test it

An alternative structure for an app with both client and server components can be placed on top of the previous structure:

- ▶ `client`
- ▶ `server`
- ▶ `core` (or `shared`)

The `https://www.dartlang.org/tools/pub/package-layout.html` link on the Dart site contains some additional information.

See also

- ▶ You might also want to read the *Publishing and deploying your app* recipe in this chapter

Using a library from within your app

As indicated in the previous recipe, every kind of app can contain a `lib` folder, which at the very least contains the model classes. These model classes are very important because they form the backbone of your project, so they must be accessible in your entire application. You can do this by placing them at the top in a `lib` folder, or even better in the lib/model. This central position will also make them stand out and easy to find for other readers of your code.

How to do it...

Take a look at the structure of the `bank_terminal` project. The model classes `Person` and `BankAccount` are placed in the `lib\model` folder. Give your project a name in the `pubspec.yaml` file:

```
name: bank_terminal
```

Then, use the same name for the library script you created in the `lib` folder `bank_terminal.dart`, which contains the following code:

```
library bank_terminal;

import 'dart:convert';

part 'model/bank_account.dart';
part 'model/person.dart';
```

The library has the same name as your app! This is not required for the Dart script itself, but it is a common and advised practice.

Now when a `pub get` or `pub upgrade` command is performed, a `bank_terminal` folder appears in `packages`. You can then make this library available for use in your other Dart scripts by importing it as any hosted package you would have downloaded from the pub. For example, in `web\bank_terminal.dart` we have the following code:

```
import 'package:bank_terminal/bank_terminal.dart';
```

In this case, the model classes are made available. The project structure is shown in the following screenshot:

```
File  Edit  Refactor  Navigate  Run  Tools  Help

Files                              bank_terminal.dart
  bank_terminal                 1  library bank_terminal;
    packages                    2
      bank_terminal             3  import 'dart:convert';
      browser [0.9.0]           4
      pubspec.lock              5  part 'model/bank_account.dart';
      pubspec.yaml              6  part 'model/person.dart';
    lib                         7
      model
        bank_account.dart
        person.dart
      bank_terminal.dart [bank_terminal]
    web
      packages
      bank_terminal.css
      bank_terminal.dart
      bank_terminal.html
  Dart SDK
```

Using a library in your app

How it works...

The pub tool was designed to work this way to make it easy to use internal libraries for your app. Every script that declares a library in the `lib` folder (or its subfolders) will be picked up by the `pub get` or `pub upgrade` commands. The result is that the library with all its code is considered a separate "internal" package, and thus placed in the `packages` folder together with other packages your app depends on. This makes for a clean code model, and it also makes it easier for the pub to deploy your code.

There's more...

The pub tool can be extended to several subfolders of lib, each containing their own library file (for example, a script `model.dart` that starts with the `library` model in the `model` folder) and then one top-level library file `project_name.dart`, containing the following code as its first lines:

```
library project_name;
import 'model/model.dart';    // importing library model
import 'view/view.dart';      // importing library view
```

...

This way, the different libraries from model, view, and so on are imported into one big library, which is then imported by the app as follows:

```
import 'package:project_name/project_name.dart';
```

Microtesting your code with assert

Writing tests for your app is necessary, but it is not productive to spend much time on trivial tests. An often underestimated Dart keyword is assert, which can be used to test conditions in your code.

How to do it...

Look at the code file `microtest.dart`, where `microtest` is an internal package as seen in the previous recipe:

```
import 'package:microtest/microtest.dart';

void main() {
  Person p1 = new Person("Jim Greenfield", 178, 86.0);
  print('${p1.name} weighs ${p1.weight}' );
  // lots of other code and method calls
  // p1 = null;
  // working again with p1:
  assert(p1 is Person);
  p1.weight = 100.0;
  print('${p1.name} now weighs ${p1.weight}' );
}
```

We import the `microtest` library, which contains the definition of the `Person` class. In `main()`, we create a `Person` object p1, go through lots of code, and then want to work with p1 again, possibly in a different method of another class. How do we know that p1 still references a `Person` object? In the previous snippet, it is obvious, but it can be more difficult. If p1 was, for example, dereferenced, without assert we would get the exception **NoSuchMethodError: method not found: 'weight='**.

However, if we use the assert statement, we get a much clearer message: **AssertionError: Failed assertion: line 9 pos 9: 'p1 is Person' is not true**. You can test it by uncommenting the line p1 = null.

How it works...

The `assert` parameter is a logical condition or any expression (such as calling a function returning a Boolean value) that resolves to false or true. If its value is false, the normal execution is stopped by throwing an `AssertionError`.

Use `assert` to test any non-obvious conditions in your code; it can replace a lot of simple unit tests or unit tests that can be difficult to set up. Rest assured `assert` only works in the checked mode; it does not affect the performance of your deployed app because it is ignored in the production mode.

There's more...

Testing with `assert` is often very useful when entering a method to test conditions on parameters (preconditions), and on leaving a method testing the return value (postconditions). You can also call a `test` function (which has to return a Boolean value) from `assert` such as `assert(testfunction());`.

Unit testing a Polymer web app

A project should contain a number of automated tests that can be run after every code change to ensure that the previous functionality still works. Dart's `unittest` framework is the best tool for the job, and the Dart website has some excellent articles to get you started. However, testing Polymer web applications is a lot trickier because of the way Polymer works, as it hides HTML in shadow DOM and also because it works in an asynchronous fashion, independent of the testing code.

Getting ready

We will create some tests in the ClickCounter example (the standard web application template using the `polymer` library). You can find the code in the `polymer1` app. We include the `unittest` library in the `pubspec.yaml` file, and create a `test` folder.

How to do it...

In the `test` folder, we create a `test_polymer1.html` page; a web page that loads the Polymer component required to test this functionality. The following is the minimum content required for the component:

```html
<head>
    <title>test_polymer1</title>
    <link rel="import" href="../web/polymer1.html">
    <script type="application/dart"   src="test_polymer1.dart"></
script>
    </head>
```

test_polymer1.dart contains the test script:

```dart
import 'package:unittest/unittest.dart';
import 'dart:html';
import 'package:polymer/polymer.dart';
import '../web/clickcounter.dart';

main() {
  initPolymer();

  var _el;

  setUp((){
    _el = createElement('<click-counter>Click counter test</click-
counter>');

    document.body.append(_el);
  });

  tearDown((){
    _el.remove();
  });

  // tests:
  test('shadowroot elements are created', (){
expect(querySelector('click-counter').children, isNotNull);
expect(querySelector('click-counter').shadowRoot.text, isNotNull);
  });
  test('initial text ok', (){
      expect(querySelector('click-counter').shadowRoot.text.
contains('click count: 0'), isTrue);
    });
```

```
    // test button with text Transaction:
    test('button with id click exists', (){
var button = querySelector('click-counter').shadowRoot.
querySelector('#click');
      expect(button, isNotNull);
    });
    test('button click() increments counter', (){
ButtonElement button = querySelector('click-counter').shadowRoot.
querySelector('#click');
        button.click();
        button.click();
        button.click();
        // get counter value:
        ClickCounter cc = querySelector('click-counter');
        expect(cc.count, 3);   // after 3 clicks
    });
}

createElement(String html) =>
  new Element.html(html, treeSanitizer: new NullTreeSanitizer());

class NullTreeSanitizer implements NodeTreeSanitizer {
  void sanitizeTree(node) {}
}
```

When the script is run, the following output appears:

unittest-suite-wait-for-done

PASS: shadowroot elements are created

PASS: initial text ok

PASS: button with id click exists

PASS: button click() increments counter

All 4 tests passed.

unittest-suite-success

How it works...

The test web page loads the Polymer component, and the test script loads the `unittest` and `polymer` packages and component classes (`clickcounter.dart`). In `main()`, we load the `polymer` package with `initPolymer()`; in `setup()`, we use a helper method `createElement()`, with an HTML string containing the `polymer` tag `<clickcounter>` as argument to instantiate the Polymer component and add it to the page. This was done in order to avoid the default HTML sanitization `createElement()`, which uses a null sanitizer instead of the built-in sanitizer (refer to *Chapter 5, Handling Web Applications,* for more information on this topic). Then, we start testing, for example:

▸ `expect(querySelector('click-counter').children, isNotNull);` so that the Polymer component tree is created

▸ `var button = querySelector('click-counter').shadowRoot.` `querySelector('#click');` `expect(button, isNotNull);` so that the button with the ID `'click'` is created

▸ `expect(querySelector('click-counter').shadowRoot.text.` `contains('click count: 0'), isTrue);` so that the text initially displayed is `'click count: 0'`.

Notice how we have to dig into `shadowRoot` of the Polymer component to get this information as follows:

▸ Verify that after clicking the button three times invoked by `button.click()`, our count property has the value 3:

```
ClickCounter cc = querySelector('click-counter');
expect(cc.count, 3);
```

See also

▸ To discover more information about the Dart `unittest` library, refer to the book *Learning Dart, Ivo Balbaert, Dzenan Ridjanovic, Packt Publishing,* or the excellent articles at `https://www.dartlang.org/articles/writing-unit-tests-for-pub-packages/` and `https://www.dartlang.org/articles/dart-unit-tests/`. These should help give you further background knowledge and information on how to extend the use of Dart Unittest in your own work.

Adding logging to your app

Every production app needs a logger functionality that allows you to output log messages at varying levels of severity (information/warning/debug) to the (web browser's debug) console or a file. This recipe will enable you to do just that quickly and easily.

Getting ready

Use the logging package developed by the Dart team available from pub for this purpose. Add it to your pubspec.yaml file, and add the code line import 'package:logging/logging. dart'; to your code. See it in action in bank_terminal_polymer. We add the import to the code of the Polymer component and model class BankAccount.

How to do it...

1. In web\bank_account.dart, we have at the top level the following code:

```
import 'package:logging/logging.dart';
final Logger log = new Logger('Bank Account');
```

2. We change the constructor to the following code:

```
BankAccount.created() : super.created() {
    setupLogger();
    log.info('Bank Account component is created');
}
```

setupLogger() **is the place where you can define the format of your logs, the following code presents a minimal format:**

```
setupLogger() {
    // Set up logger.
    Logger.root.level = Level.ALL;
    Logger.root.onRecord.listen((LogRecord rec) {
print('${rec.level.name}: ${rec.time}: ${rec.message}');
    });
}
```

3. In checkAmount(), we add the following warning message:

```
checkAmount(String in_amount) {
    try {
      amount = double.parse(in_amount);
    } on FormatException catch(ex) {
      log.warning("Amount $in_amount is not a double!");
      return false;
    }
    return true;
}
```

4. In the `model` class in `lib\bank_account.dart` file, we add an `"info"` message when the `BankAccount` object is created: `log.info('Bank Account is created')`, and in the `transact` method, we add `"severe message"` when the balance becomes negative:

```
transact(double amount) {
    balance += amount;
    if (amount < 0 && (-amount) > balance) {
      log.severe("Balance will go negative!");
    }
    date_modified = new DateTime.now();
}
```

5. If we then run the app, input an amount `50q`, and then an amount `-5000`, which will make our balance negative. This means we will get the following console output:

INFO: 2014-04-28 11:27:33.525: Bank Account component is created

FINE: 2014-04-28 11:27:33.551: [Instance of '_Binding']: bindProperties: [value] to [bank-account].[Symbol("bac")]

FINE: 2014-04-28 11:27:33.557: [bank-account] cancelUnbindAll

FINE: 2014-04-28 11:27:33.561: [bank-app] cancelUnbindAll

INFO: 2014-04-28 11:27:33.561: Bank Account is created

FINE: 2014-04-28 11:27:39.172: >>> [bank-account]: dispatch enter

INFO: 2014-04-28 11:27:39.176: <<< [bank-account]: dispatch enter

WARNING: 2014-04-28 11:27:44.089: Amount 50qs is not a double!

SEVERE: 2014-04-28 11:29:02.778: Balance will go negative!

INFO: 2014-04-28 11:29:02.778: <<< [bank-account]: dispatch transact

How it works...

The object of the `Logging` class must first be configured; otherwise, nothing happens. This is done in `setupLogger()`, which does the following things:

▶ It sets the level of the messages (choose between SHOUT, SEVERE, WARNING, INFO, CONFIG, FINE, FINER, FINEST, ALL, or OFF, or predefine your own).

▶ It sets up an event handler to listen for the onRecord stream. This processes objects of type `LogRecord`, which have access to the name, time, message, and stacktrace. Then, you code what you want to do with this event, print it to the console, write it in a file, send it in a mail, and so on.

There's more...

The following remarks tell you what to do in some special cases. To quickly display errors in a web app, you can add the following code in your code:

```
window.console.error('Something bad occurred');
```

If you want to log something asynchronously, use this snippet:

```
Future futr = doAsync();
futr.then((result) {
  log.fine('This result came back: $result');
  processResult(result);
})
.catchError((e, stackTrace) => log.severe('Something went wrong - ',
e, stackTrace));
```

Documenting your app

A project needs to be documented so that future developers can change and expand it. From release 1.2 onwards, the docgen tool is provided as an API Documentation Generator, which generates and serves documentation for the Dart SDK and packages, as well as for your applications. This recipe is designed to show you how to best document the application you have built.

Getting ready

Run pub get on your project before running the docgen tool. We will illustrate this with the bank_terminal_polymer app.

How to do it...

1. In a command-line session at the top level of your app, run:

   ```
   docgen .
   ```

2. When the documentation is generated, issue the following command:

   ```
   docgen --serve .
   ```

This installs the `dartdoc-viewer` tool and starts up a local web server for your docs, which you can access via the URL `http://localhost:8080`. The following is a screenshot from the `BankAccount` class documentation (you can change the view with the **Options** menu):

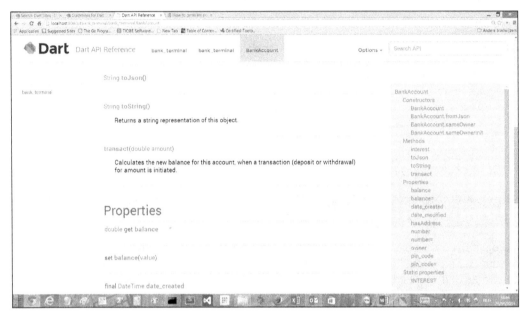

Viewing documentation

How it works...

The command creates a `docs` folder in your app, and writes JSON files with the API information in them for your app's `lib` folder, as well as for every imported package and the Dart SDK. Dartdoc comments (`/** ... */`) are included.

There's more...

To make the docs available from an intranet web server or from an Internet web server, perform the following steps:

1. Copy `dartdoc-viewer` (compiled to JavaScript) onto the server.
2. Copy the generated files to a `docs` directory under the main URL.

Also, private declarations are ignored unless the flag `--include-private` is used. Various other options are documented at `https://www.dartlang.org/tools/docgen/#options`.

A command that specifies the output folder and does not generate docs for the SDK and packages will be as follows:

```
docgen --out out/doc/api --no-include-sdk --no-include-dependent-packages
--compile lib/app.dart
```

Profiling and benchmarking your app

One of the key success factors of Dart is its performance. The Dart VM has a built-in optimizer to increase the execution speed. This optimizer needs a certain amount of execution time before it has enough information to do its work. This is no problem for an app in production, but when testing, you must ensure this condition is met. In this recipe, we are going to focus on how to best benchmark your application.

Getting ready

The benchmark_harness package from the Dart team is built specifically for this purpose. Add it to the pubspec.yaml file and import it in your code. We will illustrate this with the template_benchmark app. Also, make sure that all the issues detected by the checked mode are solved (because these could have an effect on the execution speed) and that the app is run in the production mode (refer to the *Setting up the checked and production modes* recipe in *Chapter 1, Working with Dart Tools*).

How to do it...

Perform the following steps to get the benchmark harness working:

1. Import the benchmark library:

    ```
    import 'package:benchmark_harness/benchmark_harness.dart';
    ```

2. Define a class TemplateBenchmark with its own main() and run() methods. It is a subclass of class BenchmarkBase in the benchmark library. The benchmark is started from run():

    ```
    class TemplateBenchmark extends BenchmarkBase {
      const TemplateBenchmark() : super("Template");

      static void main() {
        new TemplateBenchmark().report();
      }

      void run() {
         fib(20);
      }
    ```

```
// recursive algorithms:
  int fib(int i) {
    if (i < 2) return i;
    return fib(i-1) + fib(i-2);
  }

// int fib(n) => n<2 ? n : fib(n-2) + fib(n-1);

// iterative algorithm:
//  int fib(int i){
//    int a = 0; int b = 1;
//    for (int n=a; n < b; n++) {
//        a = a + b; b = a;
//    }
//    return a;
//  }

void setup() { }
void teardown() { }
}
```

3. The following code starts the whole benchmark machinery:

```
main() {
    TemplateBenchmark.main();
}
```

4. If we benchmark the Fibonacci algorithm for the two recursive implementations (with if and with the ternary operators) and the iterative algorithm, we get the following results:

Template(RunTime): 482.392667631452 us.

Template(RunTime): 498.00796812749 us.

Template(RunTime): 0.2441818187589752 us.

As we expected, the iterative algorithm performs orders of magnitude better than working recursively.

How it works...

Create a new benchmark by extending the `BenchmarkBase` class (here, `TemplateBenchmark`). The benchmarked code is called from the `run()` method within this subclass. The `setup()` and `teardown()` function code are run before and after the benchmark to prepare for the benchmark or clean up after it. These are not taken into account for the benchmark itself. The top-level `main()` function runs the benchmark by calling `main()` from the subclass of `BenchmarkBase`.

See also

▶ Refer to the new Observatory tool to profile Dart apps at `https://www.dartlang.org/tools/observatory/`

Publishing and deploying your app

There comes a point in time where you consider your app to be production ready, and you are eager to hand it over to your clients or users. If it is a web app in the Dart world at this moment in time, this means compiling to JavaScript. Luckily, the pub tool will take care of this stage in your app's life, so that your app can be deployed successfully.

Getting ready

This is pretty straightforward. To prepare, you need to run and test your application in both the checked and production modes.

How to do it...

Run the `pub build` command (see the *Compiling your app to JavaScript* recipe in *Chapter 1, Working with Dart Tools*), either from the command line or in Dart Editor. This creates the `build` folder with the subfolder `bin` or `web`, respectively, for a command-line or web application. The `build` folder contains complete deliverable files. The files generated in there can be deployed like any static content. Upload the JavaScript files together with the web pages and resources to any production web server.

How it works...

The `pub build` command is Dart's optimized command to create the deployment assets. It performs tree shaking so that only the code that is necessary during execution is retained, that is, functions, classes, and libraries that are not called are excluded from the produced `.js` file. The minification process further reduces the size of the file by replacing the names of variables, functions, and so on with shorter names and moving the code around to use a few lines.

There's more...

Some application hosting sites to run your app in the cloud are as follows:

> ▶ Heroku is a Platform as a Service for cloud-hosted web apps. It doesn't yet officially support the Dart runtime, but it can already be used to do just that. Refer to `http://blog.sethladd.com/2012/08/running-dart-in-cloud-with-heroku.html` and the Dart server code lab at `https://www.dartlang.org/codelabs/deploy` for more information.

> ▶ DartVoid at `http://www.dartvoid.com/` using the Vane middleware framework; it comes with support for MongoDB.

> ▶ Google itself offers the possibility of running a Dart server on Google Compute Engine (refer to `http://alexpaluzzi.com/tag/dartlang/`) and on Google's other cloud virtual machines in the future.

Once your app is ready to be shared with other developers, it can also be published to the pub repository (`pub.dartlang.org`). This is done with the `pub publish` command; this will verify the contents of your `pubspec.yaml` configuration file and the app's folder structure. For more detailed information, refer to `https://www.dartlang.org/tools/pub/publishing.html`.

Using different settings in the checked and production modes

Often the development and deployment environments are different. For example, the app has to connect to a different database or a different mail server in either environment to use a mocked service in development and the real service in production, or something like that. How can we use different setups in both modes, or achieve a kind of precompiler directive-like functionality?

How to do it...

Perform the following steps to use different settings:

1. Add a transformers section to `pubspec.yaml` with an environment line that specifies a map of the settings, names and values, as follows (see the code in `dev_prod_settings`):

```
transformers: # or dev_transformers
- $dart2js:
      environment: {PROD: "true", DB: "MongoPROD"}
```

2. You can, for example, get the value of the DB setting from `const String.fromEnvironment('DB')`, as you can see in the following code:

```
import 'dart:html';

void main() {
  print('PROD: ${const String.fromEnvironment('PROD')}');
  bool prod = const String.fromEnvironment('PROD') == 'true';
  if (prod) {
// do production things
window.alert("I am in Production!");
      connectDB(const String.fromEnvironment('DB'));
  }
  else {  // do developer / test things }
  log('In production, I do not exist');
}

log(String msg) {
  if (const String.fromEnvironment('DEBUG') != null) {
    print('debug: $msg');
  }
}

connectDB(String con) {
  // open a database connection
}
```

3. When run in the Dart VM (and in the checked mode), the console gives `PROD: null` as an output when run as JavaScript in Chrome; an alert dialog appears and the console in the **Developer Tools** shows **PROD: true**.

How it works...

The import initializer option requires a manual code change in order to switch the environment. The transformers option uses environment declarations that are provided by the surrounding system compiling or running the Dart program. This is better because it only requires changing the configuration file `pubspec.yaml`. However, at the moment, it is only defined for dart2js, in order to deploy to JavaScript.

Make sure that the environment is indented; otherwise, you may get the error `"transformers" must have a single key: the transformer identifier`.

3
Working with Data Types

In this chapter, we will cover the following recipes:

- ▶ Concatenating strings
- ▶ Using regular expressions
- ▶ Strings and Unicode
- ▶ Using complex numbers
- ▶ Creating an enum
- ▶ Flattening a list
- ▶ Generating a random number within a range
- ▶ Retrieving a random element from a list
- ▶ Working with dates and times
- ▶ Improving performance in numerical computations
- ▶ Using SIMD for enhanced performance

Introduction

This chapter is about working with the different data types Dart has to offer. The basic data types available are `var` (stores any object); `num` (stores any number type); `int`, `double`, `String`, `bool`, `List` (arrays); and `Map` (associative arrays). All of these data types are declared in the `dart:core` library. We will talk about strings, random numbers, complex numbers, dates and times, enums, and lists. We will cover a lot of tricks to help you out in specific circumstances. To get a quick overview of all the data types in Dart, refer to `https://www.dartlang.org/docs/dart-up-and-running/contents/ch02.html#built-in-types`.

Concatenating strings

Concatenation can be done in a variety of ways in Dart (refer to the `concat_trim_strings` file, and download it from `www.packtpub.com/support`).

How to do it...

Strings can be concatenated as follows:

```
String s1 = "Dart", s2 = "Cook", s3 = "Book";
var res = "Dart" " Cook" "Book";           (1)
res = "Dart"   " Cook"
             "Book";          (2)
res = s1 + " " + s2 + s3;          (3)
res = "$s1 $s2$s3";          (4)
res = [s1, " ", s2, s3].join();          (5)

var sb = new StringBuffer();          (6)
sb.writeAll([s1, " ", s2, s3]);
res = sb.toString();
print(res); // Dart CookBook
```

How it works...

Adjacent string literals are taken together as one string as shown in line (1), even if they are on different lines as shown in line (2). The + operator does the same thing (3), as well as string interpolation (4), which is the preferred way. Still there is another way to add `join()` to `List<String>` as shown in line (5). The most efficient way, especially if you want to apply the + operator in a for loop, is to work with `StringBuffer` as shown in line (6); the concatenation only happens when `toString()` is called.

So if you have to glue a large number of strings together, use `StringBuffer`. Avoid concatenation using +. This will save you memory and will execute the file much faster.

There's more...

The `writeAll` method can take an optional separator argument, as in `sb.writeAll([s1, " ", s2, s3],'-');`, resulting in `Dart- -Cook-Book`.

Using regular expressions

Regular expressions are an indispensable tool in every programming language to search for matching patterns in strings. Dart has the `RegExp` class from `dart:core`, which uses the same syntax and semantics as JavaScript.

How to do it...

We use `RegExp` in the following code (see `using_regexp.dart`) to quickly determine whether a credit card number seems valid:

```
var visa = new RegExp(r"^(?:4[0-9]{12}(?:[0-9]{3})?)$");
var visa_in_text = new RegExp(r"\b4[0-9]{12}(?:[0-9]{3})?\b");
var input = "4457418557635128";
var text = "Does this text mention a VISA 4457418557635128 number?";

void main() {
  print(visa.pattern);
  // is there a visa pattern match in input?
  if (visa.hasMatch(input)) {
    print("Could be a VISA number");
  }
  // does string input contain pattern visa?
  if (input.contains(visa)) {
    print("Could be a VISA number");
  }
  // find all matches:
  var matches = visa_in_text.allMatches(text);
  for (var m in matches) {
    print(m.group(0));
  }
}
```

```
    visa_in_text.allMatches(text).forEach((m) => print(m[0]));
    // let's hide the number:
    print(text.replaceAll(visa_in_text, 'XXXXXXXXXXXXXXXX'));
    print(visa.isCaseSensitive);
    print(visa.isMultiLine);
}
```

The previous code gives the following output:

```
F:\Dartiverse\ADartCookbook\book\Chapter 3 - Datatypes\code\using_regexp\bin>
 using_regexp.dart
^(?:4[0-9]{12}(?:[0-9]{3})?)$
Could be a VISA number
Could be a VISA number
4457418557635128
4457418557635128
Does this text mention a VISA XXXXXXXXXXXXXXXX number?
true
false
```

How it works...

Credit card numbers are just a sequence of 13 to 16 digits, with one to four specific digits at the start that identify the card company. A regular expression is specified as a raw string r"...", where ... is the pattern. The hasMatch code tells you whether there is a match or not, and allMatches produces a collection you can walk through. In most cases, the convenience method for a single match, firstMatch is what you need. The allMatches.length part gives you the number of matches. The for loop can also be written more functionally as visa_in_text.allMatches(text).forEach((m) => print(m[0]));.

There's more...

To further verify the card number before calling the credit card verification service, you should code the Luhn algorithm (http://en.wikipedia.org/wiki/Luhn_algorithm). The class RegExp implements Perl-style regular expressions. However, it lacks a number of advanced features such as named capturing groups or conditionals.

 Refer to https://api.dartlang.org/apidocs/channels/stable/dartdoc-viewer/dart:core.RegExp for all the details on Dart. For more information on the regular expression syntax itself, refer to http://www.regular-expressions.info/refquick.html.

Strings and Unicode

Dart Strings are immutable sequences of UTF-16 code units. UTF-16 combines surrogate pairs, and if you decode these, you get Unicode code points. Unicode terminology is terse, but Dart does a good job of exposing the different parts.

How to do it...

We will see the different methods to perform action on strings with special characters in unicode.dart:

```dart
String country = "Egypt";
String city = "Zürich";
String japanese = "日本語"; // nihongo meaning 'Japanese'

void main() {
  print('Unicode escapes: \uFE18'); //  the □ symbol
  print(country[0]);                 // E
  print(country.codeUnitAt(0));      // 69
  print(country.codeUnits);          // [69, 103, 121, 112, 116]
  print(country.runes.toList());     // [69, 103, 121, 112, 116]
  print(new String.fromCharCode(69)); // E
  print(new String.fromCharCodes([69, 103, 121, 112, 116])); // Egypt
  print(city[1]);                    // ü
  print(city.codeUnitAt(1));         // 252
  print(city.codeUnits);             // [90, 252, 114, 105, 99, 104]
  print(city.runes.toList());        // [90, 252, 114, 105, 99, 104]
  print(new String.fromCharCode(252)); // ü
  print(new String.fromCharCodes([90, 252, 114, 105, 99, 104])); //
Zürich
  print(japanese[0]);                // 日
  print(japanese.codeUnitAt(0));     // 26085
  print(japanese.codeUnits);         // [26085, 26412, 35486]
  print(japanese.runes.toList());    // [26085, 26412, 35486]
  print(new String.fromCharCode(35486)); // 語
  print(new String.fromCharCodes([26085, 26412, 35486]));
// 日本語
}
```

How it works...

Within a string, Unicode characters can be escaped by using \u. The index operator [] on a string gives you the string representation of the UTF-16 code unit. These are also accessible as integers representing code points (also called `runes`) through the `codeUnitAt()` or `codeUnits` methods. The static member `charCode(s)` can take UTF-16 code units or `runes`. They work in the following way; if the char-code value is 16 bits (a single UTF-16 code unit), it is copied literally. Otherwise, it is of length 2 and the code units form a surrogate pair.

There's more...

The `dart:convert` code contains a UTF-8 encoder/decoder that transforms between strings and bytes. The `utf8encoding.dart` file shows how you can use these methods, as shown in the following code:

```dart
import 'dart:convert' show UTF8;

String str = "Acción"; // Spanish for 'Action'

void main() {
List<int> encoded = UTF8.encode(str);
  print(encoded); // [65, 99, 99, 105, 195, 179, 110]
  // The UTF8 code units are reinterpreted as
  // Latin-1 code points (a subset of Unicode code points).
  String latin1String = new String.fromCharCodes(encoded);
  print(latin1String); // AcciÃ³n
  print(latin1String.codeUnits);
// [65, 99, 99, 105, 195, 179, 110]
  var string = UTF8.decode(encoded);
  print(string); // Acción
}
```

Using complex numbers

Dart has no built-in type for complex numbers, but it is easy to build your own. The `complex_numbers` library (based on similar libraries by Tiago de Jesus and Adam Singer) provides constructors, utility methods, and four arithmetic operations both defined as operators and static methods.

How to do it...

We now define a ComplexNumber class, containing all utility methods for normal usage:

```
library complex_numbers;

import 'dart:math' as math;

class ComplexNumber {
  num _real;
  num _imag;

// 1- Here we define different ways to build a complex number:
  // constructors:
    ComplexNumber([this._real = 0, this._imag = 0]);
    ComplexNumber.im(num imag) : this(0, imag);
    ComplexNumber.re(num real) : this(real, 0);

// 2- The normal utility methods to get and set the real and
// imaginary part, to get the absolute value and the angle, to      //
compare two complex numbers:
  num get real => _real;
  set real(num value) => _real = value;

  num get imag => _imag;
  set imag(num value) => _imag = value;

  num get abs => math.sqrt(real * real + imag * imag);

  num get angle => math.atan2(imag, real);

  bool operator ==(other) {
    if (!(other is ComplexNumber)) {
      return false;
    }
    return this.real == other.real && this.imag == other.imag;
  }

  String toString() {
    if (_imag >= 0) {
      return '${_real} + ${_imag}i';
    }
    return '${_real} - ${_imag.abs()}i';
  }
```

```
// 3- operator overloading:
// The basic operations for adding, multiplying, subtraction and    //
division are defined as overloading of the operators +, *, - and /
   ComplexNumber operator +(ComplexNumber x) {
     return new ComplexNumber(_real + x.real, _imag + x.imag);
   }


   ComplexNumber operator -(var x) {
     if (x is ComplexNumber) {
return new ComplexNumber(this.real - x.real, this.imag - x.imag);
     } else if (x is num) {
       _real -= x;
       return this;
     }
     throw 'Not a number';
   }


   ComplexNumber operator *(var x) {
     if (x is ComplexNumber) {
       num realAux = (this.real * x.real - this.imag * x.imag);
       num imagAux = (this.imag * x.real + this.real * x.imag);

       return new ComplexNumber(realAux, imagAux);
     } else if (x is num) {
       return new ComplexNumber(this.real * x, this.imag * x);
     }
     throw 'Not a number';
   }


   ComplexNumber operator /(var x) {
     if (x is ComplexNumber) {
num realAux = (this.real * x.real + this.imag * x.imag) / (x.real *
x.real + x.imag * x.imag);
num imagAux = (this.imag * x.real - this.real * x.imag) / (x.real *
x.real + x.imag * x.imag);
       return new ComplexNumber(realAux, imagAux);
     } else if (x is num) {
       return new ComplexNumber(this.real / x, this.imag / x);
     }
     throw 'Not a number';
   }


// 4- Here we define the same operations as methods:
   static ComplexNumber add(ComplexNumber c1, ComplexNumber c2)        {
```

```
      num rr = c1.real + c2.real;
      num ii = c1.imag + c2.imag;
      return new ComplexNumber(rr, ii);
  }

  static ComplexNumber subtract(ComplexNumber c1, ComplexNumber c2)
  {
      num rr = c1.real - c2.real;
      num ii = c1.imag - c2.imag;
      return new ComplexNumber(rr, ii);
  }

  static ComplexNumber multiply(ComplexNumber c1, ComplexNumber c2)
  {
      num rr = c1.real * c2.real - c1.imag * c2.imag;
      num ii = c1.real * c2.imag + c1.imag * c2.real;
      return new ComplexNumber(rr, ii);
  }

  static ComplexNumber divide(ComplexNumber c1, ComplexNumber c2)
  {
num real = (c1.real * c2.real + c1.imag * c2.imag) / (c2.real *
c2.real + c2.imag * c2.imag);
num imag = (c1.imag * c2.real - c1.real * c2.imag) /  (c2.real *
c2.real + c2.imag * c2.imag);
      return new ComplexNumber(real, imag);
  }
}
```

How it works...

The `ComplexNumber` class is built using standard Dart functionalities:

- ▶ Private getters for real and imaginary parts to return their values and setters to change them
- ▶ A constructor with two optional arguments and two named constructors for a complex number, respectively, without real or imaginary parts
- ▶ Some utility methods such as `toString()` and overloading of `==`
- ▶ Operator overloading for +, -, *, and /
- ▶ The same operations implemented as static methods taking two complex numbers

There's more...

Keep an eye on the pub package `math-expressions` by Frederik Leonhardt, as evaluation of expressions with complex numbers is one of its goals.

Creating an enum

Enum does not exist in Dart as a built-in type. Enums provide additional type checking and thus, help enhance code maintainability. So what alternative do we have? Look at the code in project `enum`, where we want to differentiate the degree of an issue reported to us (we distinguish between the following levels: TRIVIAL, REGULAR, IMPORTANT, and CRITICAL).

How to do it...

The first way to achieve the creating an enum functionality is shown in `enum1.dart`:

```
class IssueDegree {
  final _value;
  const IssueDegree(this._value);
  toString() => 'Enum.$_value';

  static const TRIVIAL = const IssueDegree('TRIVIAL');
  static const REGULAR = const IssueDegree('REGULAR');
  static const IMPORTANT = const IssueDegree('IMPORTANT');
  static const CRITICAL = const IssueDegree('CRITICAL');
}

void main() {
  var issueLevel = IssueDegree.IMPORTANT;
  // Warning and NoSuchMethodError for IssueLevel2:
  // There is no such getter ALARM in IssueDegree
  // var issueLevel2 = IssueDegree.ALARM;

    switch (issueLevel) {
      case IssueDegree.TRIVIAL:
        print("Ok, I'll sort it out during lunch");
        break;
      case IssueDegree.REGULAR:
        print("We'll assign it to Ellen, our programmer");
        break;
      case IssueDegree.IMPORTANT:
```

```
        print("Let's discuss it in a meeting tomorrow morning");
        break;
      case IssueDegree.CRITICAL:
        print('Warn the Boss!');
        break;
    }
  }
```

This snippet prints **Let's discuss it in a meeting tomorrow morning**.

An alternative way, shown in enum2.dart, is to define the enum behavior in an abstract class and then to implement that, as shown in the following code:

```
import 'enum_abstract_class.dart';

class IssueDegree<String> extends Enum<String> {

   const IssueDegree(String val) : super (val);

static const IssueDegree TRIVIAL = const IssueDegree('TRIV');
static const IssueDegree REGULAR = const IssueDegree('REG');
static const IssueDegree IMPORTANT = const IssueDegree('IMP');
static const IssueDegree CRITICAL = const IssueDegree('CRIT');
}

main() {
  assert(IssueDegree.REGULAR is IssueDegree);
  // switch code
}
```

The switch code of the first example also works for this implementation. To simplify the code, the const values can also be defined outside the class, as in enum3.dart. Then, it is no longer needed to precede them with the enum class name, as shown in the following code:

```
import 'enum_abstract_class.dart';

const IssueDegree TRIVIAL = const IssueDegree('TRIV');
const IssueDegree REGULAR = const IssueDegree('REG');
const IssueDegree IMPORTANT = const IssueDegree('IMP');
const IssueDegree CRITICAL = const IssueDegree('CRIT');

class IssueDegree<String> extends Enum<String> {
   const IssueDegree(String val) : super (val);
}

main() {
```

```
    assert(REGULAR is IssueDegree);

    var issueLevel = IMPORTANT;
       switch (issueLevel) {
         case TRIVIAL:
            print("Ok, I'll sort it out during lunch");
          break;
       // rest of the code
    }
```

How it works...

The first option uses an `enum` class with a `const` constructor to set a private `_value`; the class contains the different values as constants. The constants can only be defined inside the class, and you get autocompletion (in Dart Editor or other editors with the Dart plugin) for them for free! In this way, you can use this enum-like class in a switch, and both dartanalyzer and the runtime point out the error to you if a non-existent value is used. The `enum_class.dart` file provides the template code for this case; make sure you create the constant values, as shown in the following code:

```
class Enum {
    final _value;
    const Enum(this._value);
    toString() => 'Enum.$_value';

    static const VAL1 = const Enum('VAL1');
    static const VAL2 = const Enum('VAL2');
    static const VAL3 = const Enum('VAL3');
    static const VAL4 = const Enum('VAL4');
    static const VAL5 = const Enum('VAL5');
}
```

The second way uses an abstract class `Enum` (defined in `enum_abstract_class.dart`) that takes a generic parameter `<T>`, as shown in the following code:

```
abstract class Enum<T> {
    final T _value;
    const Enum(this._value);
    T get value => _value;
}
```

Making the values top-level constants simplifies the code.

There's more...

The Ecma TC52 Dart Standards Committee has investigated a proposal for enums that will be discussed in September 2014 (refer to `http://www.infoq.com/news/2014/07/ecma-dart-google`), so providing built-in support for enums probably will be implemented in a future Dart version.

Flattening a list

A list can contain other lists as elements. This is effectively a two-dimensional list or array. Flattening means making a single list with all sublist items contained in it. Take a look at the different possibilities in `flatten_list.dart`.

How to do it...

We show three ways to flatten a list in the following code:

```
List lst = [[1.5, 3.14, 45.3], ['m', 'pi', '7'], [true, false, true]];
// flattening lst must give the following resulting List flat:
// [1.5, 3.14, 45.3, m, pi, 7, true, false, true]

void main() {
  // 1- using forEach and addAll:
  var flat = [];
  lst.forEach((e) => flat.addAll(e));
  print(flat);
  // 2- using Iterable.expand:
  flat = lst.expand((i) => i).toList();
  // 3- more nesting levels, work recursively:
  lst = [[1.5, 3.14, 45.3], ['m', 'pi', '7'], "Dart", [true, false,
true]];
  print(flatten(lst));
}
```

How it works...

The simplest method uses a combination of `forEach` and `addAll`. The second method uses the fact that `List` implements `Iterable`, and so has the `expand` method. The `expand` method is used here with an identity function as its argument; every element is returned without applying a function.

Using `expand` does not work if the list contains `ints` (or `Strings`, `doubles`, and so on) as single list elements, or if there are multiple levels of nesting. In that case, we will have to work recursively, as implemented in the `flatten` method:

```
Iterable flatten(Iterable iterable)
  => iterable.expand((e) => e is List ? flatten(e) : [e]);
```

There's more...

Why would you want to flatten a list of lists? There may be application needs to do this, for example, when you use two-dimensional lists or matrices in the game logic, but an obvious reason is that working with a list of lists is much more expensive performance wise.

Generating a random number within a range

You may have often wondered how to generate a random number from within a certain range. This is exactly what we will look at in this recipe; we will obtain a random number that resides in an interval between a minimum (min) and maximum (max) value.

How to do it...

This is simple; look at how it is done in `random_range.dart`:

```dart
import 'dart:math';

var now = new DateTime.now();
Random rnd = new Random();
Random rnd2 = new Random(now.millisecondsSinceEpoch);

void main() {
  int min = 13, max = 42;
  int r = min + rnd.nextInt(max - min);
  print("$r is in the range of $min and $max"); // e.g. 31
  // used as a function nextInter:
  print("${nextInter(min, max)}"); // for example: 17

  int r2 = min + rnd2.nextInt(max - min);
  print("$r2 is in the range of $min and $max"); // e.g. 33
}
```

How it works...

The `Random` class in `dart:math` has a method `nextInt(int max)`, which returns a random positive integer between 0 and max (not included). There is no built-in function for our question but it is very easy, as shown in the previous example. If you need this often, use a function `nextInter` for it, as shown in the following code:

```
int nextInter(int min, int max) {
    Random rnd = new Random();
    return min + rnd.nextInt(max - min);
}
```

The variable `rnd2` shows another constructor of `Random`, which takes an integer as a seed for the pseudo-random calculation of `nextInt`. Using a seed makes for better randomness, and should be used if you need many random values.

Getting a random element from a list

For certain applications such as games, it is necessary to have a means to retrieve a random element from a collection in Dart. This recipe will show you a simple way to do this.

How to do it...

This is easy to do; refer to the `random_list.dart` file:

```
import 'dart:math';

Random rnd = new Random();
var lst = ['Bill','Joe','Jennifer','Louis','Samantha'];

void main() {
    var element = lst[rnd.nextInt(lst.length)];
    print(element); // e.g. 'Louis'
    element = randomListItem(lst);
    print(element); // e.g. 'Samantha'
}
```

How it works...

We generate a random index number based on the list length and use it to retrieve a random element from the list. If you need this often, use the one-line function `randomListItem` for it, as shown in the following code:

```
randomListItem(List lst) => lst[rnd.nextInt(lst.length)];
```

See also

▸   Consult the previous recipe for more information about the use of `Random`

Working with dates and times

Proper date-time handling is needed in almost every data context. What does Dart give us to ease working with dates and times? Dart has the excellent built-in classes `DateTime` and `Duration` in `dart:core`. As a few of its many uses, you can do the following:

▸   Compare and calculate with date times

▸   Get every part of a date-time

▸   Work with different time zones

▸   Measure timespans with `Stopwatch`

However, the `DateTime` class does not provide internationalization; for this purpose, you need to use the `intl` package from the Dart team.

How to do it...

The following are some useful techniques (try them out in `date_time.dart`):

▸   Formatting dates (from `DateTime` to a string) to standard formats, but also to any format using the package `intl`, as shown in the following code:

```
import 'package:intl/intl.dart';
import 'package:intl/date_symbol_data_local.dart';

    print(now.toIso8601String()); // 2014-05-08T14:03:21.238
    print(now.toLocal());         // 2014-05-08 14:03:21.238
    print(now.toString());        // 2014-05-08 14:03:21.238
    print(now.toUtc());           // 2014-05-08 12:03:21.238Z
    // using intl to format:
    var formatter = new DateFormat('yyyy-MM-dd');
    String formatted = formatter.format(now);
    print(formatted); // 2014-05-08
    print(new DateFormat("EEEE").format(now)); // Thursday
    print(new DateFormat("yMMMMEEEEd").format(now));          //
Thursday, May 8, 2014
    print(new DateFormat("y-MM-E-d").format(now));            //
2014-05-Thu-8
    print(new DateFormat("jms").format(now)); // 2:19:08 PM
```

```
  print(new DateFormat('dd/MMM/y HH:mm:ss').format(now));      //
08/May/2014 14:39:07
   // locale data:
   initializeDateFormatting("fr_FR", null).then(formatDates);
// …
}

formatDates (var d) {
    print(new DateFormat("EEEEE", 'fr_FR').format(now));        //
jeudi
    print(new DateFormat("yMMMMEEEEd", 'fr_FR').format(now)); //
jeudi 8 mai 2014
    print(new DateFormat("y-MM-E-d", 'fr_FR').format(now));    //
2014-05-jeu.-8
}
```

▸ Parsing dates (from a string to a `DateTime`) when the given string is not in one of the acceptable date formats; an exception is thrown and caught as shown in the following code:

```
  try {
    DateTime dt = DateTime.parse("2014-05-08T15+02:00");
  } on FormatException catch(e) {
    print('FormatException: $e');
  }
```

▸ Working with timezone information:

```
print(now.toLocal());// time in local timezone
print(now.toUtc());  // time in Coordinated Universal Time
print(now.timeZoneName);    // Romance (zomertijd)
print(now.timeZoneOffset); // 2:00:00.000000
```

▸ Finding the last day of the month can be done as follows:

```
  var date = new DateTime(2014,6,0);
  print(date.day);  // 31
  // more general:
var lastDayDateTime = (now.month < 12) ?            new
DateTime(now.year, now.month + 1, 0)                 : new
DateTime(now.year + 1, 1, 0);
  print(lastDayDateTime.day); // 31
```

How it works...

Formatting a `DateTime` instance can be done with a few `to...` methods from `dart:core`, such as `toLocal()` to get the time in the local time zones (as defined by your machine). However, `intl` gives you much more flexibility; make a `DateFormat` object with the specific format string as an argument, and then call the `format` method to get a formatted string back.

For example, `d` gives the day number, `E` gives the weekday in an abbreviated form, `EE` gives the full day's name, `M` gives the month number, `y` gives the year, `H` gives the hour (0-24), `j` gives the hour (0-12) with AM or PM, `m` gives the minute, and so on. Many format combinations are possible (and you can build your own).

 For a complete overview of format combinations, refer to
https://api.dartlang.org/apidocs/channels/
stable/dartdoc-viewer/intl/intl.DateFormat.

If you want formatting for a particular locale (such as be_NL, cs_CZ, de_DE, and so on), you must first load the specific locale data by importing `date_symbol_data_local.dart` and then calling `initializeDateFormatting`. The first parameter is the specific locale. If you give it the value `null`, all the available locale data is loaded, as shown in the following code:

```
initializeDateFormatting("fr_FR", null).then(formatDates);
```

Next, when constructing the `DateFormat` object, the locale (such as `'fr_FR'`) has to be given as the second parameter:

```
new DateFormat("yMMMMEEEEd", 'fr_FR')
```

The `formatDates` method shows the following code in action:

```
formatDates (var d) {
    print(new DateFormat("EEEEE", 'fr_FR').format(now)); // jeudi
    print(new DateFormat("yMMMMEEEEd", 'fr_FR').format(now)); // jeudi
8 mai 2014
    print(new DateFormat("y-MM-E-d", 'fr_FR').format(now)); // 2014-
05-jeu.-8
}
```

Parsing a well-formed string into a `DateTime` string is done with the static `DateTime.parse` method, which takes the string and produces `DateTime`. The input format must conform to an ISO 8601 format. If the input format cannot be parsed, `FormatException` is thrown, so use try/catch to handle this.

The `toUTC` option gives you the time in **Coordinated Universal Time** (**UTC**) format, which is for all practical purposes identical to **Greenwich Mean Time** (**GMT**). Use `timeZoneName` to get an abbreviated name of the time zone for the `DateTime` object. The difference between UTC and the time zone of a `DateTime` object is calculated by calling `timeZoneOffset`.

To find the last day of the month, giving a day value of zero for the next month returns the previous month's last day.

There's more...

Be aware that a `DateTime` object is always in the local time zone, unless explicitly created in the UTC time zone with the `DateTime.utc` constructor; this can be done as follows:

```
DateTime moonLanding  = new DateTime.utc(1969, DateTime.JULY, 20);
```

In this constructor, only the year is required, all the other date and time parts are optional.

If you have other `Datetime` questions, look up the API docs at `https://api.dartlang.org/apidocs/channels/stable/dartdoc-viewer/dart-core.DateTime`.

Improving performance in numerical computations

Unlike Java and C#, who have dedicated 8, 16, 32, and 64 bit signed and unsigned integer types, and 32-bit and 64-bit floats, Dart does not have bounded integer types or 32-bit floating point number types; it only has two numeric types, `int` (an arbitrarily sized integer) and `double` (conforming to the IEEE-754 spec), and their super type `num`. This was done to make the language more dynamic and easier to learn and use. However, the Dart VM does a good job of inferring the range of integers, and optimizes whenever possible. Here, we provide a number of discussions and tips to give your code the highest performance possible when it involves numerical computing.

How to do it...

The VM uses three integer types internally and switches between them behind the scenes as numbers grow and shrink in size. They are as follows:

- smi (small integer): You can think of this integer type as being 32 bit on a 32-bit machine and 64 bit on a 64-bit machine
- mint (medium integer): This integer type is always 64 bit
- bigint (big integer): The machine's RAM is the limit for this integer type

You can't use these classes in the Dart code; the VM automatically promotes an integer from smi to mint, and to bigint when necessary. However, you can get better performance if you ensure that your integer values stay in smaller ranges. For example, refer to the `integer_promotion.dart` file:

```dart
import 'dart:math';

void main() {
    int points = 42; // starts as a smi
    print(points);   // 42
    points = pow(points, 10); // becomes a mint
    print(points); // 17080198121677824
    points = pow(points, 3); // becomes a bigint
    print(points);   // 4982860305982791130999719267476828621962135732224
}
```

> Don't use the `bigint` range unless you really have to because this will result in a performance hit. If possible, stay in the smi range; if not, use the mint range.

Working with lists of numbers, numbers can be stored in an object `List()`, or in a generic type `List<int>` or `List<double>`. While the latter is better than the first, it is best to use Dart `typed lists`, which is available in the `dart:typed_data` package such as `UInt8List`, `Int64List`, or `Float32List`. So instead of using `List<double>`, which is always slower, use `Float32List` or `Floact64List`. Be careful when using web apps; not every browser supports `typed_data` yet. For example, Internet Explorer 10 supports it, but version 9 does not.

> Use typed lists when computing; calculations will run more efficiently.

Taking into account these considerations, it is advisable to benchmark a few versions of your app with different number of type usages (for example, comparing `Float32List` with `Float64List`, or even with a normal list), in order to see which one performs best in the specific context of your app.

How it works...

Advice mostly arises from the way the Dart VM can optimize working with the different numerical types. Because JavaScript can't use the exact same optimizations, dart2js sometimes works differently; refer to the next section for special advice in this case.

Small machine integers (smis) fit in a register and can be loaded and stored directly in a field instead of being fetched from memory because they never require memory allocation. That's why they are fast. However, their range depends on the CPU architecture, so assume a 31-bit range unless you require more bits. Operations with bigints cannot be optimized by the VM. Working with `doubles` is very efficient because they are unboxed, that is, they don't need to be put on the heap.

Dart-typed lists can only store numbers and not null values. They behave as an array of bounded integer and float values, each entry containing its value, and the VM optimizes their usage. Typed lists are most of the time much more compact, providing better memory and CPU cache usage; for example, if you need only 8 bits of precision, use `Int8List`. They are also faster to process when **Garbage Collection** (**GC**) occurs because they never store object references. So they don't have to be scanned by the GC.

There's more...

From a language design point of view, using the `int` and `num` types is the best; the Dart VM experts would probably want us to work only with `double` because that is where most optimizations can be done.

Working with JavaScript

In JavaScript, every number is represented as `double` (it only knows the IEEE-754 type).

If your app will be used in the compiled JavaScript form, it is better to use only the `num` type. Also, use `is num` instead of testing `is int` or `is double` because the Dart VM and dart2js behave differently here too. If you insist on using the `int` type, stay within the smi range.

In any case, use Dart-typed lists as they map trivially to JavaScript-typed arrays. However, avoid `Int64List` or `Uint64List` because dart2js does not support 64-bit integers due to lack of support of typed data in Internet Explorer 9 (causing a runtime exception if used).

Parsing numbers

Avoid extensive use of `double.parse(String s)` or even `int.parse(String s)` as at the time of writing their performance was not optimized.

See also

> ▸ Consult `http://dartogreniyorum.blogspot.be/2013/05/performance-optimization-and-dart.html`, where the use of typed data results in a performance increase by two times

> ▸ You might also want to consult the *Benchmarking your app* recipe in *Chapter 2, Structuring, Testing, and Deploying an Application*

Using SIMD for enhanced performance

A lot of modern CPUs and GPUs provide **Single Instruction Multiple Data** (**SIMD**) support. Four 32-bit data values (integers or floats) can be processed in parallel with the help of 128-bit special registers. This provides a potential speedup of 400 percent for image processing, 3D graphics, audio processing, and other numeric computation algorithms. Also, machine-learning algorithms (such as for automatic speech recognition) that use a **Gauss Mixture Model** (**GMM**) benefit from SIMD.

How to do it...

Dart lets you work with this feature by using the special SIMD x types from the `typed_data` library. It offers the following four types:

> ▸ `Int32x4`, which represents four 32-bit integer values

> ▸ `Float32x4`, which represents four single-precision floating point values

> ▸ List structures to contain the 32-bit integer values, such as `Int32x4List`

> ▸ `Float32x4List`, list structure to contain the 32-bit floating point values

Let's see some examples of SIMD operations in `simd.dart`; the different types are highlighted in the following snippet:

```dart
import 'dart:typed_data';

void main() {
  var a = new Float32x4(14.1, 6.7, 56.3, 78.41);
  var b = new Float32x4(12.3, 5.4, 81.7, 13.43);
  Float32x4 sum = new Float32x4.zero(); //
  print(sum); // [0.000000, 0.000000, 0.000000, 0.000000]
  sum = a + b;
  print(sum); // [26.400002, 12.100000, 138.000000, 91.840004]
  print(sum.z); // 138.0
  // b.y = 3.14;  // --> NoSuchMethodError
  b = b.withY(3.14);
  print(b); // [12.300000, 3.140000, 81.699997, 13.430000]
  b = b.shuffle(Float32x4.WYXZ);
  print(b); // [13.430000, 3.140000, 12.300000, 81.699997]
  // a < b; // There is no such operator in Float32x4
  Int32x4 mask = a.greaterThan(b);   // Create selection mask.
  Float32x4 c = mask.select(a, b);    // Select.
  print(c); // [14.100000, 6.700000, 56.299999, 81.699997]
  // selectively applying an operation:
  Float32x4 v = new Float32x4(22.0, 33.0, 44.0, 55.0);
  // mask = [0xFFFFFFFF, 0xFFFFFFFF, 0xFFFFFFFF, 0x0]
  mask = new Int32x4.bool(true, true, false, true);
  // r = [4.0, 9.0, 16.0, 25.0].
  Float32x4 r = v - v;
  v = mask.select(r, v);
  print(v); // [0.000000, 0.000000, 44.000000, 0.000000]
}
```

 If your application needs a list of `Float32` objects and you can deploy them on an SIMD platform, then be sure to use `Float32x4List` instead of `List<Float32x4>` to get better performance.

How it works...

The `Float32x4` object offers the standard set of arithmetic operations and more. A `Float32x4` object is in fact an immutable object with operations that create new immutable `Float32x4` objects. The `Int32x4` object is more limited, being useful for comparison, branching, and selection. In code that is optimized for these types, the values are mapped directly to SIMD registers, and operations on them compile into a single SIMD instruction with no overhead. You can think of an SIMD value as a horizontal compartment being subdivided into four lanes, respectively called **x**, **y**, **z**, and **w**, as shown in the following screenshot:

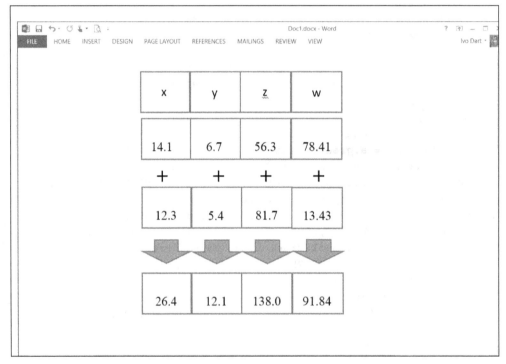

The SIMD architecture

An operation on two SIMD values happens on all the lanes simultaneously. With `.x` and other values, you can read the values of the individual lanes, but attention, this is slow. Because an SIMD value is immutable, a `b.y = value` statement is illegal. However, the `withX` methods let you do this, but again this is slow. Reordering values in one SIMD is done with a number of `shuffle` methods, where the lane order (WYXZ) indicates the new order. An SIMD instance contains four numbers, so comparisons such as `<` or `>=` cannot be defined. If you want to make `c` equal to the higher values of `a` and `b`, first you have to create a mask with the `greaterThan` operation, and then perform a `select` operation on it. An analogous masking technique is used if you want to perform an operation on some of the lanes only.

At this time, you can get this performance acceleration on all IA32/X64 platforms, and on ARM only if the processor supports NEON technology, and its implementation is pending for JavaScript. Thanks to the work of John McCutchan, Dart was the first web technology to use SIMD processing.

See also

- For more information on SIMD, refer to `http://en.wikipedia.org/wiki/SIMD`
- Dart can even beat the Java VM when using SIMD; for more information refer to `http://dartogreniyorum.blogspot.be/2013/05/dart-beats-java-in-numerical-computing.html`

4
Object Orientation

In this chapter, we will cover the following recipes:

- ► Testing and converting types
- ► Comparing two objects
- ► Using a factory constructor
- ► Building a singleton
- ► Using reflection
- ► Using mixins
- ► Using annotations
- ► Using the call method
- ► Using noSuchMethod
- ► Creating toJSON and fromJSON methods in your class
- ► Creating common classes for client and server apps

Introduction

Dart, although optionally typed, is an object-oriented language like Ruby, so it is an object. This is in contrast to JavaScript, where object orientation is not inherent in the language and was added later in different ad hoc ways. We can expect huge benefits from working with a real object-oriented language to build our client web applications. So, let's delve a bit deeper into the object-oriented nature of Dart, and find some new techniques and insights.

Testing and converting types

Everything in Dart is an object and has a type; an instance of a class descended from an object through a single inheritance chain, even null is of type Null. Type annotating a variable is not required in Dart, for example, contrary to Java. In this case, the variable is declared with `var` and is of type `dynamic`. Values sometimes have to be converted from one type to another. In order to avoid runtime type errors when the conversion fails, we can test if the value is of the type we want to cast it to before the conversion. For the code examples, refer to `types.dart`.

How to do it...

We can test and convert types with the help of the following steps:

1. We can test and show the type of an object, as shown in the following code:

```
void main() {
  var p = new Person();
  p.name = "Joe";
if (p is Person) {
    print('p is called ${p.name}');
    print('p is of type ${p.runtimeType}');             }
else {
    // p has value null and is of type Null
    print('p has value $p and is of type ${p.runtimeType}');
  }
}

class Person {
  String nmeame;
}
```

    The preceding code prints **p is of type Person**.

2. Conversion between types of variables:

    ❑   To convert everything to a string, use the `$` operator in string interpolation or the `toString()` method

    ❑   To convert a string `str` to int, use `int.parse(str)`

    ❑   To convert a string `str` to double, use `double.parse(str)`

    ❑   To handle a possible `FormatException` in the previous two conversions, use `try` / `catch`

    ❑   To convert int to double, use `toDouble()`

- ❑ To convert `double` to `int`, use `toInt()`, but truncation of the decimal part will occur

- ❑ To convert a string to `DateTime`, use `DateTime.parse(str)` with `try / catch`

- ❑ To handle a possible `FormatException` when `str` is not a recognizable date and time format

- ❑ To convert `DateTime` to a string, use `toLocal()`, `toUtc()`, or a `DateFormat` object (refer to the *Working with dates and times* recipe in *Chapter 3, Working with Data Types*)

- ❑ To convert `bool` to `int`, use the `int toInt(bool val) => val ? 1 : 0;` function

How it works...

To test if an object `p` is of a certain type, use the `is` (or its negation `is!`) operator. Because types are optional in Dart, you can only ask for `runtimeType` of an object, which is of type `Type`. The `p is Object` message is always true, and `null is T` (with T being a type) is only true if `T == null`.

The `toString()` method is a method of `Object` and returns **Instance of Type** by default, where **Type** is the class name of the object. Override this method to have more specific behaviors in your classes. In Dart, `bool` and `int` are two different types, but you can mimic C-like behavior by using a ternary operator in `toInt(bool)`.

 Conversion between types is not always safe; use `try/catch` if a `FormatException` occurs.

There's more...

There is also a shorter version, the `is` test `if (p is Person) { p.name = 'Bob'; }` can be shortened to `(p as Person).firstName = 'Bob';` with the as operator being a typecast of `p` to `Person` is done. However, you can only use this form when you are certain that `p` can be of that type; when `p` is null or not a `Person` Dart will throw an exception.

See also

- ▶ Refer to the *Working with dates and times* recipe in *Chapter 3, Working with Data Types* for date and time conversions

Comparing two objects

How can you determine whether two objects are equal or not? Basically, this is defined by objects (refer to the *How it works...* section of this recipe). Obviously, two equal objects will be of the same class (so the same type) and have the same value(s).

How to do it...

In the `comparing_objects` program, we define a class `Person`, override `==` and hashcode, and test the equality of some objects, as shown in the following code:

```
void main() {
  var p1 = new Person("Jane Wilkins", "485-56-7861", DateTime.
parse("1973-05-08"));
  var p2 = new Person("Barack Obama", "432-94-1282", DateTime.
parse("1961-08-04"));
  var p3 = p1;
  var p4 = new Person("Jane Wilkins", "485-56-7861", DateTime.
parse("1973-05-08"));

  // with == and hashCode from Object:
  // (comment out == and hashCode in class Person)
  print(p2==p1); //false: p1 and p2 are different
  print(p3==p1); //true:  p3 and p1 are the same object
  print(p4==p1); //false: p4 and p1 are different objects
  print(identical(p1, p3)); //true
  print(identical(p1, p4)); //false
  print(p1.hashCode); // 998736967
  print(p2.hashCode); // 676682609
  print(p3.hashCode); // 998736967
  // with specific == and hashCode for class Person:
  print(p2==p1); //false: p1 and p2 are different
  print(p3==p1); //true:  p3 and p1 are the same object
  print(p4==p1); //true: p4 and p1 are the same Person
  print(identical(p1, p3)); //true
  print(identical(p1, p4)); //false
  print(p1.hashCode); // 105660000000
  print(p2.hashCode); // -265428000000
  print(p3.hashCode); // 105660000000
}

class Person {
  String name;
```

```
String ssn; // social security number
DateTime birthdate;

Person(this.name, this.ssn, this.birthdate);
toString() => 'I am $name, born on $birthdate';
operator ==(Person other) => this.ssn == other.ssn;
int get hashCode => birthdate.millisecondsSinceEpoch;
}
```

How it works...

The `Object` superclass has a `bool ==(other)` method that defines the equality of objects. This returns `true` only when `this` and `other` are the same object, that is, they reference the same object in the (heap) memory. This is the default behavior, unless you override it in your classes. The `!=` operator is the negation of this. Another way to test this is the top-level identical function from `dart:core bool identical(Object a, Object b)`.

Every object has an integer `hashcode` returned by the getter `int get hashCode`. Two objects that are equal have the same hashcode, but this can differ between two runs of a program. Any subclass can have its own version to define equality between its objects.

 If you override `==` in a class, you should override `hashCode` as well for consistency.

There's more...

If you want to use instances of a class as keys in maps, then you have to overload the `==` operator and the `hashCode` method.

See also

▸ Refer to the *Working with dates and times* recipe in *Chapter 3, Working with Data Types* for date and time conversions

Using a factory constructor

Dart gives us many flexible and succinct ways to build objects through constructors:

> ▸ With optional arguments, such as in the `Person` constructor where `salary` is optional:

```
class Person{
  String name;
  num salary
  Person(this.name, {this.salary});
}
```

> ▸ With named constructors (a bonus for readable self-documenting code), for example, where a `BankAccount` for the same owner as `acc` is created:

```
BankAccount.sameOwner(BankAccount acc): owner = acc.owner;
```

> ▸ With `const` constructors, as shown in the following code:

```
class ImmutableSquare {
finalnum length;
static finalImmutableSquare ONE = const ImmutableSquare(1);
constImmutableSquare(this.length);
}
```

However, modern modular software applications require more flexible ways to build and return objects, often extracted into a factory design pattern (for more information, refer to `http://en.wikipedia.org/wiki/Factory_(object-oriented_programming)`). Dart has this pattern built right into the language with factory constructors.

How to do it...

In the `factory` program, we explore some usage examples as follows:

1. Returning an object from a cache, as shown in the following code:

```
main() {
  var sv = new Service('Credit Card Validation');
  sv.serve('Validate card number');
  Person p = new Person("S. Hawking");
  print(p); // S. Hawking
}

class Service {
  final String name;
  bool mute = false;
```

```
  // _cache is library-private, thanks to the _ in front of its
name.
    static final Map<String, Service> _cache = <String, Service>{};

    Service._internal(this.name);

    factory Service(String name) {
      if (_cache.containsKey(name)) {
        return _cache[name];
      } else {
        final serv = new Service._internal(name);
        _cache[name] = serv;
        return serv;
      }
    }

    void serve(String msg) {
        if (!mute) {
          print(msg); // Validate card number

        }
      }
    }
```

2. Creating an object from a subtype, as shown in the following code:

```
class Person {
  factory Person(name) => new Teacher(name);
}

class Teacher implements Person {
  String name;
  Teacher(this.name);
  toString() => name;
}
```

Using an `abstract` class, `abstract_factory1-3` shows you how to use a factory constructor with it:

► The factory constructor can be used with an `abstract` class, as shown in the following code:

```
void main() {
  // factory as a default implementation of an abstract class:
  Cat cat = new Animal();
  var catSound = cat.makeNoise();
```

```
    print(catSound); // Meow
}

abstract class Animal {
    String makeNoise();
    factory Animal() => new Cat();
}

class Cat implements Animal { String makeNoise() => 'Meow'; }
class Dog implements Animal { String makeNoise() => 'Woef';}
```

▶ Another example of using the factory constructor with an abstract class is shown in the following code:

```
import 'dart:math';

void main() {
    Cat an = new Animal();
    print(an.makeNoise());
}

abstract class Animal {
    // simulates computation:
    factory Animal() {
        var random = new Random();
        if (random.nextBool())
          return new Cat();
        else
          return new Dog();
    }
}

class Cat implements Animal { String makeNoise() => 'Meow'; }
class Dog implements Animal { String makeNoise() => 'Woef'; }
```

▶ The next example also illustrates how to use a factory constructor with an abstract class:

```
void main() {
    Cat cat = new Animal("cat");
    Dog dog = new Animal("dog");
    print(cat.makeNoise());
}

abstract class Animal {
```

```
    String makeNoise();
    factory Animal(String type) {
        switch(type) {
          case "cat":
            return new Cat();
          case "dog":
            return new Dog();
          default:
            throw "The '$type' is not an animal";
        }
      }
    }

    class Cat implements Animal { String makeNoise() => 'Meow'; }
    class Dog implements Animal { String makeNoise() => 'Woef'; }
```

How it works...

In the first example, we had a number of services gathered in `_cache`, but each service can be created only once through a private `_internal` constructor; every named service is unique.

In the second example, we showed that a class with a factory constructor cannot be directly extended; instead, the subtype must implement the class. In the third example, we showed three variants of using an abstract class with a factory constructor.

Why and when would you want to use a factory constructor? Sometimes, we don't want a constructor to always make a new object of the class it is in. The following are some use cases for a factory constructor; the code examples show you a usage example for all of them:

  ▸ To return an object from a cache in order to reuse it

  ▸ To create an object from a subtype of the class the constructor is in

  ▸ To limit the instances to one unique object (the singleton pattern)

  ▸ Even an abstract class can contain a factory constructor to return a default implementation of a concrete class (this is the only way an abstract class can have a constructor)

The factory constructor is invoked just as any other constructor by `new`. The consumer of the class doesn't know the constructor is really a factory, so you can refactor regular constructors into factory constructors to enhance flexibility without forcing clients to change their code. The factory could also involve much more preparation and computation, and the consumer of the class may not be aware of it; the consumer may just create a new instance. A factory invoking a private constructor is also a common pattern, as we saw in the first example.

The keyword `this` cannot be used inside a factory constructor because the constructor has no access to it.

There's more...

The factory constructor is also extensively used in standard libraries, for example, the DOM type `CustomEvent` only has factory constructors. This is because the browser has to produce these instances; the Dart object is just a wrapper. Another use case in Dart can be that you want to abstract an implementation of a certain feature. Some browsers support it natively, while others don't. You can then look into the factory to see whether the browser can handle it and then choose the right implementation according to the capabilities of the browser.

Building a singleton

In some cases, you only need one unique instance of a class because this is simply enough for the app you're working with, or perhaps to save resources. This recipe shows you how to do this in Dart.

How to do it...

The `singleton` example shows how to do this (substitute your singleton class name for `Immortal`). Use a factory constructor to implement the singleton pattern, as shown in the following code:

```
class Immortal {
    static final Immortal theOne = new Immortal._internal('Connor
MacLeod');
    String name;
    factory Immortal(name) => theOne;
    // private, named constructor
    Immortal._internal(this.name); }

main() {
    var im1 = new Immortal('Juan Ramirez');
    var im2 = new Immortal('The Kurgan');
    print(im1.name);                    // Connor MacLeod
    print(im2.name);                    // Connor MacLeod
    print(Immortal.theOne.name);    // Connor MacLeod
    assert(identical(im1, im2));
}
```

All `Immortal` instances are the same object.

How it works...

The `Immortal` class contains an object of its own type, which instantiates itself by calling the private `_internal` constructor. Because it will be unique, we declare it as static. The factory constructor always returns this instance; only one instance of the `Singleton` class (named `Immortal` here) can ever exist in the executing isolate. It has to be a factory constructor because only this type can return a value. The code can even be shortened, shown as follows:

```
class Singleton {
  factory Singleton() => const Singleton._internal_();
  const Singleton._internal_();
}
```

Using reflection

The Dart mirror-based reflection API (contained in the `dart:mirrors` library) provides a powerful set of tools to reflect on code. This means that it is possible to introspect the complete structure of a program and discover all the properties of all the objects. In this way, methods can be invoked reflectively. It will even become possible to dynamically evaluate code that was not yet specified literally in the source code. An example of this would be calling a method whose name was provided as an argument because it is looked up in the database table.

Getting ready

The part of your code that uses reflection should have the following import code:

```
import 'dart:mirrors';
```

How to do it...

To perform reflection we perform the following actions:

▶ In the `reflection` project, we use a class `Embrace` to reflect upon:

```
void main() {
    var embr = new Embrace(5);
    print(embr);   // Embraceometer reads 5
    embr.strength += 5;
    print(embr.toJson()); // {strength: 10}
    var embr2 = new Embrace(10);
    var bigHug = embr + embr2;
    // Start reflection code:
```

- Use of `MirrorSystem`, as shown in the following code:

```
final MirrorSystem ms = currentMirrorSystem();
 // Iterating through libraries
ms
   .libraries
   .forEach((Uri name, LibraryMirror libMirror){
      print('$name $libMirror');
   });
```

- Use of `InstanceMirror` and `ClassMirror`, as shown in the following code:

```
InstanceMirror im = reflect(embr);
InstanceMirror im2 = im.invoke(#toJson, []);
print(im2.reflectee); // {strength: 10}
ClassMirror cm = reflectClass(Embrace);
ClassMirror cm2 = im.type;
printAllDeclarationsOf(cm);
InstanceMirror im3 = cm.newInstance(#light, []);
print(im3.reflectee.strength);
im3.reflectee.withAffection();
}

printAllDeclarationsOf(ClassMirror cm) {
   for (var k in cm.declarations.keys)    print(MirrorSystem.
getName(k));
print(MirrorSystem.getName(m.simpleName));
}

class Embrace  {
   num _strength;
   num get strength => _strength;
   set strength(num value) => _strength=value;
   Embrace(this._strength);
   Embrace.light(): _strength=3;
   Embrace.strangle(): _strength=100;
Embrace operator +(Embrace other) =>                      new
Embrace(strength + other.strength);
   String toString() => "Embraceometer reads $strength";
   Map toJson() => {'strength': '$_strength'};

withAffection() {
     for (var no=0; no <= 3; no++) {
       for (var s=0; s <=5; s++) { strength = s; }
     }
   }
}
```

▸ Running the previous program produces the following output:

Embraceometer reads 5

{strength: 10}

dart:core LibraryMirror on 'dart.core'

dart:mirrors LibraryMirror on 'dart.mirrors'

dart:nativewrappers LibraryMirror on ''

dart:typed_data LibraryMirror on 'dart.typed_data'

dart:async LibraryMirror on 'dart.async'

dart:convert LibraryMirror on 'dart.convert'

dart:collection LibraryMirror on 'dart.collection'

dart:_internal LibraryMirror on 'dart._internal@0x1f109d24'

dart:isolate LibraryMirror on 'dart.isolate'

dart:math LibraryMirror on 'dart.math'

dart:builtin LibraryMirror on 'builtin'

dart:io LibraryMirror on 'dart.io'

file:///F:/Dartiverse/ADartCookbook/book/Chapter 4 - Object orientation/code/ reflection/bin/reflection.dart LibraryMirror on ''

{strength: 10}

_strength

strength

strength=

+

toString

toJson

withAffection

Embrace

Embrace.light

Embrace.strangle

3

How it works...

The `currentMirrorSystem` class returns a `MirrorSystem` object on the current isolate; the `libraries` getter gives you the list of libraries in the scope of the current code.

The `InstanceMirror` subclass is a representation of an instance of an object and `ClassMirror` is the representation of the class definition.

Use the top-level `reflect` method on an object to get `InstanceMirror`. This allows you to dynamically invoke code on the object producing another `InstanceMirror`; using its `reflectee` property gives you access to the actual instance.

Note that the invoke method takes as its first argument a symbol (recognizable from its # prefix) for the method name. Symbols were introduced in Dart because they survive minification.

The top-level `reflectClass` method on a class results in `ClassMirror`; the same type of object is given by calling `type` on `InstanceMirror` of that class. The `ClassMirror` class has a `declarations` getter that returns a map from the names of the declarations to the mirrors on them. Static methods can be called on `ClassMirror`.

For every type of object in Dart, there exists a corresponding mirror object. So we have `VariableMirror`, `MethodMirror`, `ClassMirror`, `LibraryMirror`, and so on. Invoking `newInstance` on a `ClassMirror` class with the name of a constructor as a symbol produces `InstanceMirror`; you can then call methods on the real object via `reflectee`.

There's more...

There are some things we should be aware of when using reflection:

▶ The mirror API is still evolving, so expect some additions and adjustments in the future. The implementation is most complete for code running in the Dart VM.

▶ Mirroring in dart2js lags a bit behind. The processes of minifying and tree shaking your app performed by dart2js will generally not detect the reflected code. So the use of reflection at runtime might fail, resulting in `noSuchMethod()` errors. To prevent this from happening, use the `Mirrors` annotation, as shown in the following code, which helps the dart2js compiler to generate a smaller code:

```
@MirrorsUsed(override:'*')
import 'dart:mirrors';
```

▶ One of the restrictions is the reflections across isolates. At the time of writing this book, reflection only works if the reflection code and the object being reflected are running in the same isolate.

▶ Suppose you have an undocumented method that returns a Future value and you want to know the properties and methods of that object without digging into the source code. Run the following code snippet:

```
import 'dart:mirrors';

undocumentedMethod().then((unknown){
        var r = reflect(unknown).type;   // ClassMirror
        var m = r.declarations;
for (var k in m.declarations.keys) print(MirrorSystem.getName(k));
});
```

See also

▶ When you want to use reflection in the code, which has to be minified and tree shaken, read the *Shrinking the size of your app* recipe in *Chapter 1, Working with Dart Tools*

Using mixins

In Dart, just like in Ruby, your classes can use mixins to assign a certain behavior to your class. Say an object must be able to store itself, so its class mixes in a class called `Persistable` that defines `save()` and `load()` methods. From then on, the original class can freely use the mixed-in methods. The mechanism is not used for specialized subclassing or is-a relationships, so it doesn't use inheritance. This is good because Dart uses a single inheritance, so you want to choose your unique direct superclass with care.

How to do it...

▶ Look at the `mixins` project; the `Embrace` class from the previous recipe needs to persist itself, so it mixes with the abstract class `Persistable`, thereby injecting the save and load behavior. Then, we can apply the `save()` method to the `embr` object, thereby executing the code of the mixin as follows:

```
void main() {
  var embr = new Embrace(5);
```

▶ Using the mixins methods, as shown in the following code:

```
    print(embr.save(embr.strength));
    print(embr is Movement); // true
    print(embr is Persistable); // true
}
```

- Mixing in `Persistable`, as shown in the following code:

```
class Embrace extends Movement with Persistable {
  // code omitted, see previous recipe
}

class Movement {
  String name;
  Movement();
  }
```

- Defining `Persistable`, as shown in the following code:

```
abstract class Persistable {
  save(var s) {
    // saving in data store
    return "You are saved with strength $s!";
  }
  load() => "You are loaded!";
}
```

The previous program produces the output **You are saved with strength 5!**

How it works...

The abstract class `Persistable` is mixed in with the keyword `with`. The class `Embrace` is a subclass of class `Movement`, `Embrace` is `Movement`; if you don't have a direct superclass, as shown in the following code:

```
class Embrace extends Object with Persistable
```

So it means that in order to use a mixin, you will always need to extend a class. Objects of the class `Embrace` are also of the mixed-in type `Persistable`.

There's more...

The class that is mixed in is usually an abstract class, but it doesn't have to be. You can also mix in several classes to give a taste of multiple inheritance, as shown in the following code:

```
class Developer extends Person with Intellectual, Addicted
```

The mixed-in class has to obey some restrictions as follows:

- It must not declare a constructor
- Its superclass is an object
- It may not contain calls to the superclass

The mixin concept very much resembles the implementation of an interface mechanism, which exists in many other languages. However, it is much more powerful because the mixed in class(es) can contain real code that can be executed, whereas interfaces can't contain code; only definitions of methods. So that's why using mixins is a good practice.

 Always examine your inheritance relationship to see if it can be better described by a mixin than with a superclass.

In Dart, you can also use the `implements` keyword; a class can implement one or more other classes. What's the difference between implementing and mixing in? Implementing means that the class provides its own code for the public methods from the class it implements, while mixing in means that the class can use the code from the `mixin` class itself.

Using annotations

Dart shares with other languages such as Java and C# the ability to attach (or annotate) variables, classes, functions, methods, and other Dart program structures with metadata words preceded by an @ sign. This is done to give more information about the structure, or indicate that it has a special characteristic or behavior. Examples are `@override`, `@deprecated`, and `@observable` (used in Polymer), so they are liberally used by the Dart team. Also, `Angular.dart` uses them abundantly. Moreover, you can also define your own annotations.

How to do it...

In the project `annotations`, we gave our `Embrace` class the metadata `@ToFix`. The `strangle` method is denoted by `@deprecated`, and we indicate with `@override` in `Embrace` that we want to override the method `consumedCalories` inherited from `Movement`, as shown in the following code:

```
const Anno = "Meta";

void main() {
  var embr = new Embrace(5);
  print(embr);
  var str = new Embrace. strangle();
}

@Anno
@ToFix("Improve the algorithms", "Bill Gates")
class Embrace {
// code ommitted, see previous recipes
```

```
  @deprecated
    Embrace.strangle(): _strength = 100;

  @override consumedCalories() { }  //        warning!


  }

class Movement {
    String Name;
    Movement();
    consumedCalories() {
      // calculation of calories
    }
}

class ToFix {
    final String note, author, date;
    const ToFix(this.note, this.author, {this.date});
}
```

How it works...

The `@deprecated` instance is used to indicate something that you no longer want users of your library to use, and that will probably stop working in a future version. When the analyzer in Dart Editor sees this annotation, it marks the code component that follows (and everywhere it is used) with a strike-through line. Moreover, it will give a warning: **'...' is deprecated**. The `@override` instance is also a good (but not necessary) indication that you want to override an inherited behavior. Here, the editor also uses this instance to point to possible bugs; if you had written `@override consumedcalories()`, then you would get the warning `Method does not override an inherited method`; so typos are eliminated.

To make your own annotations, you must make sure that it is defined as a constant expression that starts with an identifier, such as `const Anno` in the example, which could be used as `@Anno`. More specifically, it must be a reference to a compile-time constant variable or call to a constant constructor. We used the class `ToFix` to give our class the annotation `@ToFix("Improve the algorithms")`.

There's more...

Annotations are defined in Dart through the class `Annotation` in the `analyzer` library. With the reflection mirror library (see the *Using reflection* recipe), it is possible to extract metadata at runtime and use its values to influence program execution.

See also

▶   See the annotations used in `Angular.dart` in *Chapter 11, Angular Dart Recipes*

Using the call method

This is a hidden gem in Dart. It enables you to give a parameter to an object, thereby invoking the `call` method from the object's class.

How to do it...

See its usage in the `call` project, as shown in the following code:

```
var u = "Julia";

void main() {
  var embr = new Embrace(5);
```

The call method can be used in the following ways:

1. Invoke `call`, as shown in the following code:

    ```
    embr(u); // callable method!
    var m = new Mult();
    print(m(3, 4));
    }

    class Embrace {
      // see code in recipe: Using reflection
    ```

2. Define the `call` method, as shown in the following code:

    ```
    call(var user) { print("$user is called, and hugged with
    strength $strength!"); }
      }

    class Mult{
      call(int a, int b) => a * b;
    }
    ```

We get the following output on the screen:

Julia is called, and hugged with strength 5!

12

How it works...

We pass the value u to the embr object in the embr(u) call, which invokes the call method. This method defines what the instances of your class do when invoked as functions via the () syntax. The advantage of using this in a normal class is perhaps not that clear. It is more useful when making a class that in fact wants to emulate a function, such as the Mult class. An object of this call can take two integers and return their product. This example is trivial and not worth writing a special class for it, but there are cases where this ability can be put to use.

There's more...

The Mult class contains only one function. We could also have written it as a Multi function, as shown in the following code:

```
int Multi(int a, int b) => a * b;
```

We could have even invoked it with print(Multi(3, 4)); // 12.

All functions in Dart are of type Function, but we can be more specific by defining a typedef. A typedef is a way to give a name to a function's signature, that is, the type of its arguments and return type. The typedef IntOp generalizes the type of Multi, as shown in the following code:

```
typedef int IntOp(int a, int b);
Then we can write for example, when f is defined as a Function:
assert(Multi is IntOp);
f = Multi;
print(f(3, 4)); // 12
assert(f is IntOp);
```

Using noSuchMethod

When a method is called on an object, and this method does not exist in its class, or any of its superclasses in the inheritance tree, then noSuchMethod() from Object is called. The default behavior of noSuchMethod is to throw a NoSuchMethodError, **method not found: 'methodname'**. However, Dart can do more; as in some other dynamic languages, every class can implement noSuchMethod to make its behavior more adaptive and flexible. This is because of the fact that Dart is dynamically typed, so it is possible to call a method that does not exist in a dynamic variable. In Java, you get a compile time error for this. In Dart too, an error is thrown but at runtime. By using noSuchMethod(), we can circumvent this and put it to our use.

How to do it...

See `noSuchMethod` in action in the `nosuchmethod` project:

```
void main() {
  var embr = new Embrace(5);
  print(embr.missing("42", "Julia")); // is a missing method!
}

@proxy
class Embrace {
  // see code in previous recipes
  @override
  noSuchMethod(Invocation msg) => "got ${msg.memberName} "
            "with arguments ${msg.positionalArguments}";
}
```

This script gives the output **got Symbol("missing") with arguments [42, Julia]**.

How it works...

When `missing` is called and not found, `noSuchMethod` is found and executed instead. The exact signature of the method is `noSuchMethod(Invocation msg)`. When it is invoked, an object `msg` of type `Invocation` is passed to it, which contains the names of the method and its arguments. If `noSuchMethod` returns a value, that value becomes the result of the original `Invocation`. `Invocation` also has Boolean getters `isMethod`, `isAccessor`, `isGetter`, and `isSetter` to find out whether the called method was a normal method, getter, or setter. With this information being passed, we could do something more useful than just print it, as shown in the following code:

```
noSuchMethod(Invocation msg) =>
  msg.memberName == #meth1 ? Function.apply(meth2,
                        msg.positionalArguments,
                        msg.namedArguments)
        : super.noSuchMethod(msg);
```

Here, we check whether the called method was `meth1` (notice that `memberName` is of type `Symbol`) and if so, we call the `meth2` method by passing the supplied arguments. Calling `meth2` is done through the static method `apply()` in the `Function` class, which allows functions to be called in a generic fashion. Use the `@override` annotation to indicate that you are intentionally overriding a member. Use the `@proxy` annotation on the class header itself to avoid analyzer warnings if you use `noSuchMethod()` to implement every possible getter, setter, and method for a class.

There's more...

Another good reason to use `noSuchMethod` is to reduce boilerplate code when writing a lot of similar methods. To make sure that code completion still works, use the following structure:

```
abstract class Class1Api {
  method1();
  method2();
  //...
}

class Class1 implements Class1Api {
  noSuchMethod(Invocation inv) {
    //...
  }
}

main() {
  Class1 cl = new Class1();
  // cl.  // remove comment and type cl. to see method1()
          // and so on in code completion
}
```

All the methods that will implement in `noSuchMethod` are summed up in the abstract class `Class1Api`, and then the code completion list will present them. See the code in the `boilerplate.dart` file and the following screenshot:

See also

▸ See the *Using annotations* recipe in this chapter for more information on `@override` and `@proxy`

Making toJSON and fromJSON methods in your class

JavaScript Object Notation (**JSON**) is probably the most widely used data format in web applications, so it is a common requirement for a class to be able to serialize its objects to JSON strings, or reconstruct objects from JSON strings.

Getting ready

JSON is lightweight (not as verbose as XML) and text-based, so it is easily readable by humans. It starts from the notion that the state (or content) of an object is in fact like a map; the keys are the field names, and their values are the concrete data stored in the fields. For example, (see project `json/job.dart`), say we have a class `Job` defined, as shown in the following code:

```
class Job {
  String type;
  int salary;
  String company;
  Job(this.type, this.salary, this.company);
}
```

Next, we construct a job object with the following code:

```
var job = new Job("Software Developer", 7500, "Julia Computing  LLC")
;
```

Then, it can be represented as the following JSON string:

```
'{
    "type": "Software Developer",
    "salary": 7500,
    "company": "Julia Computing LLC"
}'
```

The values can themselves be lists or maps or lists of maps. For more information about JSON, refer to `http://en.wikipedia.org/wiki/JSON`.

How to do it...

▶ The following is the code to give our class JSON functionality:

```
import 'dart:convert';

class Job {
  String type;
  int salary;
  String company;
  Job(this.type, this.salary, this.company);
```

▶ The following is the code to encode or serialize data:

```
String toJson() {
  var jsm = new Map<String, Object>();
  jsm["type"] = type;
  jsm["salary"] = salary;
  jsm["company"] = company;
  var jss = JSON.encode(jsm);
  return jss;
}
```

▶ The following is the code to decode or deserialize data:

```
Job.fromJson(String jsonStr) {
  Map jsm = JSON.decode(jsonStr);
  this.type = jsm["type"];
  this.salary = jsm["salary"];
  this.company = jsm["company"];
  }
}
void main() {
 var job = new Job("Software Developer", 7500, "Julia Computing
LLC") ;
 var jsonStr = job.toJson();
 print(jsonStr);
 var job2 = new Job.fromJson(jsonStr);
 assert(job2 is Job);
 assert(job2.toJson() == jsonStr);
}
```

The output of jsonStr is **{"type":"Software Developer","salary":7500,"company":"Julia Computing LLC"}**.

The assert statements confirm that the decoded object is of type Job and is equal to the JSON string we started from.

How it works...

A JSON string can be stored in a file or database, or sent over the network to a server. So our class needs to be able to:

▶ Write its objects out in JSON format, which is also called serializing or encoding; we'll conveniently call this method `toJson()`

▶ Read a JSON string and construct an object (or many objects) from it; this is called deserializing or decoding, and we'll make a method `fromJson()` to do just this

Part of the work is done by functions in the imported `dart:convert` library, which produces and consumes JSON data, respectively:

▶ `JSON.encode()`: This serializes a Dart object into a JSON string, ready to be stored or sent over a network

▶ `JSON.decode()`: This builds Dart objects from a string containing JSON data, which is just read from storage or received over the network

These functions on `JSON` (which is an object of the class `JSONCodec`) can process data from the types `null`, `num`, `bool`, `String`, `List`, and `Map` automatically and also from a combination of these (the keys of the map need to be strings). In our `Job` class, the data is processed, as explained in the following points:

▶ `toJson()` makes the map from the object and then calls `JSON.encode()` on it to return a JSON string

▶ `fromJson()` (conveniently implemented as a named constructor) takes the JSON string, calls `JSON.decode()` to return a map, and builds the object

There's more...

If your data is not that complicated, you can build the JSON string in the code yourself, possibly as a getter, as shown in the following snippet:

```
String get toJson => '{"type": "$type", "salary": "$salary",
"company": "$company" } ';
```

 If you have to construct JSON strings literally in your code, make sure to always use double quotes to indicate strings; Dart single quotes cannot be used here.

When an object contains other objects (composition or association, such as a `BankAccount` object containing a `Person` object for the owner), the `fromJson()` and `toJson()` methods from the outer object will call the corresponding methods with the same name for all the contained objects.

If you want a more sophisticated solution that supports the encoding and decoding of arbitrary objects, look for the jsonx package on pub, by Man Hoang. This library can decode a JSON string into a strongly typed object, which gets type checking and code completion support, or encodes an arbitrary object into a JSON string. When working with JSON, it is preferred to validate it; this can be done online at http://jsonlint.com/.

Creating common classes for client and server apps

In distributed apps such as the client-server pattern, you often want to work with the same model classes on both ends. Why? Because client input needs to be validated at the client side and for this, we need the model in the client app. Data has to pass through the model before being stored so that if we want to store the data in a client database (indexed_db) as well as in a server data store, we need the model on both the sides.

How to do it...

You can see how common classes are created for client and server apps in the client_server_db app. This is a to-do application; the client is started from web/app.html and the server is started from bin/server.dart. The client stores the to-do data in indexed_db, while the server stores the data in memory. Both client and server need the model classes.

The project structure is shown in the following screenshot:

Common library

How it works...

If you want to be able to import your common model library from another package, the files must be under the `lib` directory. In this example, we see from `pubspec.yaml` that the name of the app is `client_server`. The model (with the `Task` and `Tasks` classes) has its own folder `lib/model`, which contains the model classes defined in the `shared_model` library within `lib/shared_model.dart`. The client-app `web/app.dart` uses `indexed_db`; it therefore imports a library `idb_client` to work with `indexed_db`, as shown in the following code:

```
import 'package:client_server/idb_client.dart';
```

The `idb_client` library, defined in `lib/idb_client.dart`, imports the `shared_ model` library, as shown in the following code:

```
library idb_client;

import 'package:client_server/shared_model.dart';
import 'dart:async';
import 'dart:html';
import 'dart:indexed_db';
import 'dart:convert';

part 'idb/idb.dart';
part 'view/view.dart';
```

In this way, the client app knows about the model. The server app also knows about the model by importing it (see `bin/server.dart`):

```
import 'dart:io';
import 'dart:convert';
import 'package:client_server/shared_model.dart';
// rest of code
```

There's more...

Here's another common use case for shared models; say the class has a method that performs HTTP requests; on the client, you will use `HttpRequest` from the `dart:html` library, while on the server, you will use the one from `dart:io` instead. For security reasons, both `dart:io` and `dart:html` cannot be imported in the same library, so it's a common practice to define the shared class as an abstract class, and then delegate the concrete implementation of the `HttpRequest` method to both the client and server classes, which extend the shared abstract class.

See also

► Refer to the *Structuring an application* and *Making and using a library* recipes in *Chapter 2, Structuring, Testing, and Deploying an Application* for your app

5
Handling Web Applications

In this chapter, we will cover the following recipes:

- ▶ Responsive design
- ▶ Sanitizing HTML
- ▶ Using a browser's local storage
- ▶ Using an application cache to work offline
- ▶ Preventing an onSubmit event from reloading the page
- ▶ Dynamically inserting rows in an HTML table
- ▶ Using CORS headers
- ▶ Using keyboard events
- ▶ Enabling drag-and-drop
- ▶ Enabling touch events
- ▶ Creating a Chrome app
- ▶ Structuring a game project
- ▶ Using WebGL in your app
- ▶ Authorizing OAuth2 to Google services
- ▶ Talking with JavaScript
- ▶ Using JavaScript libraries

Introduction

Web applications are what Dart was made for, so it comes as no surprise that we have a lot of questions to deal with in this area. Dart here as a client language presents itself as an alternative to JavaScript (to which it compiles), but also to CoffeeScript and TypeScript. Because the language is a higher-level one and more robust, Dart enables developers to reach a higher rate of productivity. Its structure and tooling makes possible the building of complex software systems with large teams. When running in its virtual machine, Dart delivers a very shortened app startup time, and higher performance during execution. All these enhancements make Dart a prime choice to develop browser apps. You'll find topics in this chapter that deal with safety, browser storage, all kinds of interactive events, WebGL, and of course, working together with JavaScript.

Responsive design

Nowadays, users have to interact with computer screens of all different sizes, from smartphones and tablets to laptops, desktop monitors, and TVs. To design a web application in such a way that page layouts adapt intelligently to the user's screen width resolutions is called responsive design; for example, an advanced four-column layout 1292 pixels wide, on a 1025-pixel-wide screen, that autosimplifies into two columns when viewed on a tablet or smartphone. Its significance is now broadened to encompass web applications that respond to the user's environment intelligently, but also to make the web app adapt to the user's behavior. If you do only one thing to make your app's responsive design aware, apply what you read in this topic.

How to do it...

Add the following `<meta>` tag (the so-called `viewport` tag) to the `<head>` section of your HTML pages:

```
<meta name="viewport"
      content="width=device-width, initial-scale=1.0">
```

How it works...

This will set you up for cross-device layout peace of mind. `viewport` is another word for screen width and this tag was originally devised by Apple. Setting `content` to `"width=device-width"` will query your device for its standard width and set your layout width accordingly. To be extra certain that your layout will be displayed as you intended it, you can also set the zoom level with `content="initial-scale=1"`. This will make sure that upon opening the page, your layout will be displayed properly at a 1:1 scale; no zooming will be applied. You can even prevent any zooming by adding a third attribute value `"maximum-scale=1"`. However, you must make sure that everything is readable for everybody; using this would probably hinder people with visual problems.

See also

▶ If you want to start learning more about responsive design, a nice tutorial is available at `http://www.adamkaplan.me/grid/`

Sanitizing HTML

We've all heard of (or perhaps even experienced) **cross-site scripting** (**XSS**) attacks, where evil minded attackers try to inject client-side script or SQL statements into web pages. This could be done to gain access to session cookies or database data, or to get elevated access-privileges to sensitive page content. To verify an HTML document and produce a new HTML document that preserves only whatever tags are designated safe is called sanitizing the HTML.

How to do it...

Look at the web project `sanitization`. Run the following script and see how the text content and default sanitization works:

1. See how the default sanitization works using the following code:

```
var elem1 = new Element.html('<div class="foo">content</div>');
document.body.children.add(elem1);
var elem2 = new Element.html('<script class="foo">evil content</script><p>ok?</p>');
document.body.children.add(elem2);
```

The text `content` and `ok?` from `elem1` and `elem2` are displayed, but the console gives the message **Removing disallowed element <SCRIPT>**. So a script is removed before it can do harm.

2. Sanitize using `HtmlEscape`, which is mainly used with user-generated content:

```
import 'dart:convert' show HtmlEscape;
```

In `main()`, use the following code:

```
var unsafe = '<script class="foo">evil     content</
script><p>ok?</p>';
var sanitizer = const HtmlEscape();
print(sanitizer.convert(unsafe));
```

This prints the following output to the console:

```
&lt;script class=&quot;foo&quot;&gt;evil     content&lt;&#x2F;scrip
t&gt;&lt;p&gt;ok?&lt;&#x2F;p&gt;;
```

3. Sanitize using node validation. The following code forbids the use of a `<p>` tag in node1; only `<a>` tags are allowed:

```
var html_string = '<p class="note">a note aside</p>';
var node1 = new Element.html(
        html_string,
        validator: new NodeValidatorBuilder()
            ..allowElement('a', attributes: ['href'])
        );
```

The console prints the following output:

Removing disallowed element <p>

Breaking on exception: Bad state: No elements

4. A `NullTreeSanitizer` for no validation is used as follows:

```
final allHtml = const NullTreeSanitizer();
class NullTreeSanitizer implements NodeTreeSanitizer {
        const NullTreeSanitizer();
        void sanitizeTree(Node node) {}
}
```

It can also be used as follows:

```
var elem3 = new Element.html('<p>a text</p>');
elem3.setInnerHtml(html_string, treeSanitizer: allHtml);
```

How it works...

First, we have very good news: Dart automatically sanitizes all methods through which HTML elements are constructed, such as `new Element.html()`, `Element.innerHtml()`, and a few others. With them, you can build HTML hardcoded, but also through string interpolation, which entails more risks. The default sanitization removes all scriptable elements and attributes.

If you want to escape all characters in a string so that they are transformed into HTML special characters (such as ;&#x2F for a /), use the class `HTMLEscape` from `dart:convert` as shown in the second step. The default behavior is to escape apostrophes, greater than/less than, quotes, and slashes. If your application is using untrusted HTML to put in variables, it is strongly advised to use a `validation` scheme, which only covers the syntax you expect users to feed into your app. This is possible because `Element.html()` has the following optional arguments:

```
Element.html(String html, {NodeValidator validator, NodeTreeSanitizer
treeSanitizer})
```

In step 3, only `<a>` was an allowed tag. By adding more `allowElement` rules in cascade, you can allow more tags. Using `allowHtml5()` permits all HTML5 tags.

If you want to remove all control in some cases (perhaps you are dealing with known safe HTML and need to bypass sanitization for performance reasons), you can add the class `NullTreeSanitizer` to your code, which has no control at all and defines an object `allHtml`, as shown in step 4. Then, use `setInnerHtml()` with an optional named attribute `treeSanitizer` set to `allHtml`.

Using a browser's local storage

Local storage (also called the Web Storage API) is widely supported in modern browsers. It enables the application's data to be persisted locally (on the client side) as a map-like structure: a dictionary of key-value string pairs, in fact using JSON strings to store and retrieve data. It provides our application with an offline mode of functioning when the server is not available to store the data in a database. Local storage does not expire, but every application can only access its own data up to a certain limit depending on the browser. In addition, of course, different browsers can't access each other's stores.

Look at the following example, the `local_storage.dart` file:

```
import 'dart:html';

Storage local = window.localStorage;

void main() {
   var job1 = new Job(1, "Web Developer", 6500, "Dart Unlimited") ;
```

Perform the following steps to use the browser's local storage:

1. Write to a local storage with the key `Job:1` using the following code:
   ```
   local["Job:${job1.id}"] = job1.toJson;
   ButtonElement bel = querySelector('#readls');
   bel.onClick.listen(readShowData);
   }
   ```

2. A click on the button checks to see whether the key `Job:1` can be found in the local storage, and, if so, reads the data in. This is then shown in the data `<div>`:
   ```
   readShowData(Event e) {
      var key = 'Job:1';
      if(local.containsKey(key)) {
   // read data from local storage:
         String job = local[key];
         querySelector('#data').appendText(job);
      }
   }

   class Job {
      int id;
      String type;
      int salary;
      String company;
      Job(this.id, this.type, this.salary, this.company);
      String get toJson => '{ "type": "$type", "salary": "$salary",
   "company": "$company" } ';
   }
   ```

The following screenshot depicts how data is stored in and retrieved from local storage:

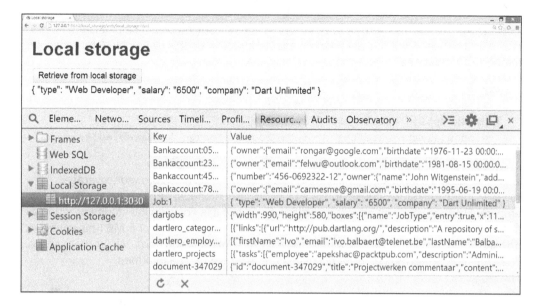

How it works...

You can store data with a certain key in the local storage from the Window class as follows using `window.localStorage[key] = data;` (both key and data are Strings).

You can retrieve it with `var data = window.localStorage[key];`.

In our code, we used the abbreviation `Storage local = window.localStorage;` because `local` is a map. You can check the existence of this piece of data in the local storage with `containsKey(key);` in Chrome (also in other browsers via **Developer Tools**). You can verify this by navigating to **Extra | Tools | Resources | Local Storage** (as shown in the previous screenshot) `window.localStorage` also has a length property; you can query whether it contains something with `isEmpty`, and you can loop through all stored values using the following code:

```
for(var key in window.localStorage.keys) {
String value = window.localStorage[key];
// more code
}
```

There's more...

Local storage can be disabled (by user action, or via an installed plugin or extension), so we must alert the user when this needs to be enabled; we can do this by catching the exception that occurs in this case:

```
try {
  window.localStorage[key] = data;
} on Exception catch (ex) {
  window.alert("Data not stored: Local storage is disabled!");
}
```

Local storage is a simple key-value store and does have good cross-browser coverage. However, it can only store strings and is a blocking (synchronous) API; this means that it can temporarily pause your web page from responding while it is doing its job storing or reading large amounts of data such as images. Moreover, it has a space limit of 5 MB (this varies with browsers); you can't detect when you are nearing this limit and you can't ask for more space. When the limit is reached, an error occurs so that the user can be informed.

 These properties make local storage only useful as a temporary data storage tool; this means it is better than cookies, but not suited for a reliable, database kind of storage.

Web storage also has another way of storing data called `sessionStorage` used in the same way, but this limits the persistence of the data to only the current browser session. So, data is lost when the browser is closed or another application is started in the same browser window.

See also

▸ For more information on the JSON format, refer to the *Making toJSON and fromJSON methods* recipe in *Chapter 4, Object Orientation in your class*

▸ A better alternative to simple local storage is IndexedDB; see the *Storing data locally in IndexedDB* recipe in *Chapter 9, Working with Databases*

Using application cache to work offline

When, for some reason, our users don't have web access or the website is down for maintenance (or even broken), our web-based applications should also work offline. The browser cache is not robust enough to be able to do this, so HTML5 has given us the mechanism of `ApplicationCache`. This cache tells the browser which files should be made available offline. The effect is that the application loads and works correctly, even when the user is offline. The files to be held in the cache are specified in a manifest file, which has a `.mf` or `.appcache` extension.

How to do it...

Look at the `appcache` application; it has a manifest file called `appcache.mf`.

1. The manifest file can be specified in every web page that has to be cached. This is done with the manifest attribute of the `<html>` tag:

   `<html manifest="appcache.mf">`

   If a page has to be cached and doesn't have the manifest attribute, it must be specified in the CACHE section of the manifest file. The manifest file has the following (minimum) content:

```
CACHE MANIFEST
# 2012-09-28:v3

CACHE:
Cached1.html
appcache.css
appcache.dart
http://dart.googlecode.com/svn/branches/bleeding_edge/dart/client/
dart.js

NETWORK:
*

FALLBACK:
/ offline.html
```

2. Run `cached1.html`. This displays the **This page is cached, and works offline!** text. Change the text to `This page has been changed!` and reload the browser. You don't see the changed text because the page is created from the application cache.

3. When the manifest file is changed (change version v1 to v2), the cache becomes invalid and the new version of the page is loaded with the **This page has been changed!** text.

4. The Dart script of the page, `appcache.dart`, should contain the following minimal code to access the cache:

```
main() {
   new AppCache(window.applicationCache);
}

class AppCache {
   ApplicationCache appCache;

   AppCache(this.appCache) {
```

```
        appCache.onUpdateReady.listen((e) => updateReady());
        appCache.onError.listen(onCacheError);
    }

    void updateReady() {
      if (appCache.status == ApplicationCache.UPDATEREADY) {
          // The browser downloaded a new app cache. Alert the user:
          appCache.swapCache();
          window.alert('A new version of this site is available.
    Please reload.');
        }
    }

    void onCacheError(Event e) {
        print('Cache error: ${e}');
        // Implement more complete error reporting to developers
    }
}
```

How it works...

The CACHE section in the manifest file enumerates all the entries that have to be cached. The NETWORK: and * options mean that to use all other resources, the user has to be online. FALLBACK specifies that offline.html will be displayed if the user is offline and a resource is inaccessible. A page is cached when either of the following is true:

▶   Its HTML tag has a manifest attribute pointing to the manifest file

▶   The page is specified in the CACHE section of the manifest file

The browser is notified when the manifest file is changed, and the user will be forced to refresh its cached resources. Adding a timestamp and/or a version number such as # 2014-05-18:v1 works fine. Changing the date or the version invalidates the cache, and the updated pages are again loaded from the server.

To access the browser's app cache from your code, use the window.applicationCache object. Make an object of the class AppCache, and alert the user when the application cache has become invalid (the status is **UPDATEREADY**) by defining an onUpdateReady listener.

There's more...

The other known states of the application cache are UNCACHED, IDLE, CHECKING, DOWNLOADING, and OBSOLETE. To log all these cache events, you could add the following listeners to the appCache constructor:

```
appCache.onCached.listen(onCacheEvent);
appCache.onChecking.listen(onCacheEvent);
appCache.onDownloading.listen(onCacheEvent);
appCache.onNoUpdate.listen(onCacheEvent);
appCache.onObsolete.listen(onCacheEvent);
appCache.onProgress.listen(onCacheEvent);
```

Provide an onCacheEvent handler using the following code:

```
void onCacheEvent(Event e) {
    print('Cache event: ${e}');
}
```

Preventing an onSubmit event from reloading the page

The default action for a submit button on a web page that contains an HTML form is to post all the form data to the server on which the application runs. What if we don't want this to happen?

How to do it...

Experiment with the submit application by performing the following steps:

1. Our web page submit.html contains the following code:

   ```
   <form id="form1" action="http://www.dartlang.org" method="POST">
     <label>Job:<input type="text" name="Job" size="75"></input>
     </label>
     <input type="submit" value="Job Search">
     </form>
   ```

   Comment out all the code in submit.dart. Run the app, enter a job name, and click on the **Job Search submit** button; the Dart site appears.

2. When the following code is added to `submit.dart`, clicking on the **no** button for a longer duration makes the Dart site appear:

```
import 'dart:html';

void main() {
  querySelector('#form1').onSubmit.listen(submit);
}

submit(Event e) {
    e.preventDefault();
  // code to be executed when button is clicked

}
```

How it works...

In the first step, when the **submit** button is pressed, the browser sees that the method is POST. This method collects the data and names from the input fields and sends it to the URL specified in `action` to be executed, which only shows the Dart site in our case.

To prevent the form from posting the data, make an event handler for the onSubmit event of the form. In this handler code, `e.preventDefault();` as the first statement will cancel the default submit action. However, the rest of the submit event handler (and even the same handler of a parent control, should there be one) is still executed on the client side.

Dynamically inserting rows in an HTML table

When displaying data coming from a database, you often don't know how many data records there will be. Our web page and the HTML table in it have to adapt dynamically. The following recipe describes how to do this.

How to do it...

Look at the `html_table` application. The web page contains two `<table>` tags:

```
<table id="data"></table>
<table id="jobdata"></table>
```

On running the app, you will be redirected to the following web page, which displays data in an HTML table:

Displaying data in an HTML table

The data is shown by the code in the `html_table.dart` file.

1. To make the code more flexible, the necessary element objects are declared up front; we use the class `Job` to insert some real data:

```
TableElement table;
TableRowElement row;
TableCellElement cell;
List<Job> jobs;

class Job {
  String type;
  int salary;
  String company;
  Job(this.type, this.salary, this.company);
}
```

The first table is shown with the preceding code.

2. Find the created table using the following query:

```
table = querySelector('#data');
```

3. Insert a row at index 0, and assign that row to a variable:

```
row = table.insertRow(0);
```

4. Insert a cell at index 0, assign that cell to a variable, and provide it with content, as shown in the following code:

```
cell = row.insertCell(0);
cell.text = 'cell 0-0';
```

5. Insert more cells with a message cascading approach and style them using the following code:

```
row.insertCell(1)
    ..text = 'cell 0-1'
    ..style.background = 'lime';
row.insertCell(2)
    ..text = 'cell 0-2'
    ..style.background = 'red';
```

6. Insert a new row at the end of the table:

```
row = table.insertRow(-1);
  row.insertCell(0).text = 'cell 1-0';
```

Here is the code to display data from a List, applying the same methods as above:

```
 var job1 = new Job("Software Developer", 7500, "Julia Computing
LLC") ;
 var job2 = new Job("Web Developer", 6500, "Dart Unlimited") ;
 var job3 = new Job("Project Manager", 10500, "Project Consulting
Inc.") ;
 jobs = new List<Job>();
 jobs
   ..add(job1)
   ..add(job2)
   ..add(job3);
table = querySelector('#jobdata');
// insert table headers:
InsertHeaders();
// inserting data:
InsertData();

InsertHeaders() {
    row = table.insertRow(-1);
    cell = row.insertCell(0);
    cell.text = "Jobtype";
    cell.style.background = 'lightblue';
```

```
      cell = row.insertCell(1);
      cell.text = "Salary";
      cell = row.insertCell(2);
      cell.text = "Company";
      cell.style.background = 'lightblue';
      }

   InsertData() {
     for (var job in jobs) {
        row = table.insertRow(-1);
        cell = row.insertCell(0);
        cell.text = job.type;
        cell = row.insertCell(1);
        cell.text = (job.salary).toString();
        cell = row.insertCell(2);
        cell.text = job.company;
      }
   }
```

7. The preceding code gets the content from the indicated cell:

    ```
    print(table.rows[1].cells[1].text); // prints 7500
    ```

How it works...

We use the methods `insertRow()` and `insertCell()` from `TableElement` and `TableRowElement`, respectively, and the properties of `TableCellElement`. Rows and columns are numbered from 0. As shown in the last line of the code, the content of specific cells can be retrieved by using an indexer `[]` on a specific row and cell.

See also...

▶   The API docs at `https://api.dartlang.org/apidocs/channels/stable/dartdoc-viewer/dart-dom-html.TableElement` will show you more useful methods

Using CORS headers

In the web application security model, the same-origin policy is an important concept. The basic principle is that content provided by unrelated websites must be strictly separated on the client side; otherwise, confidentiality or data integrity might be compromised, perhaps through cross-site scripting attacks. In other words, web pages or scripts running on pages can only access scripts or pages from the same domain as they came from; no access to other sites is allowed. For example, `http://www.example.com/dir/page2.html` cannot access `http://en.example.com/dir/other.html`. However, in a number of cases, this is too strict, as in AJAX calls with `HttpRequest` we have to load data from another server (refer to *Chapter 7, Working with Web Servers*). To make this possible, the CORS mechanism (cross-origin resource sharing) was developed, which is supported by most modern web browsers. This recipe will enable you to easily achieve this by performing the following steps.

How to do it...

The following steps show how you can configure your web server to add CORS headers:

1. When a web server sends CORS headers back in the response, the client is also allowed to send requests to servers in other domains. So in every request handling code, we must add a call to a method such as `addCorsHeaders` as shown in the following code:

```
void handleGet(HttpRequest request) {
  HttpResponse res = request.response;
  addCorsHeaders(res);
  // other code to prepare the response
  // …
  res.write(content);
  res.close();
}
```

2. Now we need to define the `addCorsHeaders` method; it contains the following code:

```
void addCorsHeaders(HttpResponse response) {
  response.headers.add('Access-Control-Allow-Origin', '*, ');
  response.headers.add('Access-Control-Allow-Methods', 'POST,
OPTIONS');
  response.headers.add('Access-Control-Allow-Headers', 'Origin,
X-Requested-With, Content-Type, Accept');
}
```

How it works...

All CORS-related headers are prefixed with `Access-Control-`. The `Access-Control-Allow-Origin` option has to be included in all valid CORS responses. The value `*` means that access is allowed from all domains. In development, this can be useful so that you can run apps from Dart Editor, which uses a 3030 port by default for its internal server. However, for a production application, you should sum up the allowed origins as follows:

- Access-Control-Allow-Origin at `http://www.example-social-network.com`
- Access-Control-Allow-Origin at `http://www.snapshot.com`

So, effectively, we name all the websites to which access is allowed. In our code, the `POST` and `OPTIONS` requests are allowed from any origin. An `OPTIONS` request is sent to get permission from the server to post data, in case the client is running from a different origin. So before the `POST` request, a so-called preflighted `OPTIONS` request is sent to determine if the actual request is allowed.

 In general, using CORS headers is not safe, and the allowed origins should be summed up. However, for development purposes, it is useful to allow them.

There's more...

Refer to `http://enable-cors.org/server.html` for more detailed information on using CORS on different platforms.

Using keyboard events

Handling keyboard events in normal web applications is not so common. However, if you are writing a web game, you'll almost certainly want to catch arrow key input, and the like. This recipe shows us how we can handle those events.

How to do it...

Look at the `keyboard` project. The web page is a copy of the page used in the *Preventing an onSubmit event* recipe, but now submit stays enabled. Suppose we also want to ensure that pressing the *Enter* key provokes `submit`, just like clicking on the **submit** button.

1. To that end, we add the following event listener to `main()`:

```
document.onKeyPress.listen(_onKeyPress);
```

2. The _onKeyPress method is as follows:

```
_onKeyPress(KeyboardEvent e){
   if (e.keyCode == KeyCode.ENTER) submit(e);
}
```

Now, pressing *Enter* will cause the form to be submitted.

How it works...

The document object from dart:html has three events to work with key input: onKeyPress, onKeyDown, and onKeyUp. They all generate a stream of KeyboardEvent objects that capture user interaction with the keyboard. However, these events are also defined for window, the parent object of document, and any Element on the page, so you can use them very specifically on a certain InputElement or <div> region.

The keyCode of the event is an integer from a list of constants, which specifies a value for every key, such as KeyCode.A, KeyCode.SPACE, and KeyCode.LEFT for the left arrow key, and so on. This lends itself very easily to a switch/case construct, as follows:

```
_onKeyPress(KeyboardEvent e){
   e.preventDefault();
   print('The charCode is ${e.charCode}');
   if (e.keyCode == KeyCode.ENTER) submit(e);
   if (e.ctrlKey) return;

   switch(e.keyCode) {
     case KeyCode.DOWN:
       // move sprite down
       break;
     case KeyCode.UP:
       // move sprite up
       break;
     case KeyCode.F1:
       // show help
       break;
   }
}
```

The event also has an integer character code getter named charCode. If the key was a special key, this can also be tested with e.ctrlKey, e.altKey, e.metaKey, e.ShiftKey, and e.altGraphKey:

```
if (e.ctrlKey) return;
```

There's more...

The Dart classes for keyboard handling try to minimize cross-browser differences (usually related to special keys), and to do a good job with as many international keyboard layouts as possible.

Enabling drag-and-drop

Imagine developing a board game and the player has to use the keyboard to move the pieces; this wouldn't be acceptable anymore. Before HTML5, drag-and-drop using the mouse was a feature that had to be implemented through an external library like Dojo or jQuery. However, HTML5 provides native browser support to make nearly every element on a web page draggable, thus allowing more user-friendly web apps. This recipe shows you how to implement drag-and-drop (abbreviated as DnD) with Dart.

How to do it...

Run the `drag_drop` project. The result is a board of images as shown in the following screenshot, where the images are draggable and you can swap an image with any other image, as shown in the following screenshot:

Drag-and-drop images

Perform the following steps to enable drag-and-drop

1. The elements that we want to drag-and-drop must get the `draggable` attribute in HTML, so in `drag_drop.html`, we indicate this for the `<div>` elements of the board:

```
<div id="tiles">
  <div id="tile1" class="pict" draggable="true"></div>
    <div id="tile2" class="pict" draggable="true"></div>
  . . .
   </div>
```

2. In the accompanying script `drag_drop.dart`, we make a class, DragnDrop, to integrate all the drag-and-drop event handling. All our `<div>` tiles have a CSS class `pict` and are hence captured in the `cols` collection. The `main()` function makes an object, dnd, and calls the `init()` method on it:

```
void main() {
  var dnd = new DragnDrop();
  dnd.init();
}

class DragnDrop {
  Element dragSource;
  Map tiles;
  var rand = new Random();
  var cols = document.querySelectorAll('.pict');
  // ...
}
```

3. The `init()` function constructs a map with images from the `img` folder in `generateMap()`. It sets up listeners for all the Dnd events of our tiles, and the images are set up as background images for the tiles via `style.setProperty` by calling `getRandomTile()`:

```
void init() {
    generateMap();
    for (var col in cols) {
      col
        ..onDragStart.listen(_onDragStart)
        ..onDragEnd.listen(_onDragEnd)
        ..onDragEnter.listen(_onDragEnter)
        ..onDragOver.listen(_onDragOver)
        ..onDragLeave.listen(_onDragLeave)
        ..onDrop.listen(_onDrop)
        ..style.setProperty("background-image", getRandomTile(),
"")
```

```
  ..style.setProperty("background-repeat", "no-repeat", "")
  ..style.setProperty("background-position", "center", "");
  }
}

void generateMap() {
  tiles = new Map();

  for (var i = 1; i <= 9; i++) {
    tiles[i] = "url(img/tiles_0$i.jpg)";
  }
}

String getRandomTile() {
    var num = rand.nextInt(10);
    var imgUrl = tiles[num];
    while (imgUrl == null) {
      num = rand.nextInt(10);
      imgUrl = tiles[num];
    }
    tiles.remove(num);
    return imgUrl;
  }
```

4. The code for each of the `Dnd` event handlers is as follows:

```
void _onDragStart(MouseEvent event) {
    Element dragTarget = event.target;
    dragTarget.classes.add('moving');
    dragSource = dragTarget;
    event.dataTransfer.effectAllowed = 'move';
    // event.dataTransfer.setData('text/html', dragTarget.
innerHtml);
  }

  void _onDragEnd(MouseEvent event) {
    Element dragTarget = event.target;
    dragTarget.classes.remove('moving');
    for (var col in cols) {
      col.classes.remove('over');
    }
  }

  void _onDragEnter(MouseEvent event) {
```

```
      Element dropTarget = event.target;
      dropTarget.classes.add('over');
    }

    void _onDragOver(MouseEvent event) {
      // This is necessary to allow us to drop.
      event.preventDefault();
      event.dataTransfer.dropEffect = 'move';
    }

    void _onDragLeave(MouseEvent event) {
      Element dropTarget = event.target;
      dropTarget.classes.remove('over');
    }

    void _onDrop(MouseEvent event) {
    // Stop the browser from redirecting and bubbling up the      //
    event:
      event.stopPropagation();
      // Don't do anything if dropping onto the same tile we're
    dragging.
      Element dropTarget = event.target;
      if (dragSource != dropTarget) {
        var swap_image = dropTarget.style.backgroundImage;
        dropTarget.style.backgroundImage = dragSource.style.
    backgroundImage;
        dragSource.style.backgroundImage = swap_image;
      }
    }
```

How it works...

Drag-and-drop makes an element on a page draggable by working with the following event life cycle: Drag, DragStart, DragEnd, DragEnter, DragLeave, DragOver, and finally Drop. They generate a stream of MouseEvents caught by the onDragEvent event handlers (where the event is Start, End, and so on). The event.target option changes for each type of event, depending on where we are in the drag-and-drop event model.

The basic requirement for an element to move is that it has the attribute draggable="true". In drag-and-drop, we can distinguish three objects:

▸ The source element is where the drag originates (this can be an image, list, link, file object, or block of HTML code)

> ▶ The data payload is what we're trying to drop

> ▶ The target element is an area to catch the drop or the drop zone, which accepts the data the user is trying to drop

Nearly everything can be drag enabled, including images, files, links, or other DOM nodes. However, not all elements can be targets, for example images, but our example shows that it is easy to work around that.

The visual effects that accompany drag-and-drop are implemented through CSS. Every tile has the CSS class `pict`, which contains the attribute `cursor: move`, which gives users a visual indicator that something is moveable.

When a drag action is initiated, `_onDragStart` is executed, adding the CSS class `moving` to our tiles. This class can be found in `drag_drop.css`:

```
.pict.moving {
  opacity: 0.25;
  -webkit-transform: scale(0.8);
  -moz-transform: scale(0.8);
  -ms-transform: scale(0.8);
  transform: scale(0.8);
}
```

We see that the opacity is reduced to 0.25 and size is scaled with factor 0.8, exactly what we see when a drag operation is started. In this example, we don't need it, but if the dragging involves HTML text, `_onDragStart` should contain the following code line:

```
event.dataTransfer.setData('text/html',   dragTarget.innerHtml);
```

The preceding code indicates what data will be transferred during the drag-and-drop process. The `dataTransfer` property is where it all happens; it stores the piece of data sent in a drag action. The `dataTransfer` option is set in the `DragStart` event and read/handled in the `Drop` event. Calling `e.dataTransfer.setData(format, data)` will set the object's content to the MIME type and the data payload will be passed as arguments.

The `_onDragEnter` function is executed when we hover over another tile; this adds the CSS class `over`, making the borderlines dashed:

```
.column.over {
  border: 2px dashed #000;
}
```

Finally, the `_onDrop` event swaps the tile images. If HTML text has to be swapped, the following lines should be added:

```
dragSource.innerHtml = dropTarget.innerHtml;
dropTarget.innerHtml = event.dataTransfer.getData('text/html');
```

The article at `http://www.html5rocks.com/en/tutorials/dnd/basics/` by Eric Bidelman is a good resource, but it uses JavaScript to explain the DnD event model. To make it easier to work with DnD in Dart, Marco Jakob developed the library `dart-html5-dnd`, available on pub. For more information on this nice package, refer to `http://code.makery.ch/dart/html5-drag-and-drop/`. DnD functionality is also implemented in the `dart:svg` library.

See also

▶ See the *Enabling touch events* recipe in this chapter to learn how to implement drag-and-drop using touch

Enabling touch events

Drag-and-drop is very handy on mobile devices where we don't have a mouse connected; we only have our fingers to interact with the screen. This recipe will show you how to add interactivity via touch events to your web app. The way to do this is very similar to the previous recipe. We will reuse the drag-and-drop example.

How to do it...

Let's look at the `touch` project as explained in the following steps:

1. Prevent zooming with the following `<meta>` tag in `touch.html`:

   ```
   <meta name="viewport"
    content="width=device-width, initial-scale=1.0, user-
   scalable=no">
   ```

   We use the same `<div>` structure, each with `class = "draggable"`, as shown in the previous recipe.

2. In `touch.dart`, we make a class, `Touch`, to contain the code specific to the touch events. An object, `touch`, is instantiated and the `init()` method is called, which prepares the board (each tile gets a different background image) and binds the touch events to event handlers:

   ```
   void main() {
     var touch = new Touch();
     touch.init();
   }

   class Touch {
   ```

```
    Element dragSource;
    Map tiles;
    var rand = new Random();
    var cols = document.querySelectorAll('.pict');

    void init() {
      generateMap();
      for (var col in cols) {

  col
      ..onTouchStart.listen(_onTouchStart)
      ..onTouchEnd.listen(_onTouchEnd)
      ..onTouchMove.listen(_onTouchMove)
      ..style.setProperty("background-image", getRandomTile(), "")
      ..style.setProperty("background-repeat", "no-repeat", "")
      ..style.setProperty("background-position", "center", "");     }
    }
```

3. The following is the code for the TouchStart event:

```
void _onTouchStart(TouchEvent event) {
  event.preventDefault(); //stop scrolling by default
  Element dragTarget = event.target; //capture drag target
  //add style to element to indicate its moving
  dragTarget.classes.add('moving');
  dragSource = dragTarget;
}
```

4. The following is the code for TouchMove:

```
  void _onTouchMove(TouchEvent event) {
    event.preventDefault();
    Element dropTarget = event.target;
    dragSource.classes.add('moving');
// Get the current x,y position of the first finger touch    //
and find the element it is over
    dropTarget = document.elementFromPoint(event.touches[0].
page.x, event.touches[0].page.y);
    // If the finger is over an element indicate that in the UI
    if (dropTarget != null) {
      dropTarget.classes.add('over');
    }
  }
```

5. The following is the code for TouchEnd:

```
void _onTouchEnd(TouchEvent event) {
  event.stopPropagation();
  event.preventDefault();
// Don't do anything if dropping onto the same tile we're      //
dragging.
  Element dropTarget = event.target;
  if (dragSource != dropTarget) {
    var swap_image = dropTarget.style.backgroundImage;
  dropTarget.style.backgroundImage = dragSource.style.
backgroundImage;
    dragSource.style.backgroundImage = swap_image;
  }
}
```

How it works...

The `meta` tag is necessary on mobile devices, and `user-scalable=no` will prevent the device from zooming in/out of the web page. We want DnD in our example and the finger gestures should not be mingled with zooming.

The three main touch events that we will have to handle in our code are `touchStart`, `touchEnd`, and `touchMove`. They are defined in `Element`, so touch can be used for nearly everything on the page. They generate a stream of `TouchEvent`s, and they contain the following three (read only) `Touch` objects:

- `touches`: These are all the current contact points with the touch surface, that is, fingers on the screen
- `changedTouches`: These are points of contact whose states changed between the previous touch event and this one
- `targetTouches`: These are all the current contact points with the surface and also all touches started on the same element which are the target of the event

This list are of type `TouchList`. A `Touch` object has, among other properties, a position given by `page.x` and `page.y`, and a target element.

The three `TouchEvent` handlers start with `e.preventDefault();` this stops the browsers default scrolling behavior. We don't want scrolling, we want dragging here. The element that is dragged is styled with `dragTarget.classes.add('moving');`. The area where the drop could take place is continually monitored in the `TouchMove` handler with the following code:

```
dropTarget = document.elementFromPoint(event.touches[0].page.x, event.
touches[0].page.y);
```

The element in that position is assigned the CSS class over. In the TouchEnd handler, the background images of the source and target element are switched.

There's more...

If you want a scenario where the element that is touched and dragged performs a certain movement, you can capture its coordinates in the TouchStart handler with the following code:

```
if (event.touches.length > 0) {
    touchStartX = event.touches[0].page.x;
}
```

In TouchMove, you move the element, probably as a function of the difference between newtouchX and touchStartX:

```
if (touchStartX != null && event.touches.length > 0) {
    int newTouchX = event.touches[0].page.x;
    if (newTouchX > touchStartX) {
     moveElement(newTouchX - touchStartX);
    }
}
```

 Alternatively, if working on a canvas element, you could start drawing by making use of the touch coordinates. See the Dart site for the complete example code for such scenarios at https://www.dartlang.org/samples/#touch_events.

See also

▸ See the *Responsive Design* recipe in this chapter for more information on the <meta> tag used

Creating a Chrome app

You can build native-like apps with the Dart web technology through Chrome apps. Such apps can be large for some browsers and appear to be part of the surrounding operating system; they run offline by default, and you can make them available from the Chrome Web Store. This recipe will show you how to start working with this type of app.

How to do it...

Perform the following steps to create a Chrome app. The code for this recipe can be found in the project `chrome_pack`:

1. Start with creating a new Dart project and choose the **Chrome packaged application** template.

2. The `Pub Get` command starts automatically, and installs the Chrome package from the pub.

3. The first thing you will notice is the presence of a new file `manifest.json`, with the following initial content:

```
{
  "name": "Chrome pack",
  "version": "1",
  "manifest_version": 2,
  "icons": {"128": "dart_icon.png"},
  "app": {
    "background": {
      "scripts": ["background.js"]
    }
  }
}
```

We don't have to change anything here, but you can add a `"description"` tag if you like.

4. The `background.js` file indicates which page the application should start with:

```
chrome.app.runtime.onLaunched.addListener(function(launchData) {
  chrome.app.window.create('chrome_pack.html', {
    'id': '_mainWindow', 'bounds': {'width': 800, 'height': 600 }
  });
});
```

5. The `chrome_pack.html` file has a <p> tag with the ID `text_id` and references the script `chrome_pack.dart`. This script first has to import the Chrome package:

```
import 'dart:html';
import 'package:chrome/chrome_app.dart' as chrome;

int boundsChange = 100;
var txtp = querySelector("#text_id");
int n = 0;
```

6. In `main()`, we get information about the platform the app is being executed in; in our case, this displays {`arch: x86-32, nacl_arch:x86-64, os: win`} and we register `rewriteText` as a `Click` event handler:

```
void main() {
  chrome.runtime.getPlatformInfo().then((var m) {
    txtp.text = m.toString();
    });
  txtp.onClick.listen(rewriteText);
}
```

7. At each click event, we show a message with the number of times clicked in the `<p>` tag and we resize the window:

```
void rewriteText(MouseEvent e) {
  txtp.text = "Hey, you clicked ${n++} times on a Chrome packaged
app!";
  resizeWindow(e);
}


void resizeWindow(MouseEvent e) {
chrome.ContentBounds bounds =  chrome.app.window.current().
getBounds();
  bounds.width += boundsChange;
  bounds.left -= boundsChange ~/ 2;
  chrome.app.window.current().setBounds(bounds);
  boundsChange *= -1;
}
```

8. We cannot run this app from Dart Editor as it is; if you try it, you get the exception **Unsupported operation: 'chrome.runtime' is not available**.

9. Instead, we have to compile it to JavaScript. Open a command window and go to the web folder of your app. The easiest way to do this is to select the web folder in Dart Editor, click on the right mouse button and select **Copy File Path**. You can paste this path on your command line after `cd` and press *Enter*. Then, type the command `dart2js chrome_pack.dart -o chrome_pack.dart.js`.

10. The option `-o` allows you to give an output file name. Alternatively, from within Dart Editor, on the Dart file navigate to **Tools | Pub Build**.

11. Now, we have to configure Chrome to install our app as a packaged app. Start `chrome://extensions` in the Chrome browser and check the **Developer mode**. Then, click on the **Load unpacked extension** button and browse to the folder containing the `manifest.json` file, and the app will be installed in Chrome, as shown in the following screenshot:

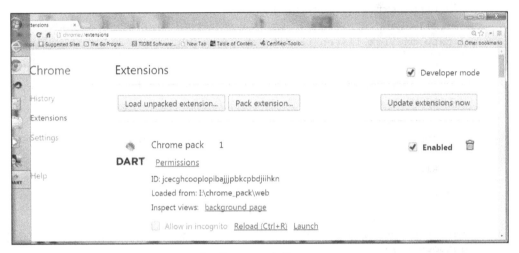

Loading an app in Chrome

12. Click on the **Launch** link to start the app, as shown in the following screenshot:

A running Chrome-packaged app

13. When you want to deploy your app to the Chrome Webstore, just click on **Pack Extension**.

14. The following are the steps to be followed when you make changes to the code:

    ❑ Save your changes

    ❑ Regenerate the JavaScript using dart2js (either from within Dart Editor or from the command line)

    ❑ Click on the **reload** button against your app's entry

How it works...

The `chrome` package was made by members of the Dart team to provide interoperability from Dart to the Chrome APIs.

The `manifest.json` file is the app's configuration file. It tells Chrome which background JavaScript file to run on starting up (app | background | scripts | `background.js`), which icons to use, which permissions the app has, and so on.

In the ninth step, `dart2js` compiles your Dart script to the JavaScript file indicated after –o. Configuring your app as a Chrome-packaged app, as shown from the tenth step to the twelfth, is straightforward.

There's more...

Chrome apps run inside a Chrome process separate from the browser, so they look like any other native application. Compared to pure web apps, they have greater access to the underlying hardware, such as the file system, USB or serial ports, socket-level protocols, and so on via the `chrome.*` API libraries.

You cannot use `window.localStorage` in this type of app, but you can use `chrome.storage` to get an API with similar features (and more); the following is a code snippet that sets a value for a key, and gets the value back:

```
chrome.storage.local.set({'key':'val'})
chrome.storage.local.get(['key'])
```

Because of the extensive use of Chrome-specific functionalities in these apps, it is generally not possible to reuse your Chrome-packaged app code in a normal web application.

See also

▶ The chrome package is documented at `http://dart-gde.github.io/chrome.dart/index.html#chrome/chrome_app`.

▶ Learn more about Chrome-packaged apps at `https://developer.chrome.com/apps/about_apps`

▶ For more information on dart2js, see the *Compiling your app to JavaScript* recipe in *Chapter 1, Working with Dart Tools*

Structuring a game project

Board games, for the greater part, have the same structure; what the user sees (the view) is a surface containing a grid of cells (model classes) that can be of different shapes. Along with a few utility classes to choose a color at random, this constitutes a solid base to build a board game. With his experience in building game projects, Dzenan Ridjanovic has extracted this game structure in the `boarding` project, which can be found at `https://github.com/dzenanr/boarding`.

How to do it...

Download the game project as a zip from the preceding URL, unzip it, and open it in Dart Editor. The code that is the starting part of a new board game can be found in the `lib` folder; the library that is boarding (in `boarding.dart`) imports the view classes `Surface` and `Shape`:

```
library boarding;

import 'dart:html';
import 'dart:math';

import 'package:boarding/boarding_model.dart';

part 'view/shape.dart';
part 'view/surface.dart';
```

The script `boarding_model.dart` declares the library `boarding_model`, which imports the model classes `Grid`, `Cell`, `Cells`, and some utility methods:

```
library boarding_model;

import 'dart:math';

part 'model/cell.dart';
```

```
part 'model/grid.dart';

part 'util/color.dart';
part 'util/random.dart';
```

By building upon these classes, you can build the specific board game you want. Concrete implementations can be found in the folder example that contains a memory game and a tic-tac-toe game (ttt). For example, the memory game start up script imports two libraries, and adds its own specific `Memory` class, which inherits from the `Grid` and `Board` classes that extend `Surface`:

```
library memory;

import 'dart:async';
import 'dart:html';
import 'package:boarding/boarding_model.dart';
import 'package:boarding/boarding.dart';

part 'model/memory.dart';
part 'view/board.dart';

playAgain(Event e) {
  window.location.reload();
}

main() {
  new Board(new Memory(4), querySelector('#canvas')).draw();
  querySelector('#play').onClick.listen(playAgain);
}
```

How it works...

The `Surface` class has a `draw()` method, which draws lines (if needed), and cells:

```
draw() {
    clear();
    if (withLines) lines();
    cells();
}
```

The classes `Circle`, `Rectangle`, `Square`, `Line`, and `Tag` (for a text) in `shape.dart` know how to draw themselves. The `Grid` class in the `model` folder knows how to construct itself with the objects of class `Cell`. The `cell.dart` file has the code for the class `Cell`, which can find out if two cells intersect, and it also has a collection of cells. Use this project as a starting point to build your own games!

There's more...

Another way of doing this is by using the `animationFrame` method from the `window` class. With this technique, we start `gameLoop` in the `main()` function and let it call itself recursively, as shown in the following code:

```
main() {
// redraw
    window.animationFrame.then(gameLoop);
}

gameLoop(num delta) {
    // animation code;
    window.animationFrame.then(gameLoop);
}
```

See also

▸ Take a look at the pub package `game_loop` from John McCutchan (`https://github.com/johnmccutchan/game_loop`). Another popular package is StageXL developed by Bernhard Pichler (`www.stagexl.org`). It is intended for Flash/ActionScript developers who want to migrate their projects as well as their skills to HTML5; visual effects, animation, sound—it's all there.

Using WebGL in your app

The HTML5 Canvas API allows you to draw in only two dimensions. Using **Web Graphics Library** (**WebGL**), you can show interactive 2D graphics and 3D graphics within any modern web browser (Internet Explorer 11 has only partial support for WebGL) without the use of plugins. WebGL elements are drawn on a canvas element, and can be combined with other HTML elements. Programs that use WebGL are a mixture of Dart (or JavaScript) code for control, and are of specific WebGL shader code. This shader code is executed on the computer's **Graphic Processing Unit** (**GPU**), allowing GPU-accelerated usage of physics effects and image processing as part of the web page canvas, so we have real parallel processing here!

WebGL provides a low-level 3D API; mastering it needs more than a recipe, probably a course or book on its own. However, this recipe will provide you with the basics in the `webgl` project and we point to some links to get further information.

Look at the code of the project `webgl`. When executed, we see a rectangular red point on a black surface. When we click on the surface, new points are shown:

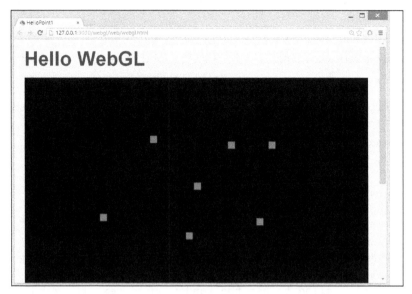

Drawing with WebGL

How to do it...

Start using WebGL by performing the following steps:

1. First, go to `http://get.webgl.org/` to determine if your browser and GPU support WebGL; you should see a spinning cube.

2. The `webgl.html` page simply defines a `<canvas>` tag on which we will draw, using the following code:

```
<canvas id="webgl" style="border: none;" width="500"
  height="500"></canvas>
```

3. To use WebGL in the code, import the `dart_webgl` package:

```
import 'dart:web_gl';
```

4. Now define the `shader` code for the drawing:

```
// Vertex shader program
var VSHADER_SOURCE = '''attribute vec4 a_Position;\n
                    void main() {\n
                    gl_Position = a_Position;\n
                    gl_PointSize = 10.0;\n
                    }\n''';
```

```
// Fragment shader program
var FSHADER_SOURCE = '''void main() {\n
gl_FragColor = vec4(1.0, 0.0, 0.0,      1.0);\n // Set the point
color
                    }\n''';
```

To set the vertex coordinates of the point to a fixed value, use the following code:

```
gl_Position = vec4(0.0, 0.0, 0.0, 1.0);
```

5. The `main()` function starts by getting a reference to the canvas and the 3D rendering context:

```
void main() {
  // Retrieve <canvas> element
  var canvas = querySelector("#webgl");
  if (canvas == null) {
    print('Failed to retrieve the <canvas> element');
  }
  // Get the rendering context for WebGL
  RenderingContext gl = canvas.getContext3d();
  if (gl == null) {
    print('Failed to get the rendering context for WebGL');
    return;
  }
}
```

6. Then, the shader code must be compiled and linked to the code:

```
// compiling the GPU code
  Shader fragShader = gl.createShader(FRAGMENT_SHADER);
  gl.shaderSource(fragShader, FSHADER_SOURCE);
  gl.compileShader(fragShader);

  Shader vertShader = gl.createShader(VERTEX_SHADER);
  gl.shaderSource(vertShader, VSHADER_SOURCE);
  gl.compileShader(vertShader);

  Program program = gl.createProgram();
  gl.attachShader(program, vertShader);
  gl.attachShader(program, fragShader);
  gl.linkProgram(program);

  if (!gl.getProgramParameter(program, LINK_STATUS)) {
    print("Could not initialise shaders");
    return;
  }
  gl.useProgram(program);
```

7. We then get an index to the location in a program of the named attribute `variable` a _Position:

```
var a_Position = gl.getAttribLocation(program,  'a_Position');
  if (a_Position < 0) {
    print('Failed to get the storage location of a_Position');
    return;
  }
```

8. We register the event handler to be called when the mouse is clicked:

```
canvas.onMouseDown.listen((ev) => click(ev, gl, canvas,  a_
Position));
```

9. Specify the color to clear `<canvas>`. Clear the canvas and draw the point:

```
gl.clearColor(0.0, 0.0, 0.0, 1.0);
gl.clear(COLOR_BUFFER_BIT);
gl.drawArrays(POINTS, 0, 1);
}
```

10. The click handler uses an array `g_points` to remember the mouse click positions:

```
List<num> g_points = new List<num>();

void click(ev, RenderingContext gl, canvas, a_Position) {
  var x = ev.clientX; // x coordinate of a mouse pointer
  var y = ev.clientY; // y coordinate of a mouse pointer
  var rect = ev.target.getBoundingClientRect();

x = ((x - rect.left) - canvas.width / 2) / (canvas.width / 2);
y = (canvas.height / 2 - (y - rect.top))/ (canvas.height / 2);

  // Store the coordinates to g_points array
  g_points.add(x);
  g_points.add(y);

  gl.clear(COLOR_BUFFER_BIT);

  var len = g_points.length;
  for (var i = 0; i < len; i += 2) {
    // Pass the position of a point to a_Position variable
gl.vertexAttrib3f(a_Position, g_points[i],
  g_points[i + 1], 0.0);
    gl.drawArrays(POINTS, 0, 1);
  }
}
```

How it works...

The shader code in the fourth step consists of a vertex shader program (to draw the shape boundaries) and fragment shader (for colors, texturing, and lighting) program; they are hard coded in strings assigned to the constants VSHADER_SOURCE and FSHADER_SOURCE.

The piece of code in the sixth step looks daunting, but don't worry, this code can simply be reused in other drawings.

Step 7 is necessary to make a connection between the a_position variable in the shader code, and the variable with the same name in Dart. Notice that the click event handler in steps 8 and 10 needs the GL context and canvas as second and third parameters.

There's more...

WebGL in itself has no built-in support to load a 3D scene defined in a regular 3D file format. The viewer code or a library such as three.dart, which is a port of Three.js (get it from the pub as three is necessary to display a 3D scene). To create content, use a regular content-creation tool and export the content to a viewer-readable format.

See also

▶ View and study the beautiful 3D solar system visualization example made by the Dart team at https://github.com/dart-lang/dart-samples/tree/master/html5/web/webgl/solar3

▶ The tutorial at http://www.learnwebgl.com was rewritten for Dart by John Thomas McDole; find it at https://github.com/jtmcdole/dart-webgl

▶ The website to find out more about WebGL at http://www.khronos.org/webgl/wiki/Main_Page

▶ If you want to read more about Shaders, visit http://aerotwist.com/tutorials/an-introduction-to-shaders-part-1/

Authorizing OAuth2 to Google services

You certainly have already seen websites where you can log in using your Google, Facebook, or Twitter account, instead of having to enter your information all over again. This service is most probably powered by OAuth2, which means (the second version of) the open (web) standard for authorization. It provides secured access to the server side of your application for clients that have been given an access token by a third-party OAuth2 authorization server. The credentials are guaranteed to be verified by the token and are not given to you as the website owner. The Dart team and community have provided us with some nice packages to easily implement this functionality.

<h1>How to do it...</h1>

If you want to use OAuth2 authentication from Google in a client app, there is the `google_oauth2_client` library. Add `google_oauth2_client` to your `pubspec.yaml` dependencies and let pub in Dart Editor install it, or invoke `pub get` in the command line. Add the following to your script, `import 'package:google_oauth2_client/google_oauth2_browser.dart';`, to start working with it in code.

Perform the following steps to use OAuth2 authentication from Google:

1. You need to register at the Google API Console site and create a Client ID by performing the following steps:

   □ Go to `https://console.developers.google.com/project` and create a project, for example, `oauth2-test`; it will be given a project ID.

   □ From the **Project Dashboard**, go to **APIs & auth, Credentials**. Click on the **Create New Client ID** button. Choose **Web application** as the type.

   □ In **Authorized JavaScript Origins**, insert the URL `http://127.0.0.1:3030`, used by the Dart Editor to launch web apps. Click on the **Create Client ID** button and a new screen appears with your client ID.

2. Add an `auth` variable initialized with the Oauth Client ID you just registered:

```
final auth = new GoogleOAuth2(
  "xxxxxxxxxxxxxxxxxx.apps.googleusercontent.com", // insert Client id
  ["openid", "email"],
  tokenLoaded:oauthReady);
```

3. Add a `Log in with Google` button in the `main()` code:

```
var logIn = new ButtonElement()
    ..text = "Log in with Google"
    ..onClick.listen((_) {
      auth.login();
});

document.body.children.add(logIn);
```

In the same way, you could also provide a logout facility:

```
var logOut = new ButtonElement()
    ..text = "Log out"
    ..onClick.listen((_) {
      auth.logout();
    });

document.body.children.add(logOut);
```

4. To see what is returned from the authentication, we add the following code:

```
void oauthReady(Token token) {
  print(token);
}
```

5. Suppose we want to use that token to access our Google+ profile data and display the user's full name. Go to the project dashboard (refer to step 2), select **Boost your app with a Google API**, then **Enable an API**, and then enable the Google+ API. Go to the API access screen and create a **Public API Access Key**. You will have to insert this value in **plus.key** in step 8.

6. Now add `google_plus_v1_api` to the `pubspec.yaml` file and add the following import line:

```
import "package:google_plus_v1_api/plus_v1_api_browser.dart"
  as plusclient;
```

7. Add `plusclient.Plus.PLUS_ME_SCOPE` after the e-mail scope in the `auth` variable.

8. Now add the following code to `oauthReady`:

```
// get the users full name
  var plus = new plusclient.Plus(auth);
  // set the API key
  plus.key = "Axxxxxxxxxxxxxxxxxxxx-x-xxxxxxxxx-x";
  plus.oauth_token = auth.token.data;
  plus.people.get("me").then((person) {
    // log the users full name to the console
    print("Hello ${person.name.givenName}  ${person.name.
familyName}");
  });
```

How it works...

Steps 3 to 5 illustrate how to make use of the OAuth client. Clicking on the **login** button will display the Google login screen, where the user has to enter their e-mail address and password, as shown in the following screenshot:

Google account login screen

A screen appears to grant access to your application, based on the scopes you specified in the `auth` variable `["openid", "email"]`. After that, the `tokenLoaded` event is fired, an oAuth token is returned, and its callback function `oauthReady` can print it out; it has the following format (sensitive data being replaced by `x`):

```
[Token type=Bearer,
data=xxx.xxxx-xxxxxxxxxxxxxxxxxxxx,
expired=false,
expiry=2014-05-24 15:46:19.445,
email=xxxxxxxxxxxxxx@gmail.com,
userId=xxxxxxxxxxxxxxxxxxxxxxx]
```

This token will be sent to your web application on the server. To summarize, the user is authenticated to your application as an existing Google account through the OAuth2 protocol.

From step 7 onwards, we use our token to log in to Google+. In step 9, `auth.token` is given to the Google+ client, and this prints out `givenName` and `familyName` from the Google+ service, for example, **Hello John Doe**.

In general, if you want to access a certain URL `urlxyz` through OAuth2 and you already have an auth token, use the following code:

```
var request = new HttpRequest();
request.onLoad.listen(...);
request.open(method, urlxyz);
auth.authenticate(request).then((request) => request.send());
```

There's more...

The Dart team has made the `oauth2` client library, which allows you to obtain OAuth2 authorization from a non-Google server. With it, a user is authenticated for your app, without having to store passwords on your website. After the user has been authenticated, your application has an `oauth2` token for that user, which can be used to access other services. To start working with it in the code, add `oauth2` to your `pubspec.yaml` dependencies and let the pub in Dart Editor install it, or invoke `pub get` on the command line. Then, add the following to your script:

```
import 'package:oauth2/oauth2.dart';
```

The way to go about this is a bit more involved, but with what you have learned now, you will be able to grasp the example code given at `http://pub.dartlang.org/packages/oauth2`.

To authenticate via OAuth2 from Facebook, Windows Live, or Google in a server-side application, use the pub package by Christophe Hurpeau.

See also

- For more detailed information on OAuth2 and Google, see the article *Using OAuth2 to access Google APIs* at `https://developers.google.com/accounts/docs/OAuth2?csw=1`
- If you want to learn more about Oauth2, refer to `http://oauth.net/2/`

Talking with JavaScript

If we take into account the enormous amount of JavaScript code and libraries that exist, and are still being developed, it is very important that we have a simple way to use JavaScript code from within Dart applications, in particular to get access from Dart to the JavaScript code that is running in the same web page. The earliest attempts used `window.postMessage`, and then a package called `js` was built. Because of the huge importance of this topic, the Dart team now has provided us with a core library, `dart:js`, to interoperate with JavaScript. This provides better performance, reduces the size of the compiled JavaScript file, and makes it also easier to use. Once `dart:js` is ready, the package `js` has been rewritten to use `dart:js` under the covers.

How to do it...

Take a look at the project `js_interop`, as explained in the following steps:

1. To start using `dart:js` in our project, we have to import it in our code:

    ```
    import 'dart:js';
    ```

2. In `js_interop.html`, we declare a Dart script, and the JavaScript program `js_interop.dart` will look into the code of `interact.js`:

    ```
    <script type="application/dart" src="js_interop.dart"></script>
    <script type="application/javascript"
      src="interact.js"></script>
    ```

3. The `interact.js` file contains the following code: a variable `jsvar`, a class `Person` with the properties `name` and `gender`, and the methods `greeting` and `sayHello`:

    ```
    var jsvar = "I want Dart";

    function Person(name, gender) {
      this.name = name;
      this.gender = gender;
      this.greeting = function(otherPerson) {
        alert('I greet you ' + otherPerson.name);
      };
    }

    Person.prototype.sayHello = function () {
      alert ('hello, I am ' + this.name );
    };
    ```

4. First, we get the contents of a JavaScript variable:

    ```
    var dart = context['jsvar'];
    print(dart);   // I want Dart
    ```

5. Then, we make a `Person` object:

    ```
    var pers1 = new JsObject(context['Person'], ['An',
      'female']);
    var pers2 = new JsObject(context['Person'], ['John',
      'male']);
    ```

6. We access and set the properties using the following code:

```
print(pers1['name']); // An
print(pers2['gender']); // male
pers2['gender'] = 'female';
print(pers2['gender']); // female
```

7. We call the methods on the `Person` object:

```
pers1.callMethod('sayHello', []);
pers2.callMethod('greeting', [pers1]);
```

The preceding steps display alert windows with the messages **hello, I am An** and **I greet you An**.

8. Now we get the global object in JavaScript (normally a window) via `context`, and display an alert window with `callMethod`:

```
context.callMethod('alert', ['Hello from Dart!']);
```

9. Use `jsify` to create a JavaScript object and array:

```
var jsMap = new JsObject.jsify({'a': 1, 'b': 2});
print(jsMap); // [object Object]
var jsArray = new JsObject.jsify([1, 2, 3]);
print(jsArray); // [1, 2, 3]
```

How it works...

The `dart:js` library provides Dart access to JavaScript objects in web applications, not in server applications. More specifically, it exposes wrapped or proxy versions of any JavaScript objects you access. This enables Dart to safely sandbox JavaScript away and prevents its problems from leaking into the Dart application. You can get and set properties and call JavaScript functions and methods on JavaScript objects, while conversions between Dart and JavaScript are taken care of as far as possible. At this moment, the bridge is not fully bidirectional; JavaScript has no access to Dart objects, but it can call Dart functions.

Inclusion of the `script` tag in the HTML `<script src="packages/browser/interop.js"></script>` code is no longer needed.

The main type of object is `JsObject` with which we can reach out to JavaScript objects; in other words, we create a Dart proxy object to the JavaScript object. To get the global object in JavaScript (which is mostly `window`), use the top-level getter function `context`; this is used in step 8. However, `context` is also used to get the values of JavaScript variables, as shown in step 4.

You can create JavaScript objects as shown in step 5. Use the `JsObject()` constructor. This takes the name of a JavaScript constructor function and the list of arguments that it needs as arguments. As shown in step 6, we can use the `[]` index operator to get the value of properties and `[] =` to set them; instead of a numerical index, we use the property name string as the key. The seventh and eighth step demonstrate that we can call a JavaScript method on an object with `callMethod`, taking the name of the method and the list of its arguments as parameters. Finally, in step 9, we see that `JsObject.jsify` turns a Dart map into a JavaScript object using the keys as properties; the same method also turns a Dart list into a JavaScript array.

There's more...

To be able to compare, we will now show the same code but rewritten with the `js` package. In `js_interop2.html`, we have the same JavaScript, but running together with the Dart script `js_interop2.dart`. We add the `js` package to our `pubspec.yaml` file as `js:any`, and let `pub get` do its magic. To make the package available to our Dart script, we add the following code to `js_interop2.dart`:

```
import 'package:js/js.dart' as js;
```

Rewriting the Dart code from `js_interop.dart` gets us the following output:

```
void main() {
  // getting a variable:
    var dart = js.context['jsvar'];
  print(dart); // I want Dart
  // making objects:
    var pers1 = new js.Proxy(js.context.Person, ['An', 'female']);
  var pers2 = new js.Proxy(js.context.Person, ['John', 'male']);
  // accessing and setting properties:
  print(pers1.name); // prints the whole object: [An, female]
  pers1.name = 'Melissa'; // change name property
  print(pers1.name); // Melissa
  // calling methods:
    pers1.sayHello.call(); // window: hello, I am Melissa
  pers2.greeting.call(pers1); // window: I greet you Melissa
  // getting the global object in JavaScript via context
  js.context.alert('Hello from Dart via JavaScript');
  // using jsify:
    var jsMap = js.map({'a': 1,'b': 2});
  print(jsMap); // [object Object]
    var jsArray = js.array([1, 2, 3]);
  print(jsArray); // [1, 2, 3]
}
```

The syntax is a bit easier than `dart:js` but because the names in the `js` package cannot be minified since it uses `dart:mirrors` and `noSuchMethod`, using this library can result in a noticeable increase in code size when compiled to JavaScript. If this is a big disadvantage for you, use `dart:js` instead. We use the `js` package in the next recipe to talk to the Google Visualizations API.

See also

▸ See the *Using JavaScript libraries* recipes for more information on how to use JavaScript libraries

▸ A small library that makes it easy to call Dart from Javascript is available at `https://github.com/jptrainor/js_bridge`, it's a thin layer around dart:js.

Using JavaScript libraries

In this recipe, we use the `js` package as an interface from our Dart script to the Google Chart JavaScript API. This gives us many rich and highly customizable ways to graphically represent data in our Dart web apps and, because it is built with HTML5/SVG, it works cross-browser (even for older IE versions) and cross-platform (also for iOS and Android).

How to do it...

Take a look at the project `googlechart`:

1. In the `<body>` tag of the HTML file, place the following:

    ```
    <div id="chart" style="width: 900px; height: 500px;"></div>
    <script type="text/javascript"
      src="https://www.google.com/jsapi"></script>
    <script type="application/dart"
      src="googlechart.dart"></script>
    ```

    The `<div>` tag with the ID `chart` is where the chart will be drawn; the code to do this is contained in `googlechart.dart`.

2. The following is the data we want to represent in a chart:

    ```
    var listData = [
                    ['Year', 'Sales', 'Expenses'],
                    ['2004',  1000,      400],
                    ['2005',  1170,      460],
                    ['2006',  660,      1120],
                    ['2007',  1030,      540]
                   ];
    ```

3. After importing the `js` package, we load the `corechart` package from the Google API and tell our code to execute the method `drawChart` when this is done:

```
import 'dart:html';
import 'package:js/js.dart' as js;

main() {
  js.context.google.load('visualization', '1', js.map(
    { 'packages': ['corechart'],
      'callback': drawChart,
    }));
}
```

4. Calling the `drawChart` method then loads the data and draws the chart:

```
void drawChart() {
  var gviz = js.context.google.visualization;
  var arrayData = js.array(listData);
  var tableData = gviz.arrayToDataTable(arrayData);
  var options = js.map({
    'title': 'Company Performance, ',
    'hAxis': {'title': 'Year', 'titleTextStyle': {'color':
      'red'}}
  });
  var chart = new js.Proxy(gviz.ColumnChart,
querySelector('#chart'));
  chart.draw(tableData, options);
}
```

Performing the previous steps gives the following output in the browser:

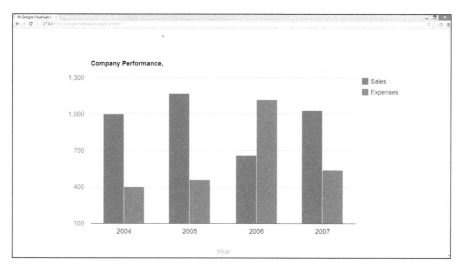

Using Google Charts with js

Also, notice that when hovering over the columns, a tooltip is shown with the exact data for that column.

How it works...

In the first step, the highlighted script tag refers to the online Google visualization libraries that have to be loaded dynamically before you can use them to draw charts. Step 2 defines the data; this could have been loaded from a file or database. In step 4, we get a reference `gviz` to the JavaScript Google Visualizations object via `js.context`. Then, the data is transformed into a JavaScript array with `js.array`; the chart options such as title, x axis, color, and so on are passed via `js.map`. Then, we construct a proxy `chart` to the JavaScript object, on which the `draw` method is invoked.

So basically, there are four steps to create a chart:

1. Load the `jsapi` library.
2. List the data.
3. Configure the options.
4. Create the chart.

See also

▶   Want to learn more about Google Charts? Then visit `https://google-developers.appspot.com/chart/interactive/docs/`, where you can find a wealth of examples. These are written in JavaScript, but with what you now know, you can easily translate them to Dart.

6

Working with Files and Streams

In this chapter, we will cover the following recipes:

- ▶ Reading and processing a file line by line
- ▶ Writing to a file
- ▶ Searching in a file
- ▶ Concatenating files
- ▶ Downloading a file
- ▶ Working with blobs
- ▶ Transforming streams

Introduction

Working with files is the bread and butter of every programming language when reaching out for data in the environment. The classes and methods dealing with this functionality can be found in the `dart:io` package, together with support for networking (sockets and HTTP). This package can only be used in Dart command-line applications, not in browser apps, so our code runs in a Dart VM.

When working with files, and I/O in general, there are two modes of operation:

- ▶ Synchronous operations, where code execution waits for the I/O result
- ▶ Asynchronous operations, where the code execution is not blocked and continues while I/O is taking place

Because the Dart VM is single threaded, a synchronous call blocks the application. So, for scalability reasons, the asynchronous way is the best practice using the `Future` and `Stream` classes from the `dart:async` package. Most methods on files come in pairs, the asynchronous and the synchronous versions, such as `copy` and `copySync`. Unless you really have to wait for the result, use the asynchronous way so that screens and apps do not appear to be blocked and can still respond.

If you need a recap, visit the tutorials at `https://www.dartlang.org/docs/tutorials/futures/` and `https://www.dartlang.org/docs/tutorials/streams/`. In this chapter, we will focus on recipes to handle files.

Reading and processing a file line by line

Files containing data in the **comma separated values** (**csv**) format are structured so that one line contains data about one object, so we need a way to read and process the file line by line. As an example, we use the data file `winequality-red.csv`, that contains 1,599 sample measurements, 12 data columns, such as **pH** and **alcohol**, per sample, separated by a semicolon (;), of which you can see the top 20 in the following screenshot:

	fixed acidi	volatile ac	citric acid	residual su	chlorides	free sulfur	total sulfu	density	pH	sulphates	alcohol	quality
2	7.4	0.7		0	1.9	0.076	11	34	0.9978	3.51	0.56	9.4	5
3	7.8	0.88		0	2.6	0.098	25	67	0.9968	3.2	0.68	9.8	5
4	7.8	0.76	0.04	2.3	0.092	15	54	0.997	3.26	0.65	9.8	5
5	11.2	0.28	0.56	1.9	0.075	17	60	0.998	3.16	0.58	9.8	6
6	7.4	0.7		0	1.9	0.076	11	34	0.9978	3.51	0.56	9.4	5
7	7.4	0.66		0	1.8	0.075	13	40	0.9978	3.51	0.56	9.4	5
8	7.9	0.6	0.06	1.6	0.069	15	59	0.9964	3.3	0.46	9.4	5
9	7.3	0.65		0	1.2	0.065	15	21	0.9946	3.39	0.47	10	7
10	7.8	0.58	0.02		2	0.073	9	18	0.9968	3.36	0.57	9.5	7
11	7.5	0.5	0.36	6.1	0.071	17	102	0.9978	3.35	0.8	10.5	5
12	6.7	0.58	0.08	1.8	0.097	15	65	0.9959	3.28	0.54	9.2	5
13	7.5	0.5	0.36	6.1	0.071	17	102	0.9978	3.35	0.8	10.5	5
14	5.6	0.615		0	1.6	0.089	16	59	0.9943	3.58	0.52	9.9	5
15	7.8	0.61	0.29	1.6	0.114	9	29	0.9974	3.26	1.56	9.1	5
16	8.9	0.62	0.18	3.8	0.176	52	145	0.9986	3.16	0.88	9.2	5
17	8.9	0.62	0.19	3.9	0.17	51	148	0.9986	3.17	0.93	9.2	5
18	8.5	0.28	0.56	1.8	0.092	35	103	0.9969	3.3	0.75	10.5	7
19	8.1	0.56	0.28	1.7	0.368	16	56	0.9968	3.11	1.28	9.3	5
20	7.4	0.59	0.08	4.4	0.086	6	29	0.9974	3.38	0.5	9	4

How to do it...

Examine the code of the command-line project `processing_lines` using the following methods:

1. Using the `readAsLines` method as shown in the following code:

```
import 'dart:io';
// for step 3:
import 'dart:async';
import 'dart:convert';

main() {
  File data= new File("../winequality-red.csv");
  data.readAsLines().then(processLines)
  .catchError((e) => handleError(e));
}

processLines(List<String> lines) {
  // process lines:
  for (var line in lines) {
  print(line);
  }
}

handleError(e) {
  print("An error $e occurred");
}
```

The previous code gives the following output:

```
"fixed acidity";"volatile acidity";"citric acid";"residual sugar";"chlorides";"free sulfur dioxide";"total sulfur dioxide";"
7.4;0.7;0;1.9;0.076;11;34;0.9978;3.51;0.56;9.4;5: 48 bytes
7.8;0.88;0;2.6;0.098;25;67;0.9968;3.2;0.68;9.8;5: 48 bytes
7.8;0.76;0.04;2.3;0.092;15;54;0.997;3.26;0.65;9.8;5: 51 bytes
11.2;0.28;0.56;1.9;0.075;17;60;0.998;3.16;0.58;9.8;6: 52 bytes
7.4;0.7;0;1.9;0.076;11;34;0.9978;3.51;0.56;9.4;5: 48 bytes
7.4;0.66;0;1.8;0.075;13;40;0.9978;3.51;0.56;9.4;5: 49 bytes
7.9;0.6;0.06;1.6;0.069;15;59;0.9964;3.3;0.46;9.4;5: 50 bytes
7.3;0.65;0;1.2;0.065;15;21;0.9946;3.39;0.47;10;7: 48 bytes
7.8;0.58;0.02;2;0.073;9;18;0.9968;3.36;0.57;9.5;7: 49 bytes
```

2. Extracting the data of each line to an object as shown in the following code:

```
processLines(List<String> lines) {
// process lines:
  for (var line in lines) {
  print(line);
  // when not header line, split line on separator:
  if (!header) {
```

```
      List<String> fields = line.split(";");
      Wine wn = new Wine();
      wn.fixed_acidity = fields[0];
      wn.volatile_acidity = fields[1];
      // extracting remaining properties
      wn.alcohol = fields[10];
      wn.quality = fields[11];
      print(wn);
      }
      header = false;
    }
  }
}
class Wine {
  var fixed_acidity;
  var volatile_acidity;
  // other properties
  var alcohol;
  var quality;

  toString() => "This wine has $fixed_acidity fixed acidity, "
  "alcohol % of $alcohol and quality $quality.";
}
```

The preceding code gives the **This wine has 6.8 fixed acidity, alcohol % of 11.3 and quality 6** output.

3. Use the openRead method as an alternative as shown in the following code:

```
main() {
  File data= new File("../winequality-red.csv");
  // using openRead:
  Stream<List<int>> input = data.openRead();
  input
  .transform(UTF8.decoder) // Decode to UTF8.
  // Convert stream to individual lines.
  .transform(const LineSplitter())
  .listen((String line) { // Callback to process results.
  print('$line: ${line.length} bytes');
  // Further processing of line, e.g. as in processLines
  }, onDone: () {
  print('File is now closed.');
  }, onError: (e) {
  print(e.toString());
  });
}
```

The previous code gives the following output:

7.8;0.88;0;2.6;0.098;25;67;0.9968;3.2;0.68;9.8;5: 48 bytes

7.8;0.76;0.04;2.3;0.092;15;54;0.997;3.26;0.65;9.8;5: 51 bytes

How it works...

In step 1, we created a `File` object reference to our data file. On this object, we call the asynchronous `readAsLinesmethod` method that returns `Future` with a return value of the type `List<String>`. Each line is read as a string, and all lines form a list. When the file is read in its entirety and this value is returned, it is executed with the callback `functionprocessLines` that effectively gets `List<String>` as its argument. In `processLines`, we can get at each line and transform or process it. If `readAsLines` returns with an error, `catchError` is fired, and `handleError` callback is executed (we could have shortened this line to `catchError(handleError);`).

For example, when the file is not found, we have the following message:

An error FileSystemException: Cannot open file, path = 'winequality-red.csv' (OS Error: The system cannot find the specified file. , errno = 2) occurred

In step 2, we split each data field. At that moment, we can create a `Wine` object for each line, start doing calculations with the data, and so on.

The `readAsLines` method takes an optional argument of the type `encoding`, such as this: `readAsLines(encoding: ASCII);` instead of ASCII, you can use LATIN1 or UTF-8.

In step 3, we see an alternative way to be used when the file is too large to fit in memory (the code line with `readAsLines` is now no longer needed). With `openRead`, the file is read in chunks as a stream of integers. In this stream, we use the `transform` method to convert to UTF-8 and then to split it into separate lines. The listen event then activates a callback function for each line read. The `onDone` option defines a callback function when the last line of the file is read in; `onError` defines an error handler. For this to work, we need to import `dart:async` and `dart:convert`. If you find the syntax used in the `listen` callback a bit too clunky, you can always write it with named event handlers as in `processing_lines2.dart` as follows:

```
// previous lines left out
.listen(processLine, onDone: close, onError: handleError);
}

processLine(line) {  print('$line: ${line.length} bytes'); }
close() { print('File is now closed.'); }
handleError(e) { print(e.toString()); }
```

The other possibilities are as follows:

▶ Use the method `readAsBytes` if you want to be able to process individual bytes in the file

▶ Use the method `readAsString` if you want to read the file in memory as one big string

▶ Use the method `readAsLinesSync` if you want to read the file in memory as one big string and wait until that is done

See also

▶ See the *Transforming streams* recipe in this chapter.

Writing to a file

In this recipe, we demonstrate the three most important ways to write to a file. You can find the code in the project `writing_files`.

How to do it...

The three ways to write to a file are discussed as follows:

1. First, we import the packages `io` and `convert` as shown in the following code:

    ```
    import 'dart:io';
    import 'dart:convert';

    void main() {
    ```

2. We can write to a file using `writeAsString` as shown in the following code:

    ```
    final filename = 'outString.txt';
    new File(filename).writeAsString('Dart is an elegant
    language').then((File file) {
    // do something with the file.
    });
    ```

3. We can write to a file using `writeAsBytes` as shown in the following code:

    ```
    final string = '你好世界';
    // Encode to UTF8.
    var encodedData = UTF8.encode(string);
    new
    File('outUTF8.txt').writeAsBytes(encodedData).then((file)
    => file.readAsBytes()).then((data) {
    // Decode to a string, and print.
    ```

```
    print(data);
    // [228, 189, 160, 229, 165, 189, 228, 184, 150, 231, 149, 140]
    print(UTF8.decode(data)); // prints '你好世界'.
  });
```

4. We can write to a file using `openWrite` as shown in the following code:

```
    var file = new File('out3.txt');
    var sink = file.openWrite();
    sink.write('File was written to at ${new DateTime.now()}\n');
    // close the IOSink to free system resources!
    sink.close();
  }
```

How it works...

Step 1 uses the asynchronous `writeAsString` method to write one (big) string to a file, and this file is then automatically closed. In the callback function called by `then`, you could, for example, send the file over the network. Step 2 shows how to write raw bytes to a file with `writeAsBytes`. This is necessary when the file contains non-readable or Unicode characters.

There's more...

What do we do when we want to write to our file in chunks? Then, we use the `openWrite` method as shown in step 3. When called on a `File` object, this creates an `IOSink` object for that file, which you can write to with any of the following methods: `write`, `writeln`, `writeCharCode`, `writeAll`. In contrast to the write methods of the previous steps, the `IOSink` object must be explicitly closed when no longer needed. The `openWrite` method takes two optional arguments as shown in the following code:

```
    file.openWrite(mode: FileMode.APPEND, encoding: ASCII);
```

The default mode is `FileMode.WRITE`.

Searching in a file

In this recipe, we demonstrate how to search for certain words in a text file. You can find the code in the `search.dart` script in the project `searching_file`. As an example text file, we use `taoprog.txt`.

How to do it...

The program is launched from the command-line in the `bin` folder (or in Dart Editor with a Managed Launch with **Script arguments** `-n search1 search2taoprog.txt`) as shown in the following screenshot:

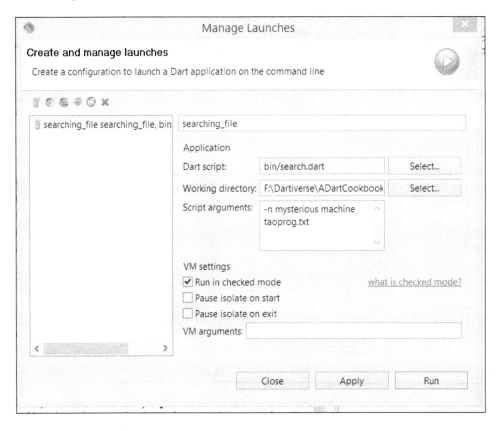

In `dart search.dart -n search1 search2 taoprog.txt`, where `search1` and `search2` are words to be searched for, there can be one or more search words. For example, let's search for *mysterious* and *machine*, in which case, the output is as follows:

```
Observatory listening on http://127.0.0.1:5623
15: Something mysterious is formed, born in the silent void.  Waiting
32: The Tao gave birth to machine language.  Machine language gave birth
90: The programmers of old were mysterious and profound.  We cannot
107: Grand Master Turing once dreamed that he was a machine.  When he
110: "I don't know whether I am Turing dreaming that I am a machine, or a
111: machine dreaming that I am Turing!"
229: seeks the simplest harmony between machine and ideas.  This is why
306: Why do you expect it from a machine that humans have constructed?
```

The flag −n is optional; if included, we see a line number printed in front of the line.

The following is the code from the script:

```
import 'dart:io';
import 'package:args/args.dart';

const HOWTOUSE = 'usage: dart search.dart [-n] search-pattern file';
const LINENO = 'line-number';
ArgResults argResults;
var searchTerms = "";
File file;
```

Perform the following steps to search in a file:

1. We can search a file using the args package as shown in the following code:

    ```
    void main(List<String> args) {
      final parser = new ArgParser()..addFlag(LINENO, negatable:
      false, abbr: 'n');
      argResults = parser.parse(args);
      if (argResults.rest.length < 2) {
        print(HOWTOUSE);
        exit(1);
      }
    }
    ```

2. We can search a file by capturing the filename and the search terms as shown in the following code:

    ```
    final strFile = argResults.rest.last;
    File file = new File(strFile);
    searchTerms = argResults.rest.sublist(0,
    argResults.rest.length  - 1);
    searchFile(file, searchTerms);
    }
    ```

3. We can search a file by reading in the file and searching, as shown in the following code:

    ```
    searchFile(File file, searchTerms) {
      file.readAsLines().then(searchLines).catchError(print);
    }
    searchLines(lines) {
      for (var i = 0; i < lines.length; i++) {
        for (var j = 0; j < searchTerms.length; j++) {
          if (lines[i].contains(searchTerms[j])) {
            printMatch(lines[i], i);
          }
    ```

```
        }
      }
    }
```

4. We can search a file by printing out the match line found as shown in the following code:

```
void printMatch(String line, int i) {
  StringBuffer sb = new StringBuffer();
  if (argResults[LINENO]) sb.write('${i + 1}: ');
  sb.write(line);
  print(sb.toString());
}
```

How it works...

In step 1, we see that the `args` package is used to parse the command-line arguments. The option `-n` is either there or not (on or off, a Boolean value), which is why it is added as a flag to the `parser` object; `negatable:false` prevents you from writing `no-n` as an argument. We parse and then test to see that we have at least two arguments (a search term and a filename). If not, the string in the constant `HOWTOUSE` is displayed as a help option. Step 2 prepares the scene; the `last` argument is the filename, the rest of the arguments given by the `sublist` method is the list of search terms.

The actual searching happens in step 3; we use the `readAsLines` method to read the file. When this is done, the callback function `searchLines` is called in a nested for loop, where each line in succession is tested for all search terms as to whether it contains the term. So `printMatch` prints the line out and also whether `-n` specified was preceded by its line number.

See also

▶ See the *Parsing command-line arguments* recipe in *Chapter 2, Structuring, Testing, and Deploying an Application*, for more information on using the `args` package at `https://pub.dartlang.org/packages/args`

▶ You can find an example that searches recursively through a folder structure at `https://code.google.com/p/dart/source/browse/branches/bleeding_edge/dart/samples/dgrep/bin/dgrep.dart`

Concatenating files

Let's suppose that we have a number of text files we want to glue together in one big file. This recipe with code in the project `concat_files` shows you how this can be done.

How to do it...

The program is launched from the command line in the `bin` folder (or in Dart Editor with a Managed Launch with `Script` arguments `file1.txt file2.txt file.txt`) as `dart concat.dart file1.txt file2.txt file.txt`, where `file1.txt` and `file2.txt` are the files to be concatenated (there can be two or more files) into `file.txt`. The following is the code to perform this:

```dart
import 'dart:io';
import 'package:args/args.dart';

ArgResults argResults;
File output;

void main(List<String> arguments) {
  final parser = new ArgParser();
  argResults = parser.parse(arguments);
  final outFile = argResults.rest.last;
  List<String> files = argResults.rest.sublist(0, argResults.
    rest.length - 1);
  if (files.isEmpty) {
    print('No files provided to concatenate!');
    exit(1);
  }
output = new File(outFile);
if (output.existsSync()) {
  output.delete();
  }
  concat(files);
  }

concat(List<String> files) {
  for (var file in files) {
  var input = new File(file);
  try {
    var content = input.readAsStringSync();
    content += "\n";
    output.writeAsStringSync(content, mode: FileMode.APPEND);
    } catch (e) {
    print("An error $e occurred");
    }
  }
}
```

How it works...

We use the `args` package to get the output file name and the files to concatenate. To start with an empty output file, we delete it when it already exists. Then, we loop over all the input files, successively reading an input file and write it to the output in the append mode. We do all these operations in the synchronous mode, because we don't want the content of the files to be mingled.

There's more...

In `concat2.dart`, which you can find within the `concat_files` folder, we see an asynchronous version that also works here—only the code in the `concat` method has to change. Have a look at the following code:

```
IOSink snk;

Future concat(List<String> files) {
snk = output.openWrite(mode: FileMode.APPEND);
   return Future.forEach(files, (file) {
      Stream<List<int>> stream = new File(file).openRead();
      return stream.transform(UTF8.decoder)
      .transform(const LineSplitter())
      .listen((line) {
      snk.write(line + "\n");
      }).asFuture().catchError((_) => _handleError(file));
   });
}


_handleError(String file) {
   FileSystemEntity.isDirectory(file).then((isDir) {
   if (isDir) {
     print('error: $file is a directory');
     } else {
     print('error: $file not found');
     }
   });
}
```

We write to an `IOSink` object `snk` using the `openWrite` method in the append mode. The `Future.forEach` method asynchronously runs the callback provided on each file. The `forEach` method runs the callback for each element in order, moving to the next element only when the Future returned by the callback completes. The stream is transformed; transformers are used here to convert the data to UTF-8 and split string values into individual lines.

See also

- ▶ Refer to the *Parsing command-line arguments* recipe, *Chapter 2, Structuring, Testing, and Deploying an Application,* for more information on using the `args` package, and the *Transforming streams* recipe in this chapter.

Downloading a file

This recipe shows you the simplest ways to download a file through code, first in a command-line application and then from a web application. As an example, we download the front page of the Learning Dart website from `http://learningdart.org`.

Getting ready

A client program (be it web or command-line) receives content, such as files or web pages, from a web server using the HTTP protocol. The `dart:html` and `dart:io` package provides us with the basic classes we need to do this, which are as follows:

- ▶ The `Uriclass` class (from `dart:core`) has all we need to parse, encode, and decode web addresses; the method `Uri.parse` is often used

- ▶ The `HttpRequest` class (from `dart:html`) has the `getString` method to fetch a file from a URL

- ▶ The `HttpClientclass` class (from `dart:io`) has all kinds of methods, such as `get` and `post`, to send a request (class `HttpClientRequest`) to a web server and get a response (class `HttpClientResponse`) back

How to do it...

1. For a web app, this is shown in `download_string.dart`, which is started from `download_string.html` (these files can be found in the `download_file` project) as shown in the following code:

```
import 'dart:html';

main() {
  HttpRequest.getString('http://learningdart.org')
   .then(processString)
   .catchError(print);
}

processString(str) {
  print(str);
}
```

2. For a command-line app in the program `download_file.dart`, we see the basic mechanism of how to do this for a command-line app as follows:

```dart
import 'dart:io';
import 'dart:convert';

var client;

main() {
  var url = Uri.parse('http://learningdart.org');
  client = new HttpClient();
  client.getUrl(url)
  .then((HttpClientRequest req) => req.close())
  .then((HttpClientResponse resp) => writeToFile(resp));
}

writeToFile(resp) {
  resp.transform(UTF8.decoder)
  .toList().then((data) {
    var body = data.join('');
    var file = new File('dart.txt');
    file.writeAsString(body).then((_) {
    client.close();
    });
  });
}
```

How it works...

For a web app, we use the `getString` method on `HttpRequest` to fetch the file from the URL as one big string, which is asynchronously passed to `processString`. It could do just about anything with the string it gets back, for example, if it were a JSON or XML string, we could parse this and get data out of it to show on our web page. So `HttpRequest` can is used to fetch data over HTTP and FTP protocols from a URL, without producing complete web page updates. This is, in fact, the way to make AJAX calls (or `XMLHttpRequest`) and as a consequence, partial page updates. We will use it in the following recipe to fetch a large blob file.

 Don't confuse this class with another class with the same name `HttpRequest` from `dart:io`, which must be used in server-side applications (we will use it extensively in the recipes of the following chapter). A web server, or more formally, an HTTP server, that listens for HTTP requests coming in on a specific host and port, generates such an object for each request it receives.

For a command-line app, first we transform the web address string to a `Uri` object with the static method parse. Then we make an `HttpClient` object and invoke the `getUrl` request on URL (the `Uri` object). This works in two steps, each returning a Future, which are:

▶ The first `.then` completes with a request object that has been made but not sent yet. In the callback, you can still change or add to the request headers or the body. A call to `close` sends the request to the server. This step serves to make the request and send it.

▶ The second `.then` completes when the response object is received from the server, and you can access headers and the body (the body is available as a stream). This step serves to process the response; here, we call `writeToFile`.

 If there is a body, it must be processed. Avoid memory leaks by calling the method `drain()`.

In `writeToFile`, we read the response data, transforming it from UTF-8 to a string (helped by the `join` method that transforms the list into a string), and write it to a file with `writeAsString`. When this finishes, the `HttpClient` object is closed; this releases the network connections that have been made.

There's more...

The following are some variations to accomplish the same thing for a command-line app:

Using pipe

The `.then` variable in the command line can be simplified to the following:

```
.then((HttpClientResponse resp) => resp.pipe(new
    File('dart.txt').openWrite()));
```

The `pipe` method on the response object can send the stream immediately to the file to be written. This will perform better when downloading bigger files.

Using the http package

An even more simplified approach can be taken using the `http` package by the Dart team, which was made to facilitate coding requests and responses (see `download_file2.dart`). Have a look at the following code:

```
import 'dart:io';
import 'package:http/http.dart' as http;

main() {
  var url = Uri.parse('http://learningdart.org');
```

```
http.get(url).then((response) {
new File('dart.txt').writeAsBytes(response.bodyBytes);
});
}
```

See also

▶   See the *Writing to a file* recipe for information on the `writeAsBytes` method

Working with blobs

In the previous recipe, in step 1, we used a client `HttpRequest` object and its method `getString`. In this recipe, we want to download a blob (binarylargeobject) file, for example, a large image, audio, or video file. But first, you need to prepare for this if you need to do more than just download a string from a URL resource to process it on the client. You need to go through the following steps (for the code, see `request_prep.dart` in the project `request_blob`).

Getting ready

1. Create an `HttpRequest` object as shown in the following code:

    ```
    import 'dart:html';

    void main() {
    var path = 'http://learningdart.org';
    var request = new HttpRequest();
    ```

2. Open it (here, with the HTTP `GET` method) as shown in the following code:

    ```
    request
    ..open('GET', path)
    ```

3. In this stage, we could also have configured its header with the `setRequestHeader()` method, for example, `request.setRequestHeader('Content-type','application/json')` when you are sending a JSON string.

4. Define a callback function, such as `requestComplete`, to execute when the response comes back; this is done in the `onLoadEnd` event as shown in the following code:

    ```
    ..onLoadEnd.listen((e) => requestComplete(request))
    ```

5. Use the `send` method to make the request as shown in the following code:

    ```
    ..send();
    }
    ```

Here, we send an empty string, because it is a GET request, but with a POST request, we could send data such as `request.send(JSON.encode(data));`.

In the callback, we test the status of the request if it is 200; if everything is OK, we can process `responseText`. Have a look at the following code:

```
requestComplete(HttpRequest request) {
  if (request.status == 200) {
    print('headers: ${request.responseHeaders}');
    print('type: ${request.responseType}');
    print('text: ${request.responseText}');
  }
  else {
    print('Request failed, status={$request.status}');
  }
}
```

How to do it...

Now, we show you how to do the same thing for a blob in `request_blob.dart` (run it from `request_blob.html`) using the following code:

```
import 'dart:html';
```

1. To make a `FileReader` object, use the following code:

   ```
   FileReader flr = new FileReader();
   ImageElement img;

   void main() {
     img = document.querySelector('#anImage');
     // var path = 'stadium.jpg';
     var path =
     'https://farm1.staticflickr.com/2/
     1418878_1e92283336_m.jpg';
   ```

2. To build the request for a blob, use the following code:

   ```
   var request = new HttpRequest();
   request
   ..open('GET', path)
   ..responseType = 'blob'
   ..overrideMimeType("image/jpg")
   ..onLoadEnd.listen((e) => requestComplete(request))
   ..send('');
   }
   ```

3. To handle the response, use the following code:

```
requestComplete(HttpRequest request) {
    if (request.status == 200 &&request.readyState == HttpRequest.
DONE) {
        Blob blob = request.response;
        flr.onLoadEnd.listen( (e) {
        img.src = flr.result;
        });
        flr.readAsDataUrl(blob);
        }
    else {
    print('Request failed, status={$request.status}');
    }
}
```

Try it out with the 5 MB file `stadium.jpg`.

How it works...

To read the blob, we will need a `FileReader` object; we constructed this in step 1. In step 2, we build the request object, which is fairly general, except that we set `responseType` and `mimeType`. In the callback function in step 3, we test with `request.readyState == HttpRequest.DONE` to be sure that the request has been fully handled. Then, we performed the following steps:

▶   We created a `Blob` object from the `Blob` class in `dart:html` and set it to the response

▶   We read the blob with the method `readAsDataUrl`

▶   When this was completed (signaled by the `onLoadEnd` event), the source of the image tag was set to the result of the `FileReader` object

Transforming streams

Listening to a stream captures the sequence of results coming from an event-like action, such as clicking on a button in a web page or opening a file with the `openRead` method. These results are data that can be processed, but the errors that occur are also part of the stream. Dart can work with streams in a very functional way, such as filtering the results with `where` or mapping the results to a new stream (for a complete list of these methods, refer to `https://api.dartlang.org/apidocs/channels/stable/dartdoc-viewer/dart:async.Stream`). To modify the incoming results, we can also use a transformer; this recipe shows you how to do this (refer to the project `transforming_stream`).

How to do it...

In our script, we have a list, `persons`, where the items are themselves lists consisting of a name and a gender. We want to walk through the list and emit a greeting message based on the gender of the person, but if the gender is unknown, we skip that person. The following code shows us how we can do this with a transformer:

```
import 'dart:async';

var persons = [
  ['Carter', 'F'],
  ['Gates',  'M'],
  ['Nuryev', 'M'],
  ['Liszt', 'U'],
  ['Besançon', 'F']
  ];

void main() {
```

We need to perform the following steps to transform the streams:

1. To make a stream from the list, use the following code:

   ```
   var stream = new Stream.fromIterable(persons);
   ```

2. To define a stream transformer, use the following code:

   ```
   var transformer = new
     StreamTransformer.fromHandlers(handleData: convert);
   ```

3. To filter and transform the stream, and listen to its output to process further, use the following code:

   ```
   stream
   .where((value) => value[1] != 'U')
   .transform(transformer)
   .listen((value) => print("$value"));
   }

   convert(value, sink) {
     // create new value from the original value
     var greeting = "Hello Mr. or Mrs. ${value[0]}";
     if (value[1] == 'F') {
       greeting = "Hello Mrs. ${value[0]}";
       }
   ```

```
      else if (value[1] == 'M') {
      greeting = "Hello Mr. ${value[0]}";
    }
   sink.add(greeting);
  }
```

After performing the preceding steps, we get the following output:

Hello Mrs. Carter

Hello Mr. Gates

Hello Mr. Nuryev

Hello Mrs. Besançon

How it works...

To turn a list into a stream, we used the `fromIterable` method as in step 1. Discarding some values from the stream can be done with `where`; see the first clause in step 3.

Step 2 details how to transform a stream. This method takes an object (here called `transformer`) of the class `StreamTransformer`, which allows you to change the contents of the stream. The constructor named `fromHandlers` takes an optional `handleData` argument that calls our callback function `convert` for each value passed from the stream. The `convert` option builds a new value based on the content of the old value and adds it in place of the old value of the `sink` variable. Only those transformed values are output on the stream, passed on to `listen`, and processed there. The `sink` option is an instance of the abstract class `StreamSink`, which is a generic destination of data and can be implemented by any data receiver.

There's more...

We have already used `transform` in this chapter when reading a file with `openRead`, as shown in the following code:

```
Stream<List<int>> input = file.openRead();
input
.transform(UTF8.decoder)
.transform(const LineSplitter())
```

The `inputStream` stream is a `List<int>` list, and thus strongly typed. First, the incoming integers are transformed into a stream of UTF-8 characters, and then the input is split into subsequent lines. Instead of transform, we could have used the `map` method on the stream as well.

HttpRequest in the browser does not support getting the response as a stream. To work along that pattern, you have to use `WebSockets` (refer to *Chapter 7, Working with Web Servers*).

See also

- Refer to the *Reading a file* recipe, the second example in the *Concatenating files* recipe, and the *Writing files* recipe for more examples on transforming streams

7
Working with Web Servers

In this chapter, we will cover the following recipes:

- ► Creating a web server
- ► Posting JSON-formatted data
- ► Receiving data on the web server
- ► Serving files with http_server
- ► Using sockets
- ► Using WebSockets
- ► Using secure sockets and servers
- ► Using a JSON web service

Introduction

Dart, besides being an excellent web programming language is, also suitable for writing server applications. In this chapter, we will specifically look at Dart's `dart:io` library to write web servers and their functionality. This library is built to work asynchronously so that the server can handle many requests at the same time (concurrently). It provides the class `HttpRequest` to write command-line clients. The Dart team also wrote the `http_server` package available from pub package manager. This package needs `dart:io` and provides some higher-level classes to make it easier to write clients and servers.

Creating a web server

The class `HttpServer` is used to write web servers; this server listens on (or binds to) a particular host and port for incoming HTTP requests. It provides event handlers (better called `request handlers` in this case) that are triggered when a request with incoming data from a web client is received.

How to do it...

We make a project called `simple_webserver` starting from the template command-line application and import `dart:io` as follows:

```
import 'dart:io';
//Define host and port:
InternetAddress HOST = InternetAddress.LOOPBACK_IP_V6;
const int PORT = 8080;

main() {
  // Starting the web server:
  HttpServer.bind(HOST, PORT)
  .then((server) {
    print('server starts listening on port
  ${server.port}');
    // Starting the request handler:
    server.listen(handleRequest);
  })
  .catchError(print);
}

handleRequest(HttpRequest req) {
  print('request coming in');
  req.response
  ..headers.contentType = new ContentType("text", "plain",
    charset: "utf-8")
  ..write(' I heard you loud and clear.')
  ..write(' Send me the data!')
  ..close();
}
```

How it works...

A web server runs on a host (either specified by a name or an IP address) and uses a port on that host to listen for requests. We define these here upfront as stated in comment 1. HOST could be a string, such as localhost, or an object of the class `InternetAddress`. The LOOPBACK schema is the same as localhost; this is used for testing on a local machine. For production purposes, use `ANY_IP_V6` to allow for incoming connections from the network. Instead of `IP_V6`, you could also use `IP_V4`, but `IP_V6` is more general and includes an `IP_V4` listener.

A port can be any valid number above 1024 that is not in use. If another program is already listening on the same port (or the server is still running), an error occurs.

Next, we use the static method `bind` to create the web server; this returns a Future object to run asynchronously. When the bind is successful, the callback `then()` is called with the new `HttpServer` object as a parameter. We print out the port to the console, so we can confirm it is running. The `catchError` function will be triggered in the case of an exception and equally prints to the console.

 Always provide error handling in the code of a server!

Next, the callback handler `handleRequest` is set up; it will be triggered for any incoming request that it accepts as a parameter. In other words when a request comes in, the server creates an `HttpRequest` object and passes it to the callback `handleRequest` of `listen()`.

In this first example, we write to its `response` object after first setting the content type in the headers and close it when we're done. The `response` object is of the class `HttpResponse`; it will contains the server's answer to the request.

To see it in action, start the server from the editor or on the command line with the following command:

```
dart simple_webserver.dart
```

This produces the following server console output:

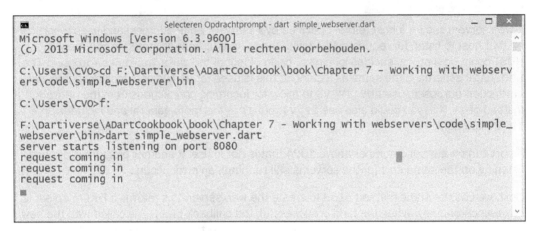

Console output from the web server

Then, start any browser with the URL `http://localhost:8080` to see the response text appear on the client as shown in the following screenshot:

The browser client shows the response

There is more...

The `HttpRequest` object also has properties that provide information about the client's request; the most important ones are as follows:

> ▸ `method`: This is derived from the way the web form was submitted. In the `<form action="http://localhost:4041"method="GET">` code, the values it can take are `GET`, `POST`, `PUT`, or `DELETE`.

> ▸ `headers`: This gives general information on the request, such as content type, content length, and date.

> ▸ `uri`: This gives the location where the request originated from.

Posting JSON-formatted data

This is a recipe for a client web app that sends a request to a web server. The request contains the form's data that is posted in the JSON format.

How to do it...

Look at the project `post_form` for the code.

1. Our form (refer the next diagram) will post data for a job in IT; we reuse the class `Job` in the *Making toJSON and fromJSON methods in your class* recipe from *Chapter 4, Object Orientation*. We keep the example short and simple, but add two new properties, `posted` and `open`. Have a look at the following code:

```
class Job {
    String type;
    int salary;
    String company;
    DateTime posted; // date of publication of job
    bool open = true; // is job still vacant ?
    Job(this.type, this.salary, this.company, this.posted);
    // toJSON and fromJSON methods
}
```

2. The `model` class is made available to the code in `post_form.dart` using the following code:

```
import '../model/job.dart';
```

3. We add our own event handler for the submit button using the following code:

```
void main() {
    querySelector("#submit").onClick.listen(submitForm);
}
```

4. The method `submitForm` makes and sends the request as follows:

```
submitForm(e) {
    e.preventDefault(); // Don't do the default submit.
    // send data to web server:
    req = new HttpRequest();
    req.onReadyStateChange.listen(onResponse);
    // POST the data to the server.
    var url = 'http://127.0.0.1:PORT';
    req.open('POST', url);
    req.send(_jobData()); // send JSON String to server
}
```

5. The `_jobData` function prepares the data to send as follows:

```
_jobData() {
    // read out data:
    InputElementicomp, isal, iposted, iopen;
    SelectElementitype;
    icomp = querySelector("#comp");
    itype = querySelector("#type");
    isal = querySelector("#sal");
    iposted = querySelector("#posted");
    iopen = querySelector("#open");
    var comp = icomp.value;
    var type = itype.value;
    varsal = isal.value.trim();
    var posted = DateTime.parse(iposted.value.trim());
    var open = iopen.value;
    // make Job object
    Job jb = new Job(type, int.parse(sal), comp, posted);
    // JSON encode object:
    return jb.toJson();
}
```

6. The `onResponse` function gets the response from the server and shows it on the screen as shown in the following code:

```
void onResponse(_) {
if (req.readyState == HttpRequest.DONE) {
    if (req.status == 200) {
        serverResponse = 'Server: ' + req.responseText;
        }
    } else if (req.status == 0) {
        // Status is 0: most likely the server isn't running.
        serverResponse = 'No server';
        }
    querySelector("#resp").text = serverResponse;
}
```

The following screenshot shows how our screen looks after sending the data:

The client sends job data

In the previous screenshot, no server is shown because there is no web server to process the request.

How it works...

In step 1, we added a `DateTime` property. Such a type is not natively serializable to JSON; the `encode` method does not know how to handle this case. We have to define this ourselves and provide a `toEncodable` closure as the second optional argument of `JSON.encode`; this returns an appropriate serialization of `DateTime`. The following code is the revised `toJson` method in the class `Job`:

```
String toJson() {
  var jsm = new Map<String, Object>();
  jsm["type"] = type;
  jsm["salary"] = salary;
  jsm["company"] = company;
  jsm["posted"] = JSON.encode(posted, toEncodable: (p){
    if(p is DateTime)
    return p.toIso8601String();
    return p;
  });
  jsm["open"] = open;
  var jss = JSON.encode(jsm);
  return jss;
}
```

The important part happens in step 4, where the `HttpRequest` object is sent; `req.open` posts the data to the URL of the server (here we test it locally with the localhost address 127.0.0.1). We also define a callback function `onResponse` for the `onReadyStateChange` event that signals when a server response comes in.

The `send()` function happens asynchronously, so it returns as soon as the request is sent; `req.send` takes the data to be sent as the argument, and this is the JSON string prepared in the function `_jobData` in step 5. This reads out the data values from the screen and makes a `Job` object with them, and JSON formats that object with `toJson`.

Finally in step 6, when the request is complete and the server responds with the OK status 200, which means success, the text response from the server is shown; otherwise it shows **No server**. The state in which the communication with the server is carried, is given by the `readyState` field. The ready state can have five possible values: `unsent`, `opened`, `headers received`, `loading`, and `done`. When the ready state changes, `HttpRequest` fires an event named `onReadyStateChange` and the `onResponse` callback function gets called.

See also

> ▶ See the *Working with blobs* recipe in *Chapter 6, Working with Files and Streams*, to learn how to make a request to download a blob file

Receiving data on the web server

In the previous recipe, we made a client app that sends its data to a web server in JSON format. In this recipe, we will make the web server that receives this data step by step, possibly process it, and then send it back to the client. You can find the code in the script `server\webserver.dart` in the project `post_form`.

How to do it...

Perform the following steps to make this work:

1. The following is the code that starts the web server:

```
import 'dart:io';

const HOST = '127.0.0.1';
const PORT = 4040;

void main() {
  HttpServer.bind(HOST, PORT).then(acceptRequests,
    onError: handleError);
}
```

2. The `acceptRequests` function describes how the web server handles incoming requests based on their method as follows:

```
void acceptRequests(server) {
  server.listen((HttpRequest req) {
    switch (req.method) {
      case 'POST':
      handlePost(req);
      break;
      case 'GET':
      handleGet(req);
      break;
      case 'OPTIONS':
      handleOptions(req);
      break;
      default: defaultHandler(req);
      }
    },
  onError: handleError, // Listen failed.
  onDone: () => print('Web server shuts down.'));
  print('Listening for GET and POST on http://$HOST:$PORT');
}
```

3. The different request handlers are shown in the following code:

```
void handlePost(HttpRequest req) {
  HttpResponse res = req.response;
  addCorsHeaders(res);
  res.statusCode = HttpStatus.OK;
  req.listen(processData, onError: handleError);
}

processData(List<int> buffer) {
  res.write('OK, I received: ');
  res.write(new String.fromCharCodes(buffer));
  // process incoming data
  res.close();
}

handleGet(HttpRequest req) { // not needed here }

void handleOptions(HttpRequest req) { // not needed here }

void addCorsHeaders(HttpResponse res) {
  res.headers.add('Access-Control-Allow-Origin', '*');
```

```
        res.headers.add('Access-Control-Allow-Methods', 'POST, OPTIONS');
        res.headers.add('Access-Control-Allow-Headers',
        'Origin, X-Requested-With, Content-Type, Accept');
    }

    void defaultHandler(HttpRequest req) {
        res = req.response;
        res.statusCode = HttpStatus.METHOD_NOT_ALLOWED;
        res.write("Unsupported request: ${req.method}.");
        res.close();
    }

    handleError(e) {
        print(e);
        // other error handling
    }
```

Run the client from the previous recipe (start `web\post_form.html`) and post a job in JSON format to the server. The web server responds with an acknowledgement and returns the data back to the client. The client shows the following response:

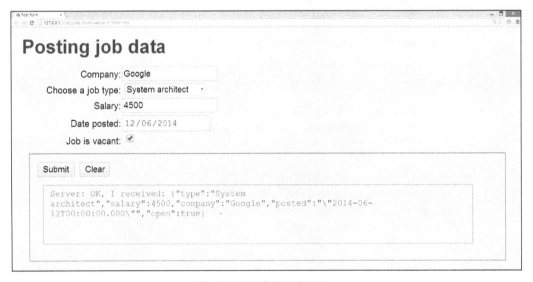

The response of the web server

How it works...

In step 1, we used an alternative way (compared to the *Making a web server* recipe) to start up the server; we give two callback functions for the `Future` object returned by `bind`:

 ▸ The first parameter is the `acceptRequests` function, which receives an `HttpServer` object as a parameter and then listens for incoming requests

 ▸ The second parameter is the optional `onError` argument with the callback function `handleError`; this is invoked when the binding fails, for example, when the port is in use

Another, more elegant way of writing this is shown in the following code:

```
HttpServer.bind(HOST, PORT)
.then(acceptRequests)
.catchError(handleError);
```

Step 2 gives us the processing of requests. For every incoming request, the server creates an `HttpRequest` object and passes it to the callback of `listen()`. So, the `HttpServer` object produces a stream of `HttpRequest` objects to be processed. Here, we see how you can use a switch/case to act differently on different kinds of requests (other request method), using the same exception-catching mechanism as in step 1. A second optional `onDone` parameter is a function that is called when the server is shut down.

In step 3, we built different request handlers. We always set the status code of the response, such as `res.statusCode = HttpStatus.OK;`; there are a lot of predefined values. See the docs for the class `HttpStatus`. In particular, you can use `HttpStatus.NOT_FOUND` in an error handler to signal a `404 File not Found` HTTP error.

One thing to notice here is that we let the server send CORS headers to the client. This allows the client to send POST requests in the event that this web server is different from the one serving the original web application. Then, the client must first send an `OPTIONS` request, but for this, we don't have to write client code; it is handled automatically by the `HttpRequest` object. For a POST request, the code in `handlePost` listens for the client's data in `req.listen`. When all of the data is received, this is passed as a `List<int>` buffer to the callback function `processData`. In our case, this makes a string from the data and writes it back to the response. The response is a data stream that the server can use to send data back to the client. Other methods of writing to this stream are `writeln()`, `writeAll()`, and `writeCharCodes()`.

At this point in the code, the real server processing of the data, such as writing to a file (for example code see the *There's more...* section) or saving in a database, will be done. Closing the response sends it to the client.

There's more...

If the server has to set the content type for the response, do this as follows before the first write to the response in `handlePost`:

```
res.headers.contentType =
new ContentType("application", "json", charset: 'utf-8');
```

Here, we make it clear that we send JSON data using the UTF-8 character set.

Writing data to a file on the server

If we wanted to write the data received from the client to a file, we could do this as follows:

▶ Add the following line to `handlePost` before `req.listen`:

```
BytesBuilder builder = new BytesBuilder();
```

▶ In the following code, we see `processData`:

```
processData(List<int> buffer) {
  builder.add(buffer);
}
```

▶ The `builder` option collects the buffered data in chunks through the `add` method until all the data is delivered. Then, the `onDone` method in `acceptRequests` is called, such as `onDone writeToFile`). In the following code, we see `writeToFile`:

```
writeToFile(builder) {
  var strJson = UTF8.decode(builder.takeBytes());
  var filename = "jobs.json";
  new File(filename).writeAsString(strJson, mode:
    FileMode.APPEND).then((_) {
    res.write('Job data was appended to file');
    res.close();
  });
}
```

See also

▶ See the *Using CORS headers* recipe in *Chapter 5, Handling Web Applications*, for more information on CORS

Serving files with http_server

One of the main functions of a web server that we take for granted is the serving of static files. We can write this functionality completely with the classes from `dart:io`, but the Dart team has written a pub package called `http_server` with the aim to simplify web server programming to provide web content. We will use `http_server` in this recipe to code a web server that serves files. You can find the code in the project `serving_files`.

How to do it...

Perform the following steps to construct a web server for server files:

1. In the first example, `serving_file.dart`, you see the code for a web server delivering a file called `Learning Dart Packt Publishing.html`:

    ```
    import 'dart:io';
    import 'package:http_server/http_server.dart';

    InternetAddress HOST = InternetAddress.LOOPBACK_IP_V6;
    const PORT = 8080;

    void main() {
      VirtualDirectory staticFiles = new VirtualDirectory('.');
      HttpServer.bind(HOST, PORT).then((server) {
        server.listen((req) {
        staticFiles.serveFile(new File('Learning Dart Packt
        Publishing.html'), req);
        });
      });
    }
    ```

    Start the server by running `bin\serving_file.dart` and open a browser with the URL `localhost:8080`. You will see the **Learning Dart** web page.

2. To serve all files from the current directory, and all its subfolders, expand the code as shown in the following code (to see `serving_curdir.dart`):

    ```
    import 'dart:io';
    import 'dart:async';
    import 'package:http_server/http_server.dart';

    InternetAddress HOST = InternetAddress.LOOPBACK_IP_V6;
    const PORT = 8080;
    VirtualDirectory staticFiles;

    void main() {
    ```

```
      staticFiles = new VirtualDirectory('.')
      ..allowDirectoryListing = true;

      runZoned( startServer, onError: handleError);
}

startServer() {
   HttpServer.bind(HOST, PORT).then((server) {
      server.listen(staticFiles.serveRequest);
      });
}

handleError(e, stackTrace) {
      print('An error occurred: $e $stackTrace');
}
```

Start the server by running `bin\serving_curdir.dart`, and open a browser with the URL `localhost:8080`. You will see a list of what's inside the bin folder as shown in the following screenshot:

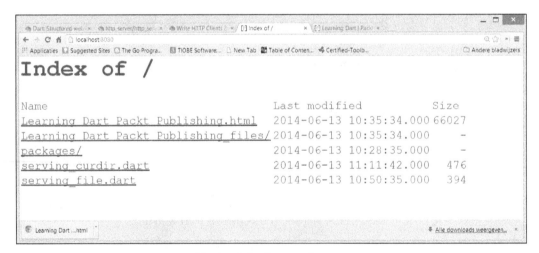

Directory listing from a web server

How it works...

In step 1, we first add the package `http_server` to our project (adding it to `pubspec.yaml` and importing it in the code). Then, we define the folder from which serving will take place by making an object `staticFiles` from the class `VirtualDirectory`. This class handles all the details of serving files, specifying here that it will serve from the current directory. On this object, we call the method `serveFile` with a reference to the file as an argument.

In step 2, the `serveRequest` method handles a single request for any file in the current directory (the property `allowDirectoryListing` makes the content viewable). Notice that the server request handler is enveloped in a call to the method `runZoned` from `dart:async`. This is not needed to make it work, but it illustrates a way to make our code more robust. When using `runZoned`, the function given as its first argument is executed as if in a sandbox, and the second optional argument `onError` handles all uncaught exceptions, synchronous or asynchronous. You can find more details about the use of zones at `https://www.dartlang.org/articles/zones/`.

There's more...

- If you need the path to the current executing script, use the following code:
  ```
  var path = Platform.script.toFilePath();
  ```

- If you need the path to the web folder, use the following code:
  ```
  final HTTP_ROOT_PATH =
    Platform.script.resolve('web').toFilePath();
  ```

- You can point a virtual directory to that path in order to start serving files from that folder using the following code:
  ```
  final virDir = new VirtualDirectory(HTTP_ROOT_PATH);
  ```

Together, the classes `HttpServer`, `VirtualDirectory`, and `Platform` are sufficient to implement a basic web server. When different responses are needed according to the URL, the class `Router` (see the *Using WebSockets* recipe) can simplify the code.

 Use the pub package `path` and its cross-platform methods, such as `join` and `split` if you need to manipulate the path to certain folders or files. In particular, `toUri()` and `fromUri()` are useful when converting between a URI and a path.

Using sockets

At a somewhat lower level in the OSI model than HTTP clients and servers, we find sockets. They also enable interprocess communications across a network between clients and servers and are implemented on top of the TCP/IP. The classes that offer that functionality can be again found in `dart:io` as follows:

- `Socket`: This is used by a client to establish a connection to a server
- `ServerSocket`: This is used by a server to accept client connections

How to do it...

The following steps will show you how to make a server socket work:

1. The following is the code for the server (see the project `sockets`, `socket_server.dart`):

    ```
    import 'dart:io';
    import 'dart:convert';

    InternetAddress HOST = InternetAddress.LOOPBACK_IP_V6;
    const PORT = 7654;

    void main() {
      ServerSocket.bind(HOST, PORT)
      .then((ServerSocket srv) {
        print('serversocket is ready');
        srv.listen(handleClient);
      })
            .catchError(print);
      );
    }

    void handleClient(Socket client){
      print('Connection from: '
      '${client.remoteAddress.address}:${client.remotePort}');
      // data from client:
      client.transform(UTF8.decoder).listen(print);
      // data to client:
      client.write("Hello from Simple Socket Server!\n");
      client.close();
    }
    ```

    Start the server by running `bin\socket_server.dart`.

2. The following is the code for a client (see the project `sockets`, `socket_client.dart`):

    ```
    import 'dart:io';

    InternetAddress HOST = InternetAddress.LOOPBACK_IP_V6;
    const PORT = 7654;

    void main() {
      Socket.connect("google.com", 80).then((socket) {
        print('Connected to: '
    ```

```
      '${socket.remoteAddress.address}:${socket.remotePort}');
      socket.destroy();
      });
      // prints: Connected to: 173.194.65.101:80

      Socket.connect(HOST, PORT).then((socket) {
      print(socket.runtimeType);
      // data to server:
      socket.write('Hello, World from a client!');
      // data from server:
      socket.listen(onData);
      });
  }

  onData(List<int> data) {
      print(new String.fromCharCodes(data));
  }
```

3. Start one (or more) client(s) by running `bin\socket_client.dart`.

    The following is the output from the server console:

    serversocket is ready

    Connection from: ::200:0:8017:7b01%211558873:6564

    Hello, World from a client!

    The following is the output from a client console:

    _Socket

    Hello from Simple Socket Server!

    Connected to: 74.125.136.139:80

We can see that there is two-way communication.

How it works...

In step 1, a server to handle client socket connections is created by binding `ServerSocket` to a specific TCP port that it will listen on. This `bind` method returns a Future `<ServerSocket>`. Again, we will use the `Future.then` method to register our callback so that we know when the socket has been bound to the port. Then, the server starts listening and calls `handleClient` for each incoming connection. This callback prints the remote address from the client, prints the data the client has sent, writes a message to the client, and then closes the connection.

In step 2, the client first opens a connection to www.google.com on port 80 (the port that serves web pages). After the socket is connected to the server, the IP address and port are printed to the screen. Then, the socket is shut down using socket.destroy. In the second part of this step, we connect to the local socket server, write a message to it with socket.write, and start listening to the server with socket.listen. We transform the data that comes in as a list of integers into a string that is printed out.

There's more...

Socket communication is often blocked by firewalls; if this is an issue, take a look at WebSockets in the following recipe.

Dart also supports UDP socket programming; the article by James Locum offers a detailed discussion at http://jamesslocum.com/post/77759061182.

Using WebSockets

This recipe will show you how to use WebSockets in a client-server application (both web and command-line clients) and what its advantages are. You can find the code in the project websockets.

Getting ready

HTTP is a simple request-response-based protocol, and then the connection is broken from the application's point of view until the next request. In a modern web application (for example, in online multiplayer games), the client and server are of equal importance; changes in the state of the application can take place on both sides. So, we need a bi-directional communication channel between the client(s) and the server that allows for two-way real time updates and more interaction; this is exactly what WebSockets has to offer. WebSocket connections between a browser and a server are made through a handshake request. This is a regular HTTP client request with an upgrade flag in the header, also containing a Sec-WebSocket-Key, which is a random value that has been base64 encoded. To complete the handshake, the server responds with a Sec-WebSocket-Accept response.

WebSockets are implemented in all modern browsers (Internet Explorer v10 and above), and can also be used in non-web applications. The communication takes place over TCP port 80, so it can pass unhindered through firewalls.

How to do it...

Perform the following steps to make a WebSockets server work:

1. Use the following code to set up a WebSockets server (see `websocket_server.dart`):

```
import 'dart:io';
import 'dart:async';

InternetAddress HOST = InternetAddress.ANY_IP_V6;
const PORT = 8080;

main() {
  runZoned(startWSServer, onError: handleError);
}

startWSServer() {
  HttpServer.bind(HOST, PORT)
    .then((server) {
    print('Http server started on $HOST $PORT');
    server.listen(handleRequest);
  });
}

handleError(e, stackTrace) {
  print('An error occurred: $e $stackTrace');
}

handleRequest(HttpRequest req) {
  if ( (req.uri.path == '/ws') // command-line client
  || WebSocketTransformer.isUpgradeRequest(req) // web-client
  ){
    // Upgrade a HttpRequest to a WebSocket connection.
    WebSocketTransformer.upgrade(req).then(handleWebSocket);
  }
  else {
    print("Regular ${req.method} request for: ${req.uri.path}");
    serveNonWSRequest(req);
  }
}

handleWebSocket(WebSocket socket) {
  print('Client connected!');
  socket.listen((String msg) {
    print('Message received: $msg');
```

```
          socket.add('echo from server: $msg');
          },
          onError: (err) {
          print('Bad WebSocket request $err');
          },
          onDone: () {
          print('Client disconnected');
        });
  }
  serveNonWSRequest(req) {
    var resp = req.response;
    resp.statusCode = HttpStatus.FORBIDDEN;
    resp.reasonPhrase = "WebSocket connections only";
    resp.response.close();
  }
```

2. The following code is used for a command-line WebSocket client (websocket_
    client.dart):

```dart
import 'dart:io';

const HOST = 'localhost';
const PORT = 8080;

main() {
  var wsurl = "ws://$HOST:$PORT/ws";
  WebSocket.connect(wsurl)
  //Open the websocket and attach the callbacks
  .then((socket) {
  socket.add('from client: Hello Websockets Server!');
  socket.listen(onMessage, onDone: connectionClosed);
  })
  .catchError(print);
}

void onMessage(String msg){
  print(msg);
  }

  void connectionClosed() {
  print('Connection to server closed');
}
```

If we run the server script, `websocket_server.dart`, and then start a client `websocket_client.dart`, we get the following output on the server console:

Http server started on InternetAddress('::1', IP_V6)8080   **Client connected!**   **Message received: from client: Hello Websockets Server!**

The client console prints the following output:

echo from server: Hello Websockets Server!

To make a web client, we need a web page `websocket_webclient.html` that invokes a script `websocket_webclient.dart`. The web page is kept very simple with an input field that will collect a string to send to the server and a `<div>` element that shows the response from the server as follows:

```
<h1>WebSocket Sample</h1>
<input id="input" type="text"></input>
<div id="output"></div>
<script type="application/dart"
  src="websocket_webclient.dart"></script>
```

The following is the script code:

```
import 'dart:html';

void main() {
  TextInputElement inp = querySelector('#input');
  DivElement out = querySelector('#output');

  String srvuri = 'ws://localhost:8080/ws';
  WebSocket ws = new WebSocket(srvuri);

  inp.onChange.listen((Event e){
  ws.send(inp.value.trim());
  inp.value = "";
});

ws.onOpen.listen((Event e) {
  outputMessage(out, 'Connected to server');
});

ws.onMessage.listen((MessageEvent e){
  outputMessage(out, e.data);
});

ws.onClose.listen((Event e) {
  outputMessage(out, 'Connection to server lost...');
```

```
    });

  ws.onError.first.then((_) {
    print("Failed to connect to ${ws.url}. "
    "Please rerun bin/websocket_server.dart and try again.");
    });
  }

  void outputMessage(Element e, String message){
    print(message);
    e.appendText(message);
    e.appendHtml('<br/>');
    //Make sure we 'autoscroll' the new messages
    e.scrollTop = e.scrollHeight;
  }
```

When the server runs, start the web client by opening `websocket_webclient.html`, and type in some text. The text received by the web server is echoed back and shown both on the page and in the editor console as follows:

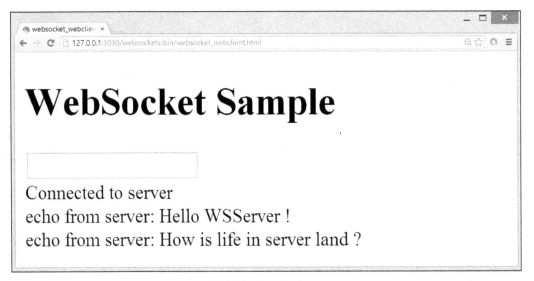

A WebSocket web client

How it works...

In step 1, the server is run in a `runZoned()` clause to add additional exception handling capabilities (see the *Serving files with http_server* recipe). We start a web server as usual. In `handleRequest`, we check whether the path of the request ends in `/ws`. In that case, we have a command-line client issuing a WebSocket request. A web client making a WebSocket request will add an upgrade flag in the headers. For this, we can test it with the `isUpgradeRequest` method of the `WebSocketTransformer` class. If that is the case, we call the `upgrade` method on the same class, and when done, we call the `handleWebSocket` method. This starts listening for client connections, prints out any client message in the server console, and echoes this back to the client. If the message was a JSON string, we could have decoded it before it starts listening to client connections with `socket.map((string) => JSON.decode(string))`.

In the case of a normal HTTP request, `serveNonWSRequest` is used to block it, but of course, we could do normal web request handling as well.

The command-line client in step 2 uses the `WebSocket` class from `dart:io`. It connects to a WebSocket server with a `ws://` URL as a parameter to the `connect` method. Then, it can write to the socket with `add` and receive messages on the socket with `listen`.

The web client in step 3 uses the `WebSocket` class from `dart:html`. Calling its constructor with the URI of the server opens the web socket connection. The `send` method called on this instance sends the client data (here, the text of the input field) to the server. When the response from the server can be read from the socket, the `onMessage` event is fired and shows the response. Other useful events of the `WebSocket` instance are:

- onOpen: This is called when the connection is made
- onClose: This is called when the socket is no longer available (because the server was shut down or a network connection failure)
- onError: This is called when an error occurs during the client-server dialog

There's more...

The pub package `route` can be used to associate callbacks with URL patterns. In this recipe, instead of testing the `/ws` pattern, we could have used `Router` from the package `route` to do that for us. We import this package, and then `startWSServer` will contain the following code:

```
import 'package:route/server.dart' show Router;

startWSServer() {
  HttpServer.bind(HOST, PORT).then((server) {
  print('Http server started on $HOST $PORT');
  Router router = new Router(server);
```

```
router.serve('/ws').transform(new WebSocketTransformer()).
    listen(handleWebSocket);
  });
}
```

As a more general example of how routing can be useful, consider the following example. Let's suppose our clients search for stock data with URLs ending with /stocks and /stocks/ GOOG. Then, we can define pattern1 and pattern2 as instances of the class UrlPattern with a regular expression containing the following pattern:

```
// Pattern for all stocks(plural).
final stocksUrl = new UrlPattern(r'/stocks\/?');
// Pattern for a single stock('/stock/GOOG', for example).
final stockUrl = new UrlPattern(r'/stock/(\d+)\/?');
```

Our router instance will then bind the callback functions serveStocks and serveStock to those patterns through the serve method:

```
var router = new Router(server)
..serve(stocksUrl, method: 'GET').listen(serveStocks)
..serve(stockUrl, method: 'GET').listen(serveStock)
  // all other possible patterns and method combinations
..defaultStream.listen(serveNotFound);
```

As shown in the first example, patterns can also be simple strings like /stockdata.

See also

- ▶ Look at the *Serving files with http_server* recipe for more information on runZoned
- ▶ The Dart website has a very good tutorial on a search app implemented with WebSockets and Dartiverse Search, at https://www.dartlang.org/docs/ dart-up-and-running/contents/ch05.html

Using secure sockets and servers

In this recipe, we describe the steps to make your web server encrypt its communication with clients using **Secure Sockets Layer** (**SSL**) on the HTTPS protocol.

Getting ready

Dart uses SSL/TSL security; it relies on X.509 certificates to validate servers and (optionally) clients. The server provides a certificate that will verify itself as a trusted server to the client. When the client accepts the certificate, symmetric session keys will be exchanged and used to encrypt the communications between the server and the client. So, in order for your server to provide a secured connection, it has to have a security certificate installed, provided by a **Certificate Authority (CA)**.

Dart uses a **Network Security Services (NSS)** database to store the server's private key and certificate. For our example, we will use the test certificate database in the subfolder `pkcert`, which is also provided as an illustration in the tutorial at `https://www.dartlang.org/docs/tutorials/httpserver/`.

You can set up an NSS key database yourself to create certificates for test purposes. James Locum provides a detailed description on how to do this at `http://jamesslocum.com/post/70003236123`.

How to do it...

The program `secure_server.dart` shows us the code needed to start a secure server; perform the following steps to use secure sockets and service:

1. Import the dart:io package as follows:

```
import 'dart:io';

InternetAddress HOST = InternetAddress.LOOPBACK_IP_V6;
const int PORT = 8080;

main() {
```

2. Read the certificate using the following code:

```
var testcertDb =
  Platform.script.resolve('pkcert').toFilePath();
SecureSocket.initialize(database: testcertDb, password:
  'dartdart');
```

3. Start the HTTP server with the certificate using the following code:

```
HttpServer.bindSecure(HOST, PORT, certificateName:
  'localhost_cert').then((server) {
  print('Secure Server listening');
  server.listen((HttpRequest req) {
    print('Request for ${req.uri.path}');
    var resp = req.response;
    resp.write("Don't worry: I encrypt your messages!");
```

```
      resp.close();
    });
  });
}
```

4. If we now use the URL `https://localhost:8080` in a browser, we first get a screen warning us that this connection is not trusted (because it is only a test certificate). If we continue, we see the response of the server in the browser's screen as shown in the following screenshot:

A secure socket connection

The following is the code for a secure command-line client (`secure_client.dart`):

```
import 'dart:io';

InternetAddress HOST = InternetAddress.LOOPBACK_IP_V6;
const int PORT = 4777;
SecureSocket socket;

void main() {
  SecureSocket.connect(HOST, PORT, onBadCertificate:
    (X509Certificate c) {
    print("Certificate WARNING: ${c.issuer}:${c.subject}");
    return true;
    }).then(handleSecureSocket);
}

handleSecureSocket(SecureSocket ss) {
  // send to server:
  ss.write("From client: can you encrypt me server?");
  // read from server:
  ss.listen((List data) {
  String msg = new String.fromCharCodes(data).trim();
  print(msg);
  });
}
```

The client console gives the following output:

Certificate WARNING: CN=myauthority:CN=localhost

How it works...

In step 1, we read the certificate. The first line with `Platform.script` finds the path to the folder `pkcert`, where the certificate database is located. Then we call the `initialize` method on the class `SecureSocket`, providing the certificate. In step 2, the secure server is started by binding to a host and port and providing the name of the certificate. Step 3 shows us a browser connecting to the secure server.

In step 4, we see how a command-line client can connect to the secure server by calling `SecureSocket.connect()`. This needs an `onBadCertificate` callback, which must return a Boolean value that indicates whether to accept or reject a bad certificate. The test certificate will trigger this callback, so we need to return `true` in order to use this certificate. With respect to the `write` and `listen` methods of `SecureSocket`, let's write to and read from the secure server.

See also

▸ Refer to the *Getting information from the operating system* recipe in *Chapter 1, Working with Dart Tools*, for more details about the `Platform` class

▸ For more information about certificates and creating them, refer to `https://help.ubuntu.com/12.04/serverguide/certificates-and-security.html`

Using a JSON web service

In this recipe, we make a browser app ask data from a web service (Yahoo stock data) in JSON format, decode that data, and dynamically build up the web page showing the data.

Getting ready

This is what the URL we will use will look like: `http://query.yahooapis.com/v1/public/yql?q=SELECT`.

To get the data, we use the **Yahoo Query Language** (**YQL**), `q=` indicating the start of the query represented by `SELECT`. Suppose we want to look up stock data for Yahoo, Google, Apple, and Microsoft, the selected query will be of the following form:

```
select * from yahoo.finance.quotes where symbol
  in(YHOO,AAPL,GOOG,CMSFT)
  &env=http://datatables.org/Falltables.env&format=json
```

How to do it...

Look at the code in `stockviewer_dart`:

```dart
import 'dart:html';
import 'dart:convert';

main() {
  LoadData();
}
```

1. Call the web server asynchronously using the following code:

```dart
void LoadData() {
  var stock = "GOOG";
  var request =
    "http://query.yahooapis.com/v1/public/
    yql?q=select%20*%20from%20yahoo.finance.quotes%20"
  "where%20symbol%20in%20(%22$stock%22)%0A%09%09"
    "&env=http%3A%2F%2Fdatatables.org%2Falltables.
    env&format=json";
  var result =
    HttpRequest.getString(request).then(OnDataLoaded);
}
```

2. Web service responses callback as shown in the following code:

```dart
void OnDataLoaded(String response) {
  String json = response.substring(response.indexOf("symbol")
    - 2, response.length - 3);
  Map data = JSON.decode(json);
  var table = CreateTable();
  var props = data.keys;
  props.forEach((prop) => ProcessStockEntry(prop, data,
    table));
  document.body.nodes.add(table);
}
```

3. Create the HTML table with the data as shown in the following code:

```
TableElement CreateTable() {
   TableElement table = new TableElement();
   var tBody = table.createTBody();
   return table;
}

void ProcessStockEntry(String prop, Map data, TableElement
   table) {
   String value = data["$prop"];
   var row = table.insertRow(-1);   // Add new row to our table
   var propCell = row.insertCell(0); // Add new cell for
     property
   String prophtml = '$prop:';
   propCell.setInnerHtml(prophtml);
   var valueCell = row.insertCell(1); // Add new cell for the
     value
   String valuehtml = '$value';
   valueCell.setInnerHtml(valuehtml);
}
```

The browser shows the stock data as shown in the following screenshot:

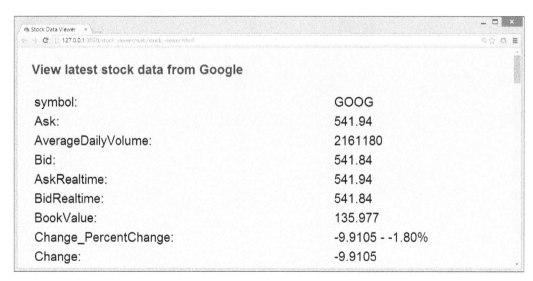

Stock data from the JSON web service

How it works...

In step 1, the request string is URI encoded, and the stock symbol we want is inserted. Then, the web server is called with the `getString` method from `HttpRequest`. Step 2 shows the code that analyzes the response when this has arrived. We extracted the map with the stock data (starting with the symbol) and decoded that JSON string into the map data. We then created an HTML table, and for each of the properties in the stock data (`Ask`, `AverageDailyVolume`, `Bid`, and so on), we inserted a table row with the key and the data in step 3.

See also

▶ See the *Downloading a file* recipe for more information on the `getString` method

8
Working with Futures, Tasks, and Isolates

In this chapter, we will cover the following recipes:

- Writing a game loop
- Error handling with Futures
- Scheduling tasks using Futures
- Running a recurring function
- Using isolates in the Dart VM
- Using isolates in web apps
- Using multiple cores with isolates
- Using the Worker Task framework

Introduction

The `Future` class from `dart:async` lies in the basis of all asynchronous programming in Dart. A Future is, in fact, a computation that is deferred; it represents an object whose value will be available sometime in the future. It is not available immediately, because the function that returns its value depends on some kind of input/output and is, thus, unpredictable by nature. Here are some examples: a time-consuming computation, reading in a big dataset, and searching through a number of websites.

In the two previous chapters, quite a lot of recipes used Futures; in *Chapter 6, Working with Files and Streams*, we had the following recipes using Futures:

- *Reading and processing a file line by line*
- *Concatenating files the asynchronous way*
- *Downloading a file*

In the preceding chapter, we used Futures in the following recipes:

- *Making a web server*
- *Receiving data on the web server*
- *Using sockets*

In this chapter, we will concentrate on how to write elegant code for Futures and combine their possibilities with the execution of tasks and isolates to enhance the performance of our apps.

Dart runs single-threaded, so it uses, by default, only one CPU on a multi-core machine; if you want concurrency, you must use isolates. In the second part of the chapter, you will find recipes featuring isolates, Dart's mechanism to provide concurrency and parallelism in applications.

Writing a game loop

In game apps, the refresh rate of the screen is vital; it must be high enough to ensure agreeable and realistic gameplay. Refreshing means periodically redrawing the screen. This recipe shows you how to build that in your app. It is illustrated in the code of `gameloop`, a simple version of the well-known memory game that uses the `boarding` package by Dzenan Ridzanovic. The goal is to click quickly enough to get identical pairs of the colored squares. Start it by running `game.html` (don't use `pub serve` for the launch, select **Run** and then **Manage Launches**, and in **Pub Settings**, uncheck **use pub serve to serve the application**).

How to do it...

1. The game starts off in `main()` of `game.dart` (only the relevant parts of the code are shown here):

```
import'dart:async';
import 'dart:html';
// ... other code
part'model/memory.dart';
part'view/board.dart';

main() {
    new Board(new Memory(4), querySelector('#canvas')).draw();
}
```

2. In the constructor of the `Board` class, the game loop is started with the call to `window.animationFrame`:

```
class Board extends Surface {
  // code left out

  Board(Memory memory, CanvasElement canvas) :
    this.memory = memory,
  super(memory, canvas) {
    // code left out
    querySelector('#canvas').onMouseDown.listen((MouseEvent e) {
    // code left out
    if (memory.recalled) { // game over
    new Timer(const Duration(milliseconds: 5000), ()
      =>memory.hide());
    }
  else if (cell.twin.hidden) {
  new Timer(const Duration(milliseconds: 800), ()
    =>cell.hidden = true);
  }
});

  window.animationFrame.then(gameLoop);
  }
```

3. And here is the `gameloop` method itself:

```
voidgameLoop(num delta) {
  draw();
  window.animationFrame.then(gameLoop);
}
void draw() {
  super.draw();
  if (memory.recalled) { // game over
  // code left out
  }
}
```

How it works...

In step 1, the game is started by instantiating an object of the `Board` class (from `view/board.dart`) and calling the `draw` method on it. In step 2, the most important statement is the last one in the constructor, `window.animationFrame.then(gameLoop);`.

This method of the `Window` class in `dart:html` returns a Future that completes just before the window is about to repaint, so this is the right time to redraw our screen.

> Use `animationFrame` to do this, because the animation then uses a consistent frame rate, and thus, looks smoother, and it also works at the screen's refresh rate. Don't use `Future` or `Timer` to draw frames; use `Timer` only if you have to code for a browser that does not support `animationFrame`!

This is done in the callback method `gameloop` in step 3; first `draw()` is executed, then `window.animationFrame`, and then (`gameLoop`). So, this recursively calls `gameloop` again and again. This way, we are sure that the animation will continue.

There's more...

We also see how the class `Timer` from `dart:async` is used. For example, in the end-of-game condition (memory is recalled), the colored pattern is hidden from sight after 5 seconds by the following `Timer` object:

```
new Timer(const Duration(milliseconds: 5000), () =>memory.hide());
```

After this duration of time, the anonymous callback function, `() =>memory.hide()`, is executed. Use the named constructor, `Timer.periodic`, with the same arguments to execute a callback function periodically.

See also

▶ Refer to the *Running a recurring function* recipe in this chapter to find out more about the `Timer` class

Error handling with Futures

This recipe shows you how to handle errors comprehensively when working with Futures. The accompanying code `future_errors.dart` (inside the bin map in the `future_errors` project) illustrates the different possibilities; however, this is not a real project, so it is not meant to be run as is.

Getting ready

When the function that returns a `Future` value completes successfully (calls back) signaled in the code by `then`, a callback function `handleValue` is executed that receives the value returned. If an error condition took place, the callback `handleError` handles it. Let's say this function is `getFuture()`, with Future as the result and a return value of type T, then this becomes equivalent to the following code:

```
Future<T> future = getFuture();
future.then(handleValue)
.catchError(handleError);

handleValue(val) {
   // processing the value
}

handleError(err) {
   // handling the error
}
```

The highlighted code is sometimes also written as follows, only to make the return values explicit:

```
future.then( (val) =>handleValue(val) )
.catchError( (err) =>handleError(err) );
```

When there is no return value, this can also be written as shown in the following code:

```
future.then( () =>nextStep() )
```

When the return value doesn't matter in the code, this can be written with an _ in place of that value, as shown in the following code:

```
future.then( (_) =>nextStep(_) )
```

But, in any case, we prefer to write succinct code, as follows:

```
future.then(nextStep)
```

The `then` and `catcherror` objects are chained as they are called, but that doesn't mean that they are both executed. Only one executes completely; compare it to the try-catch block in synchronous code. The `catcherror` object can even catch an error thrown in `handleValue`.

This is quite an elegant mechanism, but what do we do when the code gets a little more complicated?

How to do it...

Let's see the different ways you can work with Futures in action:

▸ **Chaining Futures**: Let's suppose we have a number of steps that each will return a Future and so run asynchronously, but the steps have to execute in a certain order. We could chain these as shown in the following code:

```
firstStep()
    .then((_) =>secondStep())
    .then((_) =>thirdStep())
    .then((_) =>fourthStep())
    .catchError(handleError);
```

▸ **Concurrent Futures**: If, on the other hand, all the steps return a value of the type T, and their order of execution is not important, you can use the static method of Future, wait, as shown in the following code:

```
List futs = [firstStep(), secondStep(), thirdStep(),
fourthStep()];
Future.wait(futs)
.then((_) =>processValues(_))
.catchError(handleError);
```

▸ Run the script wait_error.dart to see what happens when an error occurs in one of the steps (either by throw or a Future.error call):

```
import'dart:async';

main() {
  Future<int> a = new Future(() {
  print('a');
  return 1;
});
Future<int> b = new Future.error('Error occured in b!');
Future<int> c = new Future(() {
  print('c');
  return 3;
});
Future<int> d = new Future(() {
  print('d');
  return 4;
});

Future.wait([a, b, c, d]).then((List<int> values) =>
print(values)).catchError(print);
```

```
  print('happy end');
}
```

The output is as follows:

happy end

a

c

d

Error occurred in b!

▶ The following code helps to catch a specific error or more than one error:

```
firstStep()
.then((_) =>secondStep())
    // more .then( steps )
.catchError(handleArgumentError,
test: (e) => e is ArgumentError)
.catchError(handleFormatException,
test: (e) => e is FormatException)
.catchError(handleRangeError,
test: (e) => e is RangeError)
.catchError(handleException, test: (e) => e is Exception);
```

▶ Often, you want to execute a method that does a cleanup after asynchronous processing no matter whether this processing succeeds or ends in an error. In that case, use whenComplete:

```
firstStep()
.then((_) =>secondStep())
.catchError(handleError)
.whenComplete(cleanup);
```

With respect to handling synchronous and asynchronous errors, let's suppose that we want to call a function mixedFunction, with a synchronous call to synFunc that could throw an exception and an asynchronous call to asynFunc that could do likewise, as shown in the following code:

```
mixedFunction(data) {
  var var2 = new Var2();
  var var1 = synFunc(data);         // Could throw error.
  return var2.asynFunc().then(processResult);   // Could throw error.
}
```

If we call this function mixedFunction(data).catchError(handleError);, then catchError cannot catch an error thrown by synFunc. To solve this, they call in a Future. sync, function as shown in the following code:

```
mixedFunction(data) {
  return new Future.sync(() {
    var var1 = synFunc(data);           // Could throw error.
    return var1.asynFunc().then(processResult);  // Could throw error.
  });
}
```

That way, catchError can catch both synchronous and asynchronous errors.

How it works...

In variation 1, catchError will handle all errors that occur in any of the executed steps. For variation 2, we make a list with all the steps. The Future.wait option will do exactly as its name says: it will wait until all of the steps are completed. But they are executed in no particular order, so they can run concurrently. All of the functions are triggered without first waiting for any particular function to complete. When they are all done, their return values are collected in a list (here called val) and can be processed. Again, catchError handles any possible error that occurs in any of the steps.

In the case of an error, the List value is not returned; we see that, in the example on wait_ error, **happy end** is first printed, then a, c, and d complete, and then the error from b is caught; if d also throws an error, only the b error is caught. The catchError function doesn't know in which step the error occurred unless that is explicitly conveyed in the error.

In the same way as in the catch block, we can also test in catchError when a specific exception occurs using its second optional test argument, where you test the type of the exception. This is shown in variation 3; be sure then, to test for a general exception as the last clause. This scenario will certainly be useful if a number of different exceptions can occur and we want a specific treatment for each of them.

Analogous to the optional finally clause in a try statement, asynchronous processing can have a whenComplete handler as in variation 4, which always executes whether there is an error or not. Use it to clean up and close files, databases, and network connections, and so on.

Finally, in variation 5, the normal catchError function won't work, because it can only handle exceptions arising from asynchronous code execution. Use Future.synchere, which is able to return the result or error from both synchronous and asynchronous method calls.

Scheduling tasks using Futures

The Dart VM is single-threaded, so all of an app's code runs in one thread, also called the main isolate. This is because `main()` is the function where Dart code starts executing an isolate, because Dart's concurrency model is based on isolates as separate processes that exchange messages. We will talk about isolates in depth in the coming recipes, but if your code doesn't start a new isolate, all of it runs in one isolate. But, in this one isolate, you can have lots of asynchronous pieces of code (let's call them tasks) running at the same time; in what order do they execute, and can we influence that order? It turns out that a better understanding of Dart's event loop and task queuing mechanism enables us to do that. This recipe will clarify Dart's scheduling mechanism and give you hints and tips for an ordered execution of tasks.

How to do it...

Have a look at the program `tasks_scheduling.dart` (the tasks are numbered consecutively and according to the way they are started):

```
import 'dart:async';

main() {
  print('1) main task #1');
  scheduleMicrotask(() => print('2) microtask #1'));
  newFuture.delayed(new Duration(seconds:1),
  () =>print('3) future #1 (delayed)'));
  new Future(() => print('4) future #2'));
  print('5) main task #2');
  scheduleMicrotask(() => print('6) microtask #2'));
  new Future(() => print('7) future #3'))
  .then((_) => print('8) future #4'))
  .then((_) => print('9) future #5'))
  .whenComplete(cleanup);
  scheduleMicrotask(() => print('11) microtask #3'));
  print('12) main task #3');
}

cleanup() {
  print('10) whenComplete #6');
}
```

The following screenshot shows the output of the program, the order of which is explained in the next section:

```
1) main task #1
5) main task #2
12) main task #3
2) microtask #1
6) microtask #2
11) microtask #3
4) future #2
7) future #3
8) future #4
9) future #5
10) whenComplete #6
3) future #1 (delayed)
```

How it works...

The main isolate proceeds as follows:

1. First the code in `main()` is executed, line after line and synchronously.

2. Then the `event-loop` mechanism kicks in, and this looks at the two queues in the system in the following order:

    ❑   First, it takes a look at the microtask queue this queue is for all tasks that need to be executed before the event queue, for example, the changes that have to be done internally before the DOM starts rendering the modified screen. All of the tasks in this queue are executed before going to the following step.

    ❑   Then, the event queue is handled, here, the tasks of all outside events, such as mouse events, drawing events, I/O, timers, messages between Dart isolates, and so on, are scheduled. Of course, in each queue, the tasks are handled one by one in the *first in first out* order.

While the event-loop is handling the microtask queue, no work is done on the event-queue, so the app can't draw or react to user events and seems effectively blocked. So, keep the microtask queue as short as possible. Preferably, put your tasks on the event queue.

In principle, when both queues are empty, the app can exit. Tasks (these are pieces of code to run later, asynchronously) can be scheduled using the following classes and methods from `dart:async`:

1. Make a new Future object with a function to execute; this is appended to the event queue.

2. With `Future.delayed`, you can specify the execution of a function to occur after a certain duration; this also goes to the event queue.

3. Call the top-level `scheduleMicrotask()` function, which appends an item to the microtask queue.

 Don't use a `Timer` class to schedule a task; this class has no facilities to catch exceptions, so an error during a timer task will blow up your app.

Chaining Futures in a series of `then` statements effectively ensures that they are executed in that order (see step 1 of the previous recipe). Also, a `whencomplete` clause will execute immediately after all the previous `then` statements.

So this is the order of execution: main(), then à microtask queue, then event queue, and then delayed tasks.

 As a general best practice, don't put a compute-intensive task on either queue, but create that task in a separate isolate (or worker for a web app).

See also

▶ See the upcoming recipes about isolates in this chapter, such as *Using isolates in web apps* and *Using multiple cores with isolates*

Running a recurring function

Let's suppose your code needs to run a certain function periodically at a certain interval. This recipe shows how you can do this very easily.

How to do it...

Look at the following code of `recurring_function.dart`:

```
import 'dart:async';

var count = 0;
```

```
   const TIMEOUT = const Duration(seconds: 5);
   const MS = const Duration(milliseconds: 1);

   void main() {
      // 1. Running a function repeatedly:
      const PERIOD = const Duration(seconds:2);
      newTimer.periodic(PERIOD, repeatMe);
      // 3. Running a function once after some time:
      const AFTER70MS = const Duration(milliseconds:70);
      new Timer(AFTER70MS, () => print('this was quick!'));
      // 4. Running a function asap:
      Timer.run(() => print('I ran asap!'));
      // 5. Calculating a period and provoking a timeout:
      startTimeout(500);
   }

   repeatMe(Timer t) {
      print("I have a repetetive job, and I'm active is ${t.isActive}!");
      count++;
      // 2. Stop the repetition:
      if (count==4 &&t.isActive) {
      t.cancel();
      print("I'm active is ${t.isActive} now");
      }
   }

   startTimeout([intvariableMS ]) {
      var duration = variableMS   == null ? TIMEOUT : MS * variableMS;
      return new Timer(duration, handleTimeout);
   }

   handleTimeout() {
      print('I was timed out!');
   }
```

The following is the output from this code; if you need help figuring out the order, read the next section:

I ran asap!

this was quick!

I was timed out!

I have a repetetive job, and I'm active is true!

I have a repetetive job, and I'm active is true!

I have a repetetive job, and I'm active is true!

I have a repetetive job, and I'm active is true!

I'm active is false now

How it works...

The `Timer` class from `dart:async` gives us this functionality through the `periodic` named constructor as shown in comment 1. This takes two arguments, a `Duration` object and a function (here `repeatMe`) to run, which has the timer as the single parameter. This comes in handy to stop the repetition, which is shown in comment 2 with the `cancel()` method after 4 repetitions. The `isActive` property can be used to test whether the repetition is still going on. Comment 3 shows how to run a function only once after a time interval; just use the normal `Timer` constructor with the same arguments, but the callback doesn't have a `Timer` parameter. To run a function as soon as the event-loop mechanism permits, use the static `run` method as shown in comment 4. A negative or zero duration is equivalent to calling `run`. Comment 5 shows that a `Timer` class can also be useful to stop a running function or even the entire app.

There's more...

The durations or periods don't have to be constant from the start; they can be calculated before starting the `Timer`. Timers can also be used in web applications, but for drawing purposes, use `window.animationFrame`. When your app is compiled to JavaScript, the finest time granularity that the browser can give you is 4 milliseconds.

See also

- Refer to the *Writing a game-loop* recipe in this chapter for more information on `window.animationFrame`
- Refer to the *Exiting from an app* recipe in *Chapter 2, Structuring, Testing, and Deploying an Application*, for other alternatives to stop a running app

Using isolates in the Dart VM

Dart code runs in a single thread, in what is called a single process or isolate. In the standalone Dart VM, all code starts from `main()` and is executed in the so-called `root` isolate. To make an app more responsive or to increase its performance, you can assign parts of the code to other isolates. Moreover, because there are no shared resources between isolates, isolating third-party code increases the application's overall security. A Dart server app or command-line app can run part of its code concurrently by creating multiple isolates. If the app runs on a machine with more than one core or processor, it means these isolates can run truly in parallel. When the root isolate terminates the Dart VM exits and, with it, all isolates that are still running. Dart web apps currently can't create additional isolates, but they can create workers by adding instances of the `dart:html Worker` class, thereby adding JavaScript Web workers to the web app. In this recipe, we show you how to start up a new isolate from the main isolate and how to communicate with it using ports.

How to do it...

Examine the code in `using_spawn.dart` to create isolates with `spawn`, as shown in the following code:

```
import'dart:async';
import'dart:isolate';

main() {
  // 1- make a ReceivePort for the main isolate:
  varrecv = new ReceivePort();
  // 2- spawn a new isolate that runs the code from the echo
  // function
  // and pass it a sendPort to send messages to the main isolate
  Future<Isolate> remote = Isolate.spawn(echo, recv.sendPort);
  // 3- when the isolate is spawned (then), take the first message
  remote.then((_) =>recv.first).then((sendPort) {
  // 4- send a message to the isolate:
  sendReceive(sendPort, "Do you hear me?").then((msg) {
  // 5- listen and print the answer from the isolate
  print("MAIN: received $msg");
  // 6- send signal to end isolate:
  returnsendReceive(sendPort, "END");
  }).catchError((e) => print('Error in spawning isolate $e'));
  });
}

  // the spawned isolate:
```

```
    void echo(sender) {
    // 7- make a ReceivePort for the 2nd isolate:
    var port = new ReceivePort();
    // 8- send its sendPort to main isolate:
    sender.send(port.sendPort);
    // 9- listen to messages
    port.listen((msg) {
    var data = msg[0];
    print("ISOL: received $msg");
    SendPortreplyTo = msg[1];
    replyTo.send('Yes I hear you: $msg, echoed from spawned isolate');
    // 10- received END signal, close the ReceivePort to save
    // resources:
    if (data == "END") {
    print('ISOL: my receivePort will be closed');
    port.close();
    }
    });
    }


    Future sendReceive(SendPort port, msg) {
        ReceivePortrecv = new ReceivePort();
        port.send([msg, recv.sendPort]);
        returnrecv.first;
    }
```

This script produces the following output:

ISOL: received [Do you hear me?,SendPort]

MAIN: received Yes I hear you: [Do you hear me?,SendPort], echoed from spawned isolate

ISOL: received [END, SendPort]

ISOL: my receivePort will be closed

From the output, we see that the main isolate receives its message echoed back from the second isolate. Examine the code in using_spawnuri.dart to create isolates with spawnUri:

```
    import'dart:async';
    import'dart:isolate';

    main() {
        varrecv = new ReceivePort();
        Future<Isolate> remote =
```

```
Isolate.spawnUri(Uri.parse("echo.dart"),
["Do you hear me?"], recv.sendPort);
remote.then((_) =>recv.first).then((msg) {
print("MAIN: received $msg");
});
}
```

The following is the code from `echo.dart`:

```
import'dart:isolate';

void main(List<String>args, SendPortreplyTo) {
    replyTo.send(args[0]);
}
```

The following is the output:

MAIN: received Do you hear me?

How it works...

Isolates are defined in their own library called `dart:isolate`. They conform to the well-known actor-model: they are like separate little applications that only communicate with each other by passing asynchronous messages back and forth; in no way can they share variables in memory. The messages get received in the order in which you send them. Each isolate has its own heap, which means that all values in memory, including global variables, are available only to that isolate. Sending messages, which comes down to serializing objects across isolates, has to obey certain restrictions. The messages can contain only the following things:

► Primitive values (`null`, `bool`, `num`, `double`, and `String`)
► Instances of `SendPort`
► Lists and maps whose elements are any of these

When isolates are created via `spawn`, they are running in the same process, and then it is also possible to send objects that are copied (currently only in the Dart VM).

An isolate has one `ReceivePort` to receive messages (containing data) on; it can listen to messages. Calling the `sendport` getter on this port returns `SendPort`. All messages sent through `SendPort` are delivered to the `ReceivePort` they were created from. On `SendPort`, you use the `send` method to send messages; a `ReceivePort` uses the `listen` method to capture these messages.

For each `ReceivePort` port there can be many `SendPort`. A `ReceivePort` is meant to live for as long as there is communication, don't create a new one for every message. Because Dart does not have cross-isolate garbage collection, `ReceivePort` is not automatically garbage-collected when nobody sends messages to them anymore.

Treat `ReceivePort` like resources, and close them when they aren't used anymore.

When working with isolates, a `ReceivePort` in the main or root isolate is obligatory.

 Keeping the `ReceivePort` open will keep this main isolate alive; close it only when the program can stop.

Schematically, we could represent it as shown in the following diagram:

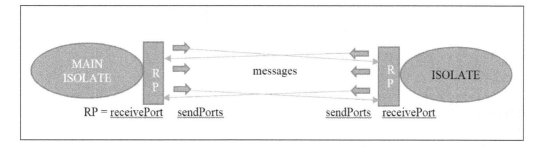

A new isolate is created in one of the following two ways:

▸ Through the static method `Isolate.spawn(fnIsolate, msg)`, the new isolate shares the same code from which it was spawned. This code must contain a top-level function or static one-argument method `fnIsolate`, which is the code the isolate will execute (in our example, the `echo` function); `msg` is a message. In step 2, `msg` is the `SendPort` of the main isolate; this is necessary because the spawned isolate will not know where to send its results.

▸ Through the static method `Isolate.spawnUri(uriOfCode, List<String>args, msg)`, the new isolate executes the code specified in the Uri `uriOfCode` (in our example, the script `echo.dart`), and passes it the argument list `args` and a message `msg` (again containing the `SendPort`).

Isolates start out by exchanging `SendPort` in order to be able to communicate. Both methods return a Future with isolate, or an error of type `IsolateSpawnException`, which must be caught. This can be done by chaining a `catchError` clause or using the optional `onError` argument of `spawn`. However, an error occurring in a spawned isolate cannot be caught by the main isolate, which is logical, because both are independent code sets being executed. You can see this for yourself by running `isolates_errors.dart`. Keep in mind the following restrictions when using `spawn` and `spawnUri`:

> ▸ Spawn works in server apps but doesn't work in Dart web apps. The browser's main isolate, the DOM isolate, does not allow this. This is meant to prevent concurrent access to the DOM.

> ▸ However, `spawnUri` does work in Dart web apps and server apps, and the isolate resulting from this invocation can itself spawn other isolates. The Dart VM translates these isolates into web workers (refer to `http://www.html5rocks.com/en/tutorials/workers/basics/`).

There's more...

So, if you have a compute-intensive task to run inside your app, then to keep your app responsive, you should put the task into its own isolate or worker. If you have many such tasks, then how many isolates should you deploy? In general, when the tasks are compute-intensive, you should use as many isolates as you expect to have cores or processors available. Additional isolates that are purely computational are redundant. But if some of them also perform asynchronous calls (such as I/O for example), then they won't use much processor time. In that case, having more isolates than processors makes sense; it all depends on the architecture of your app. In extreme cases, you could use a separate isolate for each piece of functionality or to ensure that data isn't shared.

Always benchmark your app to check whether the number of isolates are optimized for the job. You can do this as follows: in the Run Manage Launches tool, tick the choices in the VM settings, pause isolate on start, and pause isolate on exit. Then, open the observatory tool through the image button on the left-hand side of Dart Editor to the red square for termination, where you can find interesting information about allocations and performance:

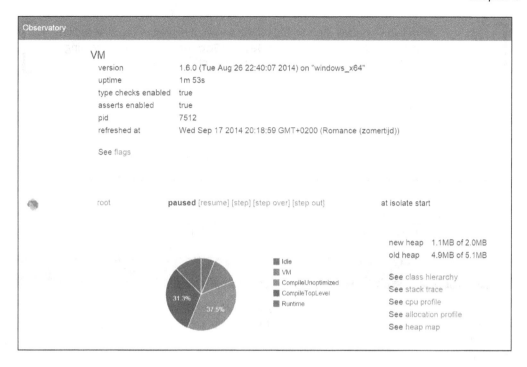

As demonstrated in the second example, `spawnUri` provides a way to dynamically (that is, in run-time) load and execute code (perhaps even an entire library). Don't confuse Futures and isolates; they are different and are also applied differently.

- An isolate is used when you want some code to truly run in parallel, such as a mini program running separately from your main program. You send isolate messages, and you can receive messages from isolates. Each isolate has its own event-loop.

- A Future is used when you want to be notified when a value is available later in the event-loop. Just asking a Future to run a function doesn't make that function run in parallel. It just schedules the function onto the event-loop to be run at a later time.

At this moment, isolates are not very lightweight in the sense of Erlang processes, where each process only consumes a small amount of memory (of the order of Kb). Evolving isolates towards that ideal is a longer-term goal of the Dart team. Also, exception handling and debugging within isolates are a bit rough or difficult; expect this to change. It is also not specified how isolates map to operating system entities such as threads or processes; this can depend on the environment and platform. Isolates haven't been extended yet to inter-VM communication.

When two Dart VMs are running on the server, it is best to use TCP sockets for communication. You can start `ServerSocket` to listen for incoming requests and use `Socket` to connect to the other server.

See also

▶ Refer to the *Using isolates in web apps* recipe for another example using `spawnUri`. Find another example of isolates in the *Using multiple cores with isolates* recipe.

▶ Refer to the *Using Sockets* recipe for more information on `Sockets` and `ServerSockets` in the next chapter.

▶ Refer to the *Profiling and benchmarking your app* recipe in *Chapter 2, Structuring, Testing, and Deploying an Application*, for more information on benchmarking.

Using isolates in web apps

In this recipe, you will learn how to use isolates in a web application in the project `using_web_isolates`. This example runs in the Dart VM embedded in a browser as well as compiled to JavaScript. In the latter case, it uses HTML5 Web workers, which runs in the background independently of other scripts without affecting the performance of the page.

How to do it...

The main isolate in `using_web_isolates.dart` runs the following code:

```
import'dart:isolate';
import'dart:html';
import'dart:async';

main() {
  Element output = querySelector('output');
  SendPortsendPort;
  ReceivePortreceivePort = new ReceivePort();
  receivePort.listen((msg) {
    if (sendPort == null) {
    sendPort = msg;
  } else {
```

```
      output.text += 'Received from isolate: $msg\n';
    }
});

String workerUri = 'worker.dart';
int counter = 0;
// start 3 isolates:
for (int i = 1; i <= 3; i++) {
  Isolate.spawnUri(Uri.parse(workerUri), [], receivePort.sendPort).
    then((isolate) {
    print('isolate spawned');
    newTimer.periodic(const Duration(seconds: 1), (t) {
      sendPort.send('From main app: ${counter++}');
      if (counter == 10) {
        sendPort.send('END');
        t.cancel();
      }
    });
  });
}
}
```

The following is the code for the isolate `worker.dart`:

```
import'dart:isolate';

main(List<String>args, SendPortsendPort) {
  ReceivePortreceivePort = new ReceivePort();
  sendPort.send(receivePort.sendPort);

  receivePort.listen((msg) {
    if (msg == 'END') receivePort.close;
    sendPort.send('ECHO: $msg');
  });
}
```

The following is the output shown on the web page:

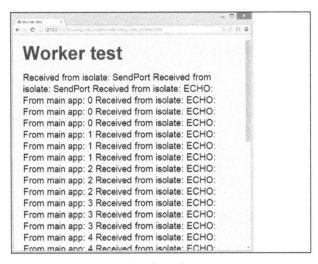

Isolates in a web app

We see the messages coming in from the three isolates. At the count of 10, the timer stops, and the isolates receive a message to shut down.

How it works...

The main isolate first sets up a `ReceivePort` and a listener to the isolates. This listener first captures the isolate's `sendPort` and then appends each message on the web page. An isolate in a web app must be started with `spawnUri`; the code sits in the script `worker.dart`. Then the root isolate starts a timer and sends each second the number of seconds passed. After 10 seconds, the timer is canceled, and an `END` message is sent.

We start three isolates, each executing the same code. The main method in the isolates code receives `List<String>args` as its first argument. This comes from the second parameter of `spawnUri`; this is a way for the main isolate to send initial data to the isolate, but here it was the empty list. Each isolate first sets up its `ReceivePort`, and sends its `sendPort` to the main isolate, so communication lines are established. Then, it starts listening and echoes back what it receives. The isolate exits when the `END` message is received. When compiling to JavaScript with `dart2js`, `.js` is automatically added to the end of the script name `worker.dart`.

See also

▸ Refer to the *Using isolates in the Dart VM* recipe for a general explanation on isolates.

Using multiple cores with isolates

In this recipe, we show you that the Dart VM uses multiple cores on a processor without having to specify anything to the VM. This allows a much better performance and throughput than if a Dart app could only use one processor.

How to do it...

Look at the following code for `many_cores.dart` (in the project `using_isolates`):

```dart
import'dart:isolate';

main() {
  int counter = 0;
  ReceivePortreceivePort = new ReceivePort();
  receivePort.listen((msg) {
    if (msg is SendPort) {
    msg.send(counter++);
  } else {
    print(msg);
    }
  });

  // starting isolates:
  for (var i = 0; i < 5; i++) {
  Isolate.spawn(runInIsolate, receivePort.sendPort);
  }
}

// code to run isolates
runInIsolate(SendPortsendPort) {
ReceivePortreceivePort = new ReceivePort();
// send own sendPort to main isolate:
sendPort.send(receivePort.sendPort);

receivePort.listen((msg) {
  var k = 0;
  var max = (5 - msg) * 500000000;
    for (var i = 0; i < max; ++i) {
    i = ++i - 1;
    k = i;
  }
```

```
    sendPort.send("I received: $msg and calculated $k");
    });
}
```

After some time, the calculated results are shown as follows:

I received: 4 and calculated 499999999

I received: 3 and calculated 999999999

I received: 2 and calculated 1499999999

I received: 1 and calculated 1999999999

I received: 0 and calculated 2499999999

The following is a screenshot of the CPU activity on an eight-core machine. It is clear that four cores are busy running the isolates corresponding to the four isolates that were spawned in the for-loop previously:

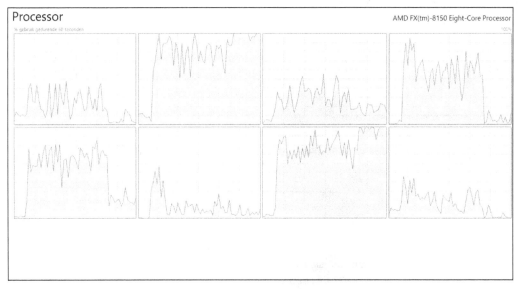

Multicore processing with isolates

How it works...

The first thing the main and other isolates do is make their ReceivePort. The isolates run the code in runInIsolate and get the port to send their results to. Have a look at the following command:

```
Isolate.spawn(runInIsolate, receivePort.sendPort);
```

The isolates send their own `sendPort` to `main`. The main isolate listens on its port; when it receives `sendPort`, it sends an integer `counter` to the isolate:

```
if (msg is SendPort) {
  msg.send(counter++);
    // other code
  }
```

The isolates listen until they receive their counter value, and then start their long-running calculation. Upon completion, the result is sent to the root isolate, where it is displayed. The program never stops because the `ReceivePort` in main is never closed.

Using the Worker Task framework

The `isolate` library only gives us the low-level, basic building blocks, so working with isolates in a realistic application environment can be challenging. Specifically for this purpose, the `worker` concurrent task executor framework was developed by Diego Rocha, available from pub package manager. It was made to abstract all the isolate managing and message passing and make concurrency in Dart as easy as possible. Worker also contains built-in error handling, so you needn't worry about that either. This recipe will show you how to use this framework so that you can concentrate on higher-level application details.

How to do it...

In the project `using_worker`, you can find a number of programs (`using_worker1` through `using_worker4`) illustrating the use of this framework. The script `using_worker.dart` illustrates the main steps, namely creating a task, creating a worker, give a task to the worker, and process the results:

```
import 'package:worker/worker.dart';

Worker worker;

void main() {
  // 1- Make a Task object:
  Task task = new HeavyTask();
  // 2- Construct a Worker object:
  worker = new Worker();
  // specifying poolSize and spawning lazy isolates or not:
  // worker = new Worker(poolSize: noIsol, spawnLazily: false);
  // 3- Give a task to the worker
  // 4- when the results return, process them
  worker.handle(task).then(processResult);
}
```

```
//5 - Task custom class must implement Task interface
classHeavyTask implements Task {

execute() {
  returnlongRunningComputation();
}

boollongRunningComputation() {
  varstopWatch = new Stopwatch();
  stopWatch.start();
  while (stopWatch.elapsedMilliseconds< 1000);
  stopWatch.stop();
  return true;
  }
}

processResult(result) {
  print(result);
  // process result
  // 4- Close the worker object(s)
  worker.close();
}
```

How it works...

First, add the package `worker` to `pubspec.yaml`, and import it in the code. A task is something that needs to be executed. This is an abstract class in the library, providing an interface for tasks and specifying that your custom `Task` class must implement the `execute` method, which returns a result. In our script the custom `Task` is `HeavyTask`, and execute simulates a long running computation using the `Stopwatch` class.

A `worker` object creates and manages a pool containing a number (`poolSize`) of isolates providing you with an easy way to perform blocking tasks concurrently. It spawns isolates lazily as Tasks are required to execute; the spawned isolates are available in a queue named `isolates`. The currently active isolates are stored in an iterable called `workingIsolates`, and the free isolates can be retrieved from an iterable called `availableIsolates`.

In the language of isolates, this is what happens; when a `Worker` instance is created, it starts listening to the `ReceivePort` of the current isolate, and a pool of isolates is created. The isolates in this pool are used to process any task passed to the worker. When a task is passed to the worker to be handled, it returns a Future. This Future will only complete when the Task is executed or when it fails to be executed.

By default, `worker` is created with `poolSize` equal to the number of processors on the machine (`Platform.numberOfProcessors`), and the isolates are spawned lazily (that is, only when needed). You can, however, change the number of isolates and also whether the isolates are spawned lazily or not using optional constructor parameters, as follows:

```
worker = new Worker(poolSize: noIsol, spawnLazily: false);
```

The work is started by handing over the task to the worker with `worker.handle(task)`. The `handle` method takes a `task`, and returns a Future object, so we process the result when it is returned with `worker.handle(task).then(processResult);`.

Also, make sure that, after the processing is done, `worker` gets closed or the program keeps running.

When executing a number of tasks, you can add them to a `List<Future>` task as shown in the following code:

```
intnoTasks = 500;
for (var i=1; i<=noTasks; i++) {
  tasks.add(worker.handle(new HeavyTask()));
}

And then process them with:
Future.wait(tasks).then(processResult);
```

This mechanism is illustrated in the `using_worker2` and `using_worker3` examples.

There's more...

Another good scenario to use isolates or use `worker` class in particular is that of a web server that has a few different services. Perhaps one of those services has to do some calculations and takes a while to respond, whereas, the others are light and respond right away. When the heavy service is requested not using isolates, all other requests are blocked, waiting to be processed, even if they are requesting one of the light services. If you do use an isolate or worker and run the heavy service in parallel, it will take roughly the same time to respond to the first request, but all the subsequent requests won't have to wait.

See also

- See the *Using isolates in the Dart VM* recipe in this chapter for background information on isolates
- See the *Error handling with Futures* recipe in this chapter for more information on how to use Futures

9
Working with Databases

In this chapter, we will cover the following recipes:

- ▶ Storing data locally with IndexedDB
- ▶ Using Lawndart to write offline web apps
- ▶ Storing data in MySQL
- ▶ Storing data in PostgreSQL
- ▶ Storing data in Oracle
- ▶ Storing data in MongoDB
- ▶ Storing data in RethinkDB

Introduction

Data is like food for applications; without it, they would have no meaning. Furthermore, data must be persisted; storing data can be done on the client, server, or both. On the client side, we look at IndexedDB and the Lawndart data manager, which provides offline data storage without having to worry whether IndexedDB is supported or not. Then, we investigate how to store data on the server in SQL as well as NoSQL database systems. By the end of this chapter, you will have a whole spectrum of choices to select the database in which you will store your app's data.

Storing data locally with IndexedDB

IndexedDB is a more robust client-side storage mechanism than local storage in a browser. Likewise, it provides offline capabilities and is based on saving and retrieving data as key-value pairs, but it lets you store significantly bigger amounts of data and allows for high performance searching using database keys. IndexedDB is supported in modern browsers, but is only partially supported in Internet Explorer above Version 10 (refer to `http://caniuse.com/#feat=indexeddb for details`).

How to do it...

You can find the code for this recipe in the `using_indexeddb` project. We use the same method from the *Posting JSON-formatted data* recipe in *Chapter 7, Working with Web Servers*, but now we only store the data locally in IndexedDB. The following is the relevant code from `using_indexeddb.dart`:

```
import 'dart:indexed_db';
void main() {
  //test if browser supports IndexedDB:
  if (!IdbFactory.supported) {
    window.alert("Sorry, this browser does not support IndexedDB");
    return;
  }
  js = new JobStore();
  //creating and opening the database:
  js.openDB();
  querySelector("#store").onClick.listen(storeData);
  }
storeData(Event e) {
  var job = _jobData();
  //writing data to IndexedDB
  js.add(job);
}
```

It is important that the data access code is isolated from the business logic code in `job.dart`. This is according to the principle of separation of concerns, which makes it a lot easier to change to another database system; only the data access code needs to be changed. The functionalities required to work with IndexedDB is found in the `JobStore` class in `jobstore_idb.dart`:

```
library store;
import 'dart:html';
import 'dart:async';
```

```
import 'dart:indexed_db';
import 'job.dart';

class JobStore {
  static const String JOB_STORE = 'jobStore';
  static const String TYPE_INDEX = 'type_index';
  Database _db;
  final List<Job> jobs = new List();

  Future openDB() {
    return window.indexedDB
    .open('JobDB',version: 1,onUpgradeNeeded: _initDb)
    .then(_loadDB)
    .catchError(print);
  }

  void _initDb(VersionChangeEvent e) {
    _db = (e.target as Request).result;
    var store = _db.createObjectStore(JOB_STORE, autoIncrement: true);
    store.createIndex(TYPE_INDEX, 'type', unique: false);
  }

  Future add(Job job) {
    // create transaction and get objectstore:
    var trans = _db.transaction(JOB_STORE, 'readwrite');
    var store = trans.objectStore(JOB_STORE);
    store.add(job.toMap())
    // called when add completes
    .then((addedKey) {
  print(addedKey);
  job.dbKey = addedKey;
  });
    return trans.completed.then((_) {
      // called when transaction completes
      jobs.add(job);
      return job;
    });
  }

Future _loadDB(Database db) {
  _db = db;
  var trans = db.transaction(JOB_STORE, 'readonly');
  var store = trans.objectStore(JOB_STORE);
```

```
    var cursors = store.openCursor(autoAdvance: true).
      asBroadcastStream();
    cursors.listen((cursor) {
      var job = new Job.fromJson(cursor.value);
      jobs.add(job);
      });

      return cursors.length.then((_) {
      return jobs.length;
    });
  }

Future update(Job job) {
  var trans = _db.transaction(JOB_STORE, 'readwrite');
  var store = trans.objectStore(JOB_STORE);
  return store.put(job.toMap());
}

Future remove(Job job) {
  var trans = _db.transaction(JOB_STORE, 'readwrite');
  var store = trans.objectStore(JOB_STORE);
  store.delete(job.dbKey);
  return trans.completed
  .then((_) {
    job.dbKey = null;
    jobs.remove(job);
  });
}

Future clear() {
  var trans = _db.transaction(JOB_STORE, 'readwrite');
  var store = trans.objectStore(JOB_STORE);
  store.clear();
  return trans.completed
  .then((_) {
    jobs.clear();
    });
  }
}
```

The following is a screenshot along with a view of the IndexedDB database in Chrome **Developer Tools**:

How it works...

Interacting with IndexedDB is implemented in the dart:indexed_db library, so we have to import it wherever needed. It is always good to test whether the browser can store data in IndexedDB. To determine whether IndexedDB is supported, use the supported getter from the IdbFactory class. All interactions with IndexedDB are asynchronous and return Futures.

As shown in the second comment, openDB() is called. The window.indexedDB.open method is the method used to open or create a new database. If the given database name and version already exist, then that database is opened. For a new database name or higher version number, the upgrade needed event is triggered. In its event handler, this lacks clarity; insert object type for the screen text term too, where the records get an automatically incremented key, is created within database JobDB. We also show how to create an index in jobstore in the type field of class Job with the createIndex method. An IndexedDB database can contain many object stores, and each store can have many indexes. Handling the possible errors when opening a database with .catchError is really important. We also keep a central Database object _db to be used in the database methods.

A common scenario is that all the records from a certain store are read into the app to show them after opening the database. This is done in `_loadDB`. If we look at the other methods (add, `update`, `remove`, and `clear`), we will see a common pattern, which all database operations must perform within a `Transaction` object. This retrieves as parameters the object store name `JOB_STORE` and a certain mode such as `readonly` or `readwrite`. Reading a number of records, such as in `_loadDB`, works through the opening cursor and then listening to it (using `listen`). Each `listen` event reads a new record through `cursor.value`, which is transformed into a `Job` object and added to the list.

An object to be stored must be given in the map format to the store's `add` method. When `autoincrement` is set to `true` for this store, the generated key number is returned as `addedKey`. When the transaction is complete (`trans.completed.then`), we add the newly created job to our list. The same pattern is followed in the `update`, `remove`, and `clear` methods, which call the methods `put`, `delete`, and `clear`, respectively, in the object store.

See also

> ▶ Refer to the *Using Browser Local Storage* recipe in *Chapter 5, Handling Web Applications*, if you want to compare local storage with IndexedDB

Using Lawndart to write offline web apps

What if the main requirement is that your app can work detached, providing universal offline key-value storage, whether IndexedDB is supported by your client's browsers or not? Then, Lawndart comes to the rescue.

Lawndart (`https://github.com/sethladd/lawndart`, but available via pub package) is not a new database, but rather a manager, which automatically chooses the best local storage mechanism available on the client. It was developed by Seth Ladd as a Dart rework of Lawnchair (`http://brian.io/lawnchair/`). You can see it in action in the project `using_lawndart`.

How to do it...

Import the Lawndart package by adding `lawndart:any` to your `pubspec.yaml` file. The following is the relevant code from the startup script `using_lawndart.dart`:

```
void main() {
  js = new JobStore();
  // 1- creating and opening the database:
```

```
  js.open();
  querySelector("#store").onClick.listen(storeData);
}

storeData(Event e) {
  var job = _jobData();
  // 2- writing data to storage
  js.add(job);
  }
```

The database specific code is isolated in jobstore_lawndart.dart:

```
library store;

import 'dart:async';
import 'package:lawndart/lawndart.dart';
import 'job.dart';

class JobStore {
  static const String JOB_DB = 'jobDb';
  static const String JOB_STORE = 'jobStore';
  final List<Job> jobs = new List();
  // 3- making a Store object:
  var _store = new Store(JOB_DB, JOB_STORE);

  Future open() {
  // 4- opening storage and retrieving all records:
  return _store.open().then(_loadDB).catchError(print);
  }

  _loadDB(_) {
  Stream dataStream = _store.all();
  return dataStream.forEach((dbjob) {
  var job = new Job.fromJson(dbjob);
  jobs.add(job);
  });
}

add(Job job) {
  // 5- storing data:
  _store.save(job.toMap(), job.dbKey.toString()).then((addedKey)     {
  jobs.add(job);
  });
}
```

```
Future update(Job job) {
    return _store.save(job.toMap(), job.dbKey.toString());
}

Future remove(Job job) {
return _store.removeByKey(job.dbKey.toString());
}

clear() {
    _store.nuke().then((_) {
        jobs.clear();
        });
    }
}
```

How it works...

Lawndart presents an asynchronous, but consistent, interface to the local storage, IndexedDB, and Web SQL. Your app simply works with an instance of the class `Store`, and the factory constructor will try IndexedDB, Web SQL, and finally, local storage. This is shown in the third comment, where an object of class `Store` is made; the object also constructs the local database needed. In the first comment, the `open` method in the `JobStore` object triggers `openmethod` on the `Store` object (fourth comment). The `_loadDB` option then reads the entire store; this is accomplished through the `all` method, which returns `Stream` of values. Adding and updating data is done by calling the `save` method on the `store` object (fifth 5). Deleting a record is done through `removeByKey`; clearing an entire database needs the `nuke` method. Notice that the code that uses Lawndart is much cleaner than IndexedDB, as shown in the previous recipe.

See also

> ▶ Cargo is another pub package developed by Joris Hermans, which accomplishes a similar goal. It is a storage package that abstracts local storage, storage on the client as well as on the server, and stores JSON files on the disk. For more information, refer to `https://pub.dartlang.org/packages/cargo`.

> ▶ The complete API documents can be found at `http://www.dartdocs.org/documentation/lawndart/`.

Storing data in MySQL

MySQL is undeniably the most popular open source SQL database. Dart can talk to MySQL using the pub package `sqljocky` by James Ots (`https://github.com/jamesots/sqljocky`). In this section, we will demonstrate how to use this driver step by step. You can see it in action in the `using_mysql` project.

Getting ready

- ▶ To get the database software, download and install the MySQL Community Server installer from `http://dev.mysql.com/downloads/mysql/`. This is straightforward. However, if you need any help with the installation, visit `http://dev.mysql.com/doc/refman/5.7/en/installing.html`.

- ▶ Run the MySQL database system by starting `mysqld` on a command prompt from the bin folder of the MySQL installation. We need to create a database and table to store data. The easiest way is to start the MySQL Workbench program, make a connection, and then click on the button **Create a new schema in the connected server**, name it `jobsdb`, and click on **apply**.

- ▶ Select the schema by double-clicking on it, and then clicking on the button on the right to the previous button **Create a new table in the active schema**. Name the table `jobs`, and create the `dbKey`, `type`, `salary`, `company`, `posted` and `open` columns; `dbKey` is the primary key. To import the driver to your application, add `sqljocky` to `pubspec.yaml` and save it. A `pub get` command is then done automatically.

How to do it...

The application starts with `using_mysql.dart`, where a `JobStore` object is created, the database is opened, records are written to the `jobs` table, and then these records are retrieved, as shown in the following code:

```
import 'job.dart';
import 'jobstore_mysql.dart';

Job job;
JobStore js;

void main() {
  js = new JobStore();
  // 1- create some jobs:
  job = new Job("Web Developer", 7500, "Google", new DateTime.now());
  js.jobs.add(job);
  job = new Job("Software Engineer", 5500, "Microsoft",
    new DateTime.now());
```

```
        js.jobs.add(job);
        job = new Job("Tester", 4500, "Mozilla", new DateTime.now());
        js.jobs.add(job);
        // 2- opening the database:
        js.open();
        // 3- storing data in database:
        js.storeData();
        // 4- retrieving and displaying data from database:
        js.readData();
    }
```

After running the preceding code, we can verify that the insertions succeeded in MySQL Workbench in the `jobs` table:

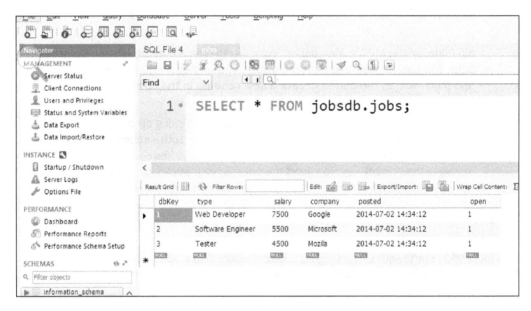

The `readData` method reads the data from the **jobs** table and prints it to the console:

dbKey: 1, type : Web Developer, salary: 7500, company: Google, posted: 2014-07-02 14:34:12.000, open: 1

dbKey: 2, type : Software Engineer, salary: 5500, company: Microsoft, posted: 2014-07-02 14:34:12.000, open: 1

dbKey: 3, type : Tester, salary: 4500, company: Mozilla, posted: 2014-07-02 14:34:12.000, open: 1

After the first run, `readData` will not show any output because it gets executed before the insertions in the database are complete; verify the output through a second run.

The interaction with MySQL through `sqljocky` takes place in the `JobStore` class in `jobstore_mysql.dart`:

```
import 'package:sqljocky/sqljocky.dart';
import 'package:options_file/options_file.dart';
import 'job.dart';

ConnectionPool pool;

class JobStore {
  final List<Job> jobs = new List();
  Job job;

  // 5- opening a connection to the database:
  open() {
    pool = getPool(new OptionsFile('connection.options'));
  }

  ConnectionPool getPool(OptionsFile options) {
    String user = options.getString('user');
    String password = options.getString('password');
    int port = options.getInt('port', 3306);
    String db = options.getString('db');
    String host = options.getString('host', 'localhost');
    return new ConnectionPool(host: host, port: port, user: user,
      password: password, db: db);
  }

  storeData() {
  for (job in jobs) {
  insert(job);
  }
}
}

// 6- inserting a record in a table:
insert(Job job) {
var jobMap = job.toMap();
pool.prepare('insert into jobs (dbKey, type, salary, company, posted,
open) values (?, ?, ?, ?, ?, ?)').then((query) {
  var params = new List();
  params.add(job.dbKey);
```

```
    params.add(job.type);
    params.add(job.salary);
    params.add(job.company);
    params.add(job.posted);
    params.add(job.open);
    return query.execute(params);
  }).then((_) {
  }).catchError(print);
}

readData() {
  pool.query('select * from jobs').then((results) {
  processJob(results);
  });
}

processJob(results) {
  results.forEach((row) {
  print('dbKey: ${row.dbKey}, type : ${row.type}, ' 'salary:
    ${row.salary}, company: ${row.company}, ' 'posted: ${row.posted},
    open: ${row.open}');
  });
}

// 7- updating a record in a table:
update(Job job) {
  var jobMap = job.toMap();
  pool.prepare('update jobs set type = ?, salary = ?, company = ?,
    posted = ?, open = ? where dbKey = ?').then((query) {
  var params = new List();
  params.add(job.dbKey);
  params.add(job.type);
  params.add(job.salary);
  params.add(job.company);
  params.add(job.posted);
  params.add(job.open);
  return query.execute(params);
  }).then((_) {
  }).catchError(print);
}

// 8- deleting a record in a table:
delete(Job job) {
  var jobMap = job.toMap();
```

```
    pool.prepare('delete from jobs where dbKey = ?').then((query) {
    var params = new List();
    params.add(job.dbKey);
    return query.execute(params);
    }).then((_) {
    }).catchError(print);
    }
}
```

How it works...

The connection information for the database is stored in the `connection.options` file. In the fifth comment, a connection to the database is opened by calling `getPool`, which returns a `ConnectionPool` object that maintains a pool of database connections. The `getPool` option takes as argument an `OptionsFile` object, from the `options_file` package, and reads the information from `connection.options`:

```
# connection.options to define how to connect to a mysql db
user=root
password=?????  # substitute your password here
# port defaults to 3306
port=3306
db=jobsdb
# host defaults to localhost
host=localhost
```

All interactions with the database work via queries. If there is a free connection in `ConnectionPool` when queries are executed, it will be used; otherwise, the query is queued until there is a free connection. As we can see in `readData`, a select query is made via `pool.query(selectStr);`. This returns a `Future` object, so the processing of the results takes place in the `then` section. This can be done using the following code:

```
    results.forEach((row) {
    print('dbKey: ${row.dbKey}, type : ${row.type}, …');
```

The preceding line can also be written as follows:

```
    results.forEach((row) {
    print('dbKey: ${row[0]}, type : ${row[1]}, …');
```

Insert, update, and `delete` queries (coded in the methods with the same name) have to first go through the `prepare` stage and then the `execute` stage. Let's see a few examples. For `insert`, this query becomes as follows (refer to the sixth comment):

```
pool.prepare('insert into jobs (dbKey, type, salary, company,
    posted, open) values (?, ?, ?, ?, ?, ?)').then((query) {})
```

An `insert` query on a table that contains an autoincrement field will return the value of that field in `${result.insertId}`. For `update`, this query becomes as follows (refer to the seventh comment):

```
pool.prepare('update jobs set type = ?, salary = ?, company = ?,
    posted = ?, open = ? where dbKey = ?').then((query) {}
```

The query for `delete` is as follows (refer to comment 8):

```
pool.prepare('delete from jobs where dbKey = ?').then((query) {}
```

The `?` character represents values to be substituted in the SQL string. These values are placed in the specified order in the `params` list, which is given as an argument to `query.execute`. A query with multiple parameter sets can be executed with `query.executeMulti()`. If you need a number of queries to be executed as a whole (or all or none succeed), use the `Transaction` class from `sqljocky` in the following format:

```
pool.startTransaction().then((trans) {
trans.query('...').then((result) {
trans.commit().then(() {...});
});
});
```

There's more...

The complete API documents can be found at `http://jamesots.github.io/sqljocky/docs/`.

Storing data in PostgreSQL

PostgreSQL is another popular open source SQL database. Dart can talk to PostgreSQL using the pub package `postgresql` by Greg Lowe (`https://github.com/xxgreg/postgresql`). In this section, we will demonstrate how to use this driver step by step. You can see it in action in the `using_postgresql` project.

Getting ready

To get the database software, download and install the PostgreSQL Server installer from `http://www.postgresql.org/download/` using the following steps:

1. The database server is configured to start automatically. We need to create a database and table to store data. The easiest way is to start the `pgAdmin` program, make a new connection, and then select **Edit**, **New Object**, and **New Database** from the menu, name it **jobsdb**, and click on **OK**.

2. Select the public schema, and again select **Edit**, **New Object**, and then **New Table**.

3. Name the table `jobs`, and create `dbKey`, `type`, `salary`, `company`, `posted`, and `open` as columns; `dbKey` is the primary key.

4. To import the driver to your application, add `postgresql` to the `pubspec.yaml` file and save it. A `pub get` command is then done automatically.

How to do it...

The application starts from `using_postgresql.dart`, where a `JobStore` object is created, the database is opened, records are written to the `jobs` table, and then these records are retrieved:

```
import 'job.dart';
import 'jobstore_postgresql.dart';

Job job;
JobStore js;

void main() {
  js = new JobStore();
  // 1- create some jobs:
  job = new Job("Web Developer", 7500, "Google", new DateTime.now());
  js.jobs.add(job);
  job = new Job("Software Engineer", 5500, "Microsoft",
    new DateTime.now());
  js.jobs.add(job);
  job = new Job("Tester", 4500, "Mozilla", new DateTime.now());
  js.jobs.add(job);
    // 2- storing data in database:
  js.openAndStore();
  // 3- retrieving and displaying data from database:
  js.openAndRead();
}
```

After running the preceding code, we can verify via pg Admin in the `jobs` table that the insertions succeeded, as shown in the following screenshot:

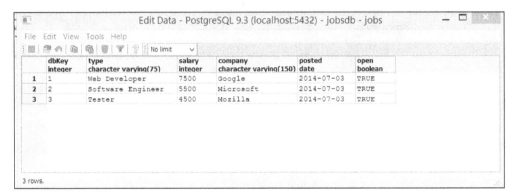

Data in PostgreSQL

The `readData` method reads the data from the `jobs` table and prints it to the console:

1 - Web Developer - 7500 - Google - 2014-07-03 00:00:00.000 true

2 - Software Engineer - 5500 - Microsoft - 2014-07-03 00:00:00.000 true

3 - Tester - 4500 - Mozilla - 2014-07-03 00:00:00.000 true

The interaction with PostgreSQL through the driver takes place in the `JobStore` class in `jobstore_postgresql.dart`:

```
library store;

import 'package:postgresql/postgresql.dart';
import 'job.dart';

class JobStore {
  final List<Job> jobs = new List();
  Job job;
  Connection conn;
  varuri = 'postgres://username:passwd@localhost:5432/jobsdb';

  // 5- opening a connection to the database:
  openAndStore() {
  connect(uri).then((_conn) {
  conn = _conn;
  storeData();
  })
  .catchError(print);
  }
```

```
storeData() {
  for (job in jobs) {
  insert(job);
}
// 6- close the database connection:
close();
}

// 7- inserting a record in a table:
insert(Job job) {
  var jobMap = job.toMap();
  conn.execute('insert into jobs values (@dbKey, @type, @salary,
    @company, @posted, @open)',
  jobMap)
  .then((_) { print('inserted'); })
  .catchError(print);
}

openAndRead() {
  connect(uri).then((_conn) {
  conn = _conn;
  readData();
})
.catchError(print);
}

// 8- reading records from a table:
readData() {
  conn.query('select * from jobs').toList().then((results) {
  processJob(results);
  close();
  });
}

// 9- working with record data:
processJob(results) {
for (var row in results) {
  // Refer to columns by nam:
  print('${row.dbKey} - ${row.type} - ${row.salary} -
    ${row.company} - ${row.posted} ${row.open}');
  // print(row[0]);    // Or by column index.
  }
}
```

```
close() { conn.close(); }

// 10- updating a record in a table:
update(Job job) {
  var jobMap = job.toMap();
  conn.execute('update jobs set type = @type, salary = @salary,
    company = @company, '
  'posted = @posted, open = @open where dbKey = @dbKey', jobMap)
  .then((_) { print('updated'); })
  .catchError(print);
}

// 11- deleting a record in a table:
delete(Job job) {
  var jobMap = job.toMap();
  conn.execute('delete from jobs where dbKey = @dbKey', jobMap)
  .then((_) { print('deleted'); })
  .catchError(print);
  }
}
```

How it works...

Obtaining a connection with a Postgres database needs a valid connection string of the following form:

```
var uri = 'postgres://username:password@localhost:5432/database';
```

This is given as an argument to the `connect` method, as shown in the fifth comment; the writing of the data in `storeData` is done in the `callback` handler, in order to be sure that we have a `Connection` object at that point. Inserting a record happens in comment 7; the values to be inserted in the `insert` SQL in the @ markers must be given through a map (here `jobMap`):

```
conn.execute('insert into jobs values (@dbKey, @type, @salary,
  @company, @posted, @open)', jobMap).then((_) { … }
```

So all the `insert`, `update`, and `delete` queries are given as string arguments to the method `conn.execute`. Strings will be escaped to prevent SQL injection vulnerabilities. After the inserts, we explicitly close the connection with `conn.close()` to save resources. Select queries are performed through `conn.query`:

```
conn.query('select * from jobs').toList().then((results) {…}
```

The processing of the results is done in the `callback` handler:

```
for (var row in results) {
  print('${row.type} - ${row.salary}');
print(row[1]);
```

Fields can be retrieved by their name or index. As always, we catch the errors with `catchError`, which at least prints the error to the console. Similar to MySQL, a connection `Pool` object can be used to avoid the overhead of obtaining a connection for each request:

```
var pool = new Pool(uri, min: 2, max: 5);
pool.start().then((_) {
print('min amount connections established.');
pool.connect().then((conn) { // Obtain connection from pool
    // … }
}
```

The connection method `runInTransaction` allows queries that need to be executed in "an all or none" way, to be bundled in a transaction.

See also

> ▶   The complete API docs can be found at `http://www.dartdocs.org/documentation/postgresql/0.2.14/index.html#postgresql`

Storing data in Oracle

Oracle is the most popular commercial SQL database. Dart can talk to Oracle using the pub package `oracledart` by Alexander Aprelev (`https://github.com/aam/oracledart`). This is a Dart native extension of C++, using the `dart_api` interface to integrate into Dart. It requires Oracle Instant Client to be present on the machine, and its OCCI binaries must be included in the PATH variable.

In this section, we will demonstrate how to use this driver step by step. You can see it in action in the project `using_oracle`.

Getting ready

To get the database software, download and execute the Oracle installer from `http://www.oracle.com/technetwork/database/enterprise-edition/downloads/index-092322.html`.

> ▸ The database server is started through the menu option **Start Database**.

> ▸ We need to create a table to store data. Start the SQL command-line terminal and paste the contents of the script `jobs.txt`. This creates the table `jobs`, together with the `dbKey`, `type`, `salary`, `company`, `posted`, and `open` columns; `dbKey` is the primary key.

> ▸ To import the driver to your application, add `oracledart` to `pubspec.yaml` and save it. A `pub get` command is then done automatically.

How to do it...

The application starts from `using_oracle.dart`, where a `JobStore` object is created, the database is opened, records are written to the `jobs` table, and then these records are retrieved. The code from `using_oracle.dart` is identical to the code from `using_postgresql.dart`, except that we now import `jobstore_oracle.dart`; so please refer to the previous recipe. The `jobstore_oracle.dart` file contains the code to talk to the database driver:

```dart
// 1- importing the driver:
import 'package:oracledart/oracledart.dart';
import 'job.dart';

class JobStore {
  final List<Job> jobs = new List();
  Job job;
  OracleConnection conn; // connection object
  OracleResultset resultset;
  OracleStatement stmt;
  var connStr = ' "(DESCRIPTION=" "(ADDRESS=(PROTOCOL=TCP)
    (HOST=oracledb)(PORT=1521))"'
  '"(CONNECT_DATA=(SERVICE_NAME=XE)(SERVER=DEDICATED)))"';

  // 2- opening a connection to the database:
  openAndStore() {
    connect("SYS", "avalon", connStr).then((oracleconnection) {
    conn = oracleconnection;
    print('connected with Oracle!');
    storeData();
```

```
    }).catchError(print);
  }

  storeData() {
  for (job in jobs) {
  insert(job);
  }
}

// 3- inserting a record in a table:
insert(Job job) {
  var jobMap = job.toMap();
  var insertSql = 'insert into jobs values (:1, :2, :3, :4, :5, :6)';
  stmt = conn.createStatement(insertSql);
  stmt.setInt(1, jobMap['dbKey']);
  stmt.setString(2, jobMap['type']);
  stmt.setInt(3, jobMap['salary']);
  stmt.setString(4, jobMap['company']);
  stmt.setString(5, jobMap['posted']);
  stmt.setString(6, jobMap['open']);
  stmt.executeQuery();
}

openAndRead() {
  connect("SYS", "avalon", connStr).then((oracleconnection) {
  conn = oracleconnection;
  readData();
  }).catchError(print);
}

// 8- reading records from a table:
readData() {
  resultset = conn.select("select * from jobs");
  processJob(resultset);
}

// 9- working with record data:
processJob(results) {
  while (resultset.next()) {
  print('dbKey: ${resultset.getInt(0)}');
  print('type:  ${resultset.getString(1)}');
  print('salary: ${resultset.getInt(2)}');
  print('company:  ${resultset.getString(3)}');
```

```
        print('posted: ${resultset.getString(4)}');
        print('open: ${resultset.getString(5)}');
      }
    }
  }
```

How it works...

First, import the `oracledart` package. The `connect` method takes the user, his/her password, and then a connection string. In its callback, an `OracleConnection` object `conn` is made available. Querying tables is done with `conn.select(selectSql)`, where `selectSql` is the selected SQL string. This returns an `OracleResultset` object that you can iterate throughout with `next()`. Values of fields can only be extracted by an index with `getInt` or `getString`.

If you need parameters in your statement, as is probably the case for insert, update, or delete statements, you first need to call `conn.createStatement(sqlStr)`, where `sqlStr` contains `:i` indicators (i equals to ith index, starting from 0). These `:i` position holders must be filled with `stmt.setInt(i, value)` or `stmt.setString(i, value)`. Then, the statement can be executed with `stmt.executeQuery()`.

There's more...

In this and the previous recipes, we discussed the SQL database servers that Dart can talk to at this time using specialized drivers. However, for example, for the popular Microsoft SQL Server there is no driver yet. In this case, we can use the pub `odbc` package by Juan Mellado (`https://code.google.com/p/dart-odbc/`). The ODBC binding is made with a Dart native extension, which makes it a bit more involved to be used, and for now it only exists in a 32-bit version.

Storing data in MongoDB

MongoDB, by the company with the same name (`http://www.mongodb.org/`), is the most popular database among the NoSQL databases. Let's look at some facts about MongoDB:

▶ MongoDB is an open source, distributed, document-oriented database; each data record is actually a document.

▶ A table is called a collection in MongoDB. Documents are stored in a JSON-like format called BSON.

▶ The most advanced driver from Dart to MongoDB is the pub package `mongo_dart` by Vadim Tsushko, Ted Sander, and Paul Evans. This recipe will show you how to create, read, update, and delete actions in a MongoDB database from a Dart app. You can see it in action in the `using_mongodb` project.

Getting ready

Install the latest production release for your system from `http://www.mongodb.org/downloads`. This is easy. However, if you need more details, refer to `http://docs.mongodb.org/manual/installation/`. Start the `mongod` server process (for example, from `c:\mongodb\bin` on Windows) before the Dart app. To make the `jobsdb` database, start a `mongo` shell and type `use jobsdb`; it's that simple. Alternatively, this can also be done via `mongo_dart`. NoSQL databases are schemaless, so the collections (which is what tables are called here) are created when the first document (or record) is inserted.

How to do it...

The application starts from `using_mongodb.dart`, where a `JobStore` object is created, the database is opened, records are written to the `jobs` table, and then these records are retrieved. The code from `using_mongodb.dart` is identical to the code from `using_postgresql.dart`, except that we now import `jobstore_mongodb.dart`; so please refer to the *Storing data in PostgreSQL* recipe. When running this script, first comment out `js.openAndRead();`. In the second run, uncomment this and comment out `js.openAndStore();`; otherwise, the reads take place before the inserts are completed. The `jobstore_mongodb.dart` code contains the code to talk to the database driver:

```
import 'package:mongo_dart/mongo_dart.dart';
import 'job.dart';

const String DEFAULT_URI = 'mongodb://127.0.0.1/';
const String DB_NAME = 'jobsdb';
const String COLLECTION_NAME = 'jobs';

class JobStore {
  final List<Job> jobs = new List();
  Job job;
  Db db;
  DbCollection jobsColl;

  JobStore() {
  // 1- make a new database
  db = new Db('${DEFAULT_URI}${DB_NAME}');
  // make a new collection
  jobsColl = db.collection(COLLECTION_NAME);
}

openAndStore() {
  db.open().then((_) {
```

```
      storeData();
    }).catchError(print);
  }

storeData() {
  for (job in jobs) {
    insert(job);
  }
}

// 2- inserting a document in a collection:
insert(Job job) {
  var jobMap = job.toMap();
  jobsColl.insert(jobMap).then((_) {
    print('inserted job: ${job.type}');
  }).catchError(print);
}

openAndRead() {
  db.open().then((_) {
    readData();
  }).catchError(print);
}

// 3- reading documents:
readData() {
  jobsColl.find().toList().then((jobList) {
    processJob(jobList);
  }).catchError(print);
}

// 4- working with document data:
processJob(jobList) {
  jobList.forEach((jobMap) {
    Job job = new Job.fromMap(jobMap);
    print('${job.dbKey} - ${job.type} - ${job.salary} - '
    '${job.company} - ${job.posted} ${job.open}');
  });
}

// 5-  updating a document:
update(Job job) {
  var jobMap = job.toMap();
```

```
      jobsColl.update({"dbKey": jobMap["dbKey"]},jobMap).then((_) {
      print('job updated');
      }).catchError(print);
    }

    // 6- deleting a document:
    delete(Job job) {
      var jobMap = job.toMap();
      jobsColl.remove(jobMap).then((_) {
      print('job updated');
      }).catchError(print);
      }
    }
```

After running the preceding script, verify in a mongo shell with `use jobsdb` and `db.jobs. find()` that the documents have been inserted, as shown in the following screenshot:

How it works...

The `mongo_dart` library makes it very easy to work with MongoDB. In comment 1, we created the `Db` and `DbCollection` objects in the constructor of `JobStore`. To manipulate documents, you have to first call the `open` method on the `Db` object.

To write a document to the collection, use the `insert` method on the `DbCollection` object, but its argument must be in the `Map` format. Reading documents is done with the `find` method. The list that is returned contains items of type `Map`, so to construct real objects, we have to make a new named constructor `fromMap` in class `Job`. Updating a document uses a method of the same name, but its first argument must be a selector to find the document that must be updated. Deleting a document uses the `remove` method.

▶ The complete API documents can be found at `http://www.dartdocs.org/documentation/mongo_dart/0.1.39/index.html#mongo_dart`

▶ Another MongoDB client by Vadim Tsushko is an object-document mapper tool called Objectory, which can be used on the client as well as the server (`https://github.com/vadimtsushko/objectory`)

Storing data in RethinkDB

RethinkDB (`http://www.rethinkdb.com/`) is a simple NoSQL database that stores JSON documents. Its main focus lies on ease of use, both for the developer, with an intuitive query language that can simulate table joins, as well as for the administrator, with friendly web tools to monitor, shard, and replicate. Another advantage is its automatic parallelization of queries. At the moment, the database system runs on OS X and a lot of Linux flavors.

We will talk to RethinkDB with a driver available on pub package called `rethinkdb_driver`, developed by William Welch (`https://github.com/billysometimes/rethinkdb`). You can see it in action in the `using_rethinkdb` project.

Getting ready

Install the latest production release for your system from `http://www.rethinkdb.com/docs/install/`. Then, perform the following steps:

1. Start the RethinkDB server by issuing the command `rethinkdb` in a terminal.

2. Then, go to `localhost:8080` in your browser — this starts an administrative UI where you can control the database server (from one machine to a cluster).

3. Click on the **Tables** tab at the top and use the **Add Database** button to create the database `jobsdb`.

4. To create the `jobs` table, click on the **Tables** tab at the top of the page and then use the **Add Table** button.

5. The table `jobs` has the columns `dbKey`, `type`, `salary`, `company`, `posted`, and `open` columns; `dbKey` is the primary key.

How to do it...

The application starts from `using_rethinkdb`, where a `JobStore` object is created, the database is opened, records are written to the `jobs` table, and then these records are retrieved. The code from `using_rethinkdb` is identical to the code from `using_postgresql.dart`, except that we now import `jobstore_rethinkdb.dart;`, so please refer to the *Storing data in PostgreSQL* recipe. The `jobstore_rethinkdb.dart` file contains the following code to talk to the database driver:

```dart
import 'package:rethinkdb_driver/rethinkdb_driver.dart';
import 'job.dart';

class JobStore {
  final List<Job> jobs = new List();
  Job job;
  Rethinkdb rdb = new Rethinkdb();
  Connection conn;

  // opening a connection to the database:
  openAndStore() {
  rdb.connect(db: "jobsdb", port:8000, host: "127.0.0.1").
    then((_conn) {
  conn = _conn;
  storeData(conn);
  }).catchError(print);
}

storeData(conn) {
  List jobsMap = new List();
  for (job in jobs) {
  var jobMap = job.toMap();
  jobsMap.add(jobMap);
}
// storing data:
rdb.table("jobs").insert(jobsMap).run(conn)
.then((response)=>print('documents inserted'))
.catchError(print);
// close the database connection:
close();
}

openAndRead() {
rdb.connect(db: "jobsdb", port:8000, host: "127.0.0.1").then((_conn) {
conn = _conn;
```

```
    readData(conn);
    }).catchError(print);
    }


    // reading documents:
    readData(conn) {
      rdb.table("jobs").getAll("1,2,3").run(conn).then((results) {
      processJob(results);
      close();
      });
    }


    // working with document data:
    processJob(results) {
    for (var row in results) {
      // Refer to columns by nam:
      print('${row.dbKey} - ${row.type} - ${row.salary} - ${row.company} -
        ${row.posted} ${row.open}');
      }
    }


    close() {
    conn.close();
    }


    // updating a document:
    update(Job job) {
      rdb.table("jobs").update({"dbKey":job.dbKey})
      .run(conn).then((response)=>print('document updated')
      ).catchError(print);
    }


    // deleting a document:
    delete(Job job) {
      rdb.table("jobs").get(job.dbKey).delete()
      .run(conn).then((response)=>print('document deleted')
      ).catchError(print);
      }
    }
```

How it works...

As always, we have to import the driver's code. Then, we define a `Rethinkdb` object on which all methods are defined, and a global `Connection` object. Opening a connection is done with the following command, where the host can also be the real name of the server. The `connect` option also takes an optional authorization key argument, `authKey`. In the `callback` handler, all document manipulation can be done using the following code:

```
rdb.connect(db: "jobsdb", port:8000, host: "127.0.0.1")
```

For example, to read documents, use the command `getAll`, which takes a list of the document keys as an argument:

```
rdb.table("jobs").getAll(keysList).run(conn).then((results) {…}
```

To insert documents, use the `insert` command:

```
rdb.table("jobs").insert(docMap).run(conn).then((results) {…}
```

The `insert` command takes a list as an argument along with its documents, where each document is in the map format. The `update` command matches documents with their arguments, and the `delete` command needs a document key as its argument.

See also

Of course, there are many other NoSQL databases. The following are a few references to other drivers:

► For CouchDB, there is the `wilt` package (https://pub.dartlang.org/packages/wilt) and the `couchclient` library (https://pub.dartlang.org/packages/couchclient)

► For Redis, you have the `redis_client` package (https://pub.dartlang.org/packages/redis_client)

► For Memcached, there is the `memcached_client` library (https://pub.dartlang.org/packages/memcached_client)

► For Riak, there is the `riak_client` package (https://pub.dartlang.org/packages/riak_client)

10
Polymer Dart Recipes

In this chapter, we will cover the following recipes:

- ▶ Data binding with polymer.dart
- ▶ Binding and repeating over a list
- ▶ Binding to a map
- ▶ Using custom attributes and template conditionals
- ▶ Binding to an input text field or a text area
- ▶ Binding to a checkbox
- ▶ Binding to radio buttons
- ▶ Binding to a selected field
- ▶ Event handling
- ▶ Polymer elements with JavaScript interop
- ▶ Extending DOM elements
- ▶ Working with custom elements
- ▶ Automatic node finding
- ▶ Internationalizing a Polymer app

Introduction

Polymer (as defined at http://www.polymer-project.org/) is a web development feature designed to fully utilize the evolving web platform on modern browsers; it modularizes the way a web client interface is defined. Web pages can now be built and composed with web components that can simply be accessed by their names. Web components are reusable chunks of styled HTML5 or extensions from native HTML tags. Moreover, they enable two-way data binding to make data from code elements visible and editable in the DOM. They can also contain code to change their behavior, either in JavaScript or Dart, through a class that backs up the components. A Polymer web component thus encapsulates structure, style, and behavior. Polymer is a library on top of web components and in some browsers that don't support web components, yet, it has been a polyfill.

Polymer.dart is the Dart port of Polymer created and supported by the Dart team. At the time of writing this, the version of polymer.dart is 0.14.0, and it is quickly aiming towards a stable production version; its main documentation page can be found at https://www.dartlang.org/polymer-dart/.

Polymer.dart runs in the following browsers: IE10, IE11, Safari 6, the latest version of Chrome, the latest version of Firefox, and the latest version of Chrome for Android. A lot has changed in the polymer.dart world since its first version, so if you need to refresh your memory, refer to https://www.dartlang.org/docs/tutorials/polymer-intro/.

Although simple, the first recipe is a complete example showing data binding and event handling to change the state of code objects. Refer to it if you need a picture of the whole machinery of programming a component. We will look at more detailed examples of how to do certain things in the following recipes.

Data binding with polymer.dart

In the first recipe, we will go through an example that shows the complete mechanics of working with a Polymer component and data binding, and at the same time emphasizes some important best practices to work with polymer.dart. You can find the code in the project bank_terminal. The app creates an object of class BankAccount (which can be found in the lib folder) and populates it with the data that is shown. You can also provide a transaction amount and the balance of the account is updated. This is depicted in the following screenshot:

How to do it...

Perform the following steps to bind data with polymer.dart:

1. First, install the `polymer` dependency in your project by adding `polymer:` `">=0.11.0 <0.12.0"` to the `pubspec.yaml` file. Save the file in the editor and run `pub get` from the command line. This has to be accompanied by an import line; in `web\bank_app.dart`, we use `import 'package:polymer/polymer.dart';` but also in `web\bank_app.html` with a `<link rel="import">` tag as the first line.

2. Also, in that file, you must indicate one or more starting points of app execution in the `transformers` section, as shown in the following code:

```
transformers:
- polymer:
entry_points:
- web/bank_terminal.html
- web/index.html
```

3. The root folder of the app contains a `build.dart` file, with the following content:

    ```
    import 'package:polymer/builder.dart';

    main() {
      build(entryPoints: ['web/bank_terminal.html']);
    }
    ```

4. The entry point `bank_terminal.html` must contain the `<script>` and `<link>` tags in the `<head>` section, in the following order:

    ```
    <script src="packages/web_components/platform.js"></script>
      <script src="packages/web_components/dart_support.js"></script>
    <!-- import the bank-app custom element -->
    <link rel="import"href="bank_app.html">
        <script type="application/dart">export
          'package:polymer/init.dart';</script>
    <script src="packages/browser/dart.js"></script>
    ```

5. The Polymer component with the name `bank-app` is instantiated in the `<body>` section of the same entry file:

    ```
    <bank-app></bank-app>
    ```

6. The component is defined in `bank_app.html` as follows:

    ```
    <link rel="import"href="packages/polymer/polymer.html">
    <polymer-element name="bank-app">
    <style>
    .auto-style1 {
      width: 25%;
      border: 1px solid #0000FF;
    }

    .auto-style2 {
      width: 107px;
    }

    .btns {
      width: 127px;
    }

    .red {
      color: red;
    }
    </style>
    <template>
    ```

```
<table class="auto-style1" on-keypress="{{enter}}">
<tr>
<td class="auto-style2">Number</td>
<td>{{bac.number}}</td>
</tr>
<tr>
<td class="auto-style2">Owner</td>
<td>{{bac.owner.name}}</td>
</tr>
<tr>
<td class="auto-style2">Starting balance</td>
<td> {{bac.balance}}</td>
</tr>
<tr>
<td class="auto-style2"> After transaction:</td>
<td> {{balance}}</td>
</tr>
<tr>
<td class="auto-style2">Amount</td>
<td><input id="amount" type="text"/></td>
</tr>
<tr>
<td>
t</td>
</tr>
</table>
</template>
<script type="application/dart" src="bank_app.dart"></script>
</polymer-element>
```

7. The code of the Polymer component can be found in `bank_app.dart`:

```
import 'dart:html';
import 'package:polymer/polymer.dart';
import 'package:bank_terminal/bank_terminal.dart';

@CustomTag('bank-app')
classBankAppextendsPolymerElement {
  @observableBankAccountbac;
  @observable double balance;
  doubleamount = 0.0;

  BankApp.created() : super.created() { }

  @override
```

```
        attached() {
          super.attached();
          varjw = new Person("John Witgenstein");
          bac = newBankAccount(jw, "456-0692322-12", 1500.0);
          balance = bac.balance;
        }

        transact(Event e, vardetail, Node target) {
          InputElementamountInput = shadowRoot.querySelector("#amount");
          if (!checkAmount(amountInput.value)) return;
          bac.transact(amount);
          balance = bac.balance;
        }

        enter(KeyboardEvent  e, vardetail, Node target) {
          if (e.keyCode == KeyCode.ENTER) {
            transact(e, detail, target);
          }
        }

      checkAmount(String in_amount) {
        try {
        amount = double.parse(in_amount);
        } onFormatExceptioncatch(ex) {
        returnfalse;
        }
        returntrue;
      }
    }
```

How it works...

The actual numbers in step 1 for the `polymer` dependency may vary, but because the changes between versions can still be significant, it is better to use explicit versions rather than any other version here in order to not break your app; you can then also upgrade it when ready after thorough testing. The `build.dart` script in step 3 ensures that the project is built whenever a file in it is saved. The `<link>` tag in step 4 imports the Polymer element `bank-app`, which lives in `bank_app.html`. The `platform.js` and `dart_support.js` files contain the so-called platform polyfills; this is the JavaScript code to make new web standards such as custom elements, shadow DOM, template elements, and HTML imports work. They are called polyfills because at a later stage the browser should provide native code for these standards. The `init.dart` script starts up polymer.dart, and `dart.js` checks whether there is a Dart VM available to run the code directly. If this is not the case, the app runs from the compiled JavaScript code. Step 5 uses the name of the Polymer element as an HTML tag.

Step 6 comprises the HTML code for the Polymer component. It defines its style (in a `<style>` tag) and structure (within a `<template>` tag) between the `<polymer-element>` tags; its starting tag has the name of the component as an attribute, which is `name="bank-app"`. We see how one-way data binding is achieved with the `{{ ... }}` syntax of the `polymer` expression, as in `<td>{{bac.number}}</td>` or `<td>{{bac.owner.name}}</td>`. The dots between the curly braces take the place of a variable from the code, whose value is shown in that place in the web page. In the code, these variables are annotated with `@published`. Event. Interaction is achieved through declarative on-event = `"{{ ... }}"` handlers, such as `on-click="{{transact}}"` in the button. Here, the dots stand for the name of a method in the code to be executed when the event happens. After `<template>`, the accompanying Dart script `bank_app.dart` is referenced through a `<script>` tag.

Finally, in step 7, we get to the Dart class that is backing up for our Polymer component and see the `BankApp` class extend `PolymerElement`; its class inherits from `PolymerElement`. The class declaration must be preceded by the annotation `@CustomTag('bank-app')` to associate it with the Polymer component. Variables that have to be visualized on the web page are annotated with `@observable`.

Override a custom element life cycle method such as `attached` to execute component-specific code. This method is executed when an element is inserted into the DOM; so it is a good place to initialize an app. It is obligatory to provide the created named constructor for your component. The constructor or any overridden method must call the superclass constructor or method first. The `transact` or `enter` method shows the signature for an event handler, `enter(KeyboardEvent e, var detail, Node target)`. The `transact` method shows how we can get the value for an input element in our Polymer component; use the `shadowRoot.querySelector` method. After the format of the input amount is checked, the `transact` method of the class `BankAccount` in the `bank_terminal` library changes the state of the `bac` object.

The name of a Polymer component must contain at least one dash (-). Notice the naming scheme; if the name of the Polymer component is `pol-comp1`:

- Then it is referenced in the HTML code as `< pol-comp1>`
- It is defined in the files `pol_comp1.html` and `pol_comp1.dart`
- Its class name is `Polcomp1`

There's more...

Polymer components can also be added dynamically via code, instead of being statically declared in the page's HTML. Suppose you want to add a component named `pol-comp1` in a `<div>` tag with an ID of `add-comp1`. You can do this with the following code:

```
querySelector('#add-comp1').children.add(new Element.tag('pol-comp1'));
```

In step 3, you could call a linter instead of an ordinary build by replacing this line, as shown in the following code:

```
main(args) {
   lint(entryPoints: ['web/index.html'], options: parseOptions(args));
}
```

This will display more extensive syntax or usage warnings in your code.

Binding and repeating over a list

In this recipe, we show you how the data of a list can be displayed in a Polymer component. So we perform data binding from the code to the UI here as well as in the following recipe. You can find the code for this recipe in the project `databinding_list`.

How to do it...

1. The script starts from `web\index.html`, where a component with the name `pol-list` is imported through the line:

   ```
   <link rel="import"href="pol_list.html">
   ```

   From this, we know that the component is defined in `pol_list.html`, and the code behind it is in a file named `pol_list.dart`. For a discussion of the other tags, see the previous recipe.

2. We define a list of companies that we want to display in the file `pol_list.dart`:

   ```
   import'dart:html';
   import'package:polymer/polymer.dart';

   @CustomTag('pol-list')
   classPollist extends PolymerElement {
      final List companies = toObservable(['Google', 'Apple',
      'Microsoft', 'Facebook']);

      Pollist.created() : super.created() {
      companies.add('HP');
   }

   addcompanies(Event e, var detail, Node target) {
      companies.add('IBM');
      companies.add('Dell');
      }
   }
   ```

3. The structure of the component is outlined in `pol_list.html`:

```
<link rel="import"href="packages/polymer/polymer.html">
<polymer-element name="pol-list">
<template>
<ul>
<template repeat="{{comp in companies}}">
<li> {{comp}} is an excellent company to work for.</li>
</template>
</ul>
<p><b>We selected {{companies.length}} companies for you. </b></p>
<button on-click="{{addcompanies}}">Add some companies</button>

</template>
<script type="application/dart"
src="pol_list.dart"></script>
</polymer-element>
```

 To register the click event handler, you must use a dash in `on-click`; the `on-click` option will result in `ReferenceError`.

The following screenshot is what the web page displays when the app is run and the button is clicked:

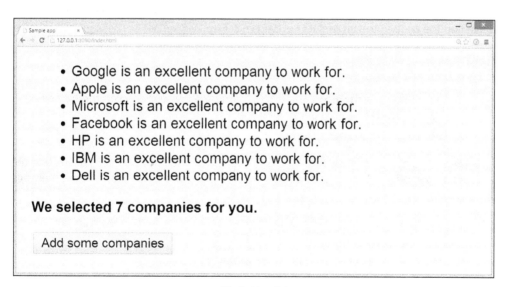

Binding to a list

How it works...

We want to view the contents of the list on our page; this is made possible in step 2 by using the `toObservable` function from the `polymer` package. This function converts a literal `List` to an `ObservableList` (`@observable` doesn't work for a list or map). However, the list is changed in the created event, which is called when the component is instantiated. Also, `companies` is changed by pressing the button, which calls the method `addcompanies`.

Step 3 shows how a template loop is created. The `<template repeat="{{item in list}}">` content `</template>` syntax means that for every item in the list the content inside the template (here, the `<li>` tag) is rendered.

From the running app, as shown in the previous screenshot, we see that whenever the observed list is changed, these changes are reflected in the web page. It also shows that the data binding syntax `{{ }}` can display properties of objects (here, `length` of the list).

There's more...

The same repeating template can be applied for every collection type, which is a type that implements `Iterable`.

Binding to a map

In this recipe, we show you how the data of a map can be displayed in a Polymer component. You can find the code in the project `databinding_map`.

How to do it...

1. The script starts with `web\index.html`, where a component with the name `pol-map` is imported through the following line:

    ```
    <link rel="import"href="pol_map.html">
    ```

    From this code, we know that the component is defined in `pol_map.html`, and the code behind it is in a file named `pol_map.dart`. For a discussion of the other tags, see the first recipe.

2. We define a map `companies`, which we want to display in the file `pol_map.dart`:

    ```
    import'dart:html';
    import'package:polymer/polymer.dart';

    @CustomTag('pol-map')
    classPolmap extends PolymerElement {
    Map companies = toObservable({1: 'Google', 2: 'Microsoft'});
    ```

```
Polmap.created() : super.created() {
    companies[3] = 'HP';
}

addcompanies(Event e, var detail, Node target) {
    companies[4] = 'Facebook';
    companies[5] = 'Apple';
    }
}
```

3. The structure of the Polymer component is outlined in `pol_map.html`:

```
<link rel="import"href="packages/polymer/polymer.html">
<polymer-element name="pol-map">
<template>
<p><b>The list of companies: </b></p>
<template repeat="{{key in companies.keys}}">
<p> {{key}}: {{companies[key]}}</p>
</template>
<button on-click="{{addcompanies}}">Add some companies</button>
<p>My favorite company is: {{companies[1]}}</p>
</template>
<script type="application/dart"
    src="pol_map.dart"></script>
</polymer-element>
```

The following screenshot is what the web page displays when the app is running and the
button is clicked:

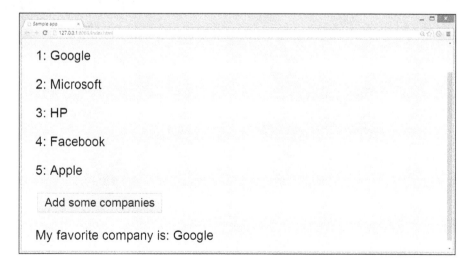

How it works...

We want to view the contents of `Map` in our page. This is made possible in step 2 by using the `toObservable` function from the `polymer` package. This function converts a literal map to an `Observable` map. However, `Map` `companies` is changed in the `created` event, which is called when the component is instantiated. Also, `companies` is changed by pressing the button, which calls the method `addcompanies`.

Step 3 shows how a template loop is created using `<template repeat="{{key in companies.keys}}"> content </template>`.

This means that for every `key` in the list `companies.keys`, the content inside the template (here, `<p>{{key}}: {{companies[key]}}</p>`) is rendered.

We could have also worked with `companies.values`, or any of the other map getters and methods such as `companies.length`. From the running app, as shown in the previous screenshot, we see that whenever the observed map is changed, these changes are reflected in the web page.

See also

 ▸ Refer to the *Binding and repeating over a list* recipe in this chapter on how to use the repeating template construct

Using custom attributes and template conditionals

In this recipe, we will explore two `polymer.dart` features:

 ▸ **Custom attributes**: Like HTML attributes for normal tags, these are attributes for your Polymer component, and they can be changed in the code

 ▸ **Template conditionals**: The UI can be controlled by declarative conditions of the form `<template if={{condition}}></template>`, where a condition is an expression involving observed or published variables

You can find the code in the project `custom_attrib`.

How to do it...

In this example, we simulate an oven, with the temperature as its attribute. We show the temperature in a textual form, and also test the temperature to display an appropriate message, as shown in the following screenshot:

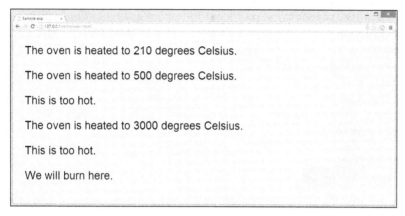

Custom attributes and template conditionals

1. The script starts with `web\index.html`, where a component with the name `pol-oven` is imported through the following line:

```
<link rel="import"href="pol_oven.html">
```

This component is used three times on the page:

```
    <body>
<pol-oven temperature="210"></pol-oven>
<pol-oven temperature="500"></pol-oven>
<pol-oven temperature="3000"></pol-oven>
</body>
```

From this code, we know that the component is defined in `pol_oven.html`, and the code behind it is in a file named `pol_oven.dart`. For a discussion of the other tags, see the first recipe.

2. The code for `pol-oven` is defined in `pol_oven.dart`:

```
import'package:polymer/polymer.dart';

@CustomTag('pol-oven')
classPoloven extends PolymerElement {
  @published int temperature = 0;

  Poloven.created() : super.created() {  }
}
```

3. The structure of the component is outlined in `pol_oven.html`:

```
<link rel="import"href="packages/polymer/polymer.html">
<polymer-element name="pol-oven">
<template>
<p>The oven is heated to {{temperature}} degrees Celsius.   </p>
<template if="{{temperature > 400}}">
<p>This is too hot. </p>
</template>
<template if="{{temperature > 1000}}">
<p>We will burn here. </p>
</template>
</template>
<script type="application/dart" src="pol_oven.dart"></script>
</polymer-element>
```

How it works...

In step 1, we see that the same component, `pol-oven`, can be used multiple times on the same page; each occurrence being a different instance of the component. Of course, a combination of different components is also possible, each time the component contains its attribute `temperature` with a different value.

In step 2, it is shown that a custom attribute must be annotated with `@published`; this means that it is not merely displayed (and updated when changed, indicated with `@ observable`), but is also an attribute to be used in the `polymer` tag.

Finally, in step 3, we see that the attribute values are displayed, but also that a piece of the UI code is displayed whether the evaluated condition is true or false. If the attribute value changes in the code, the conditional templates are automatically re-evaluated, possibly changing the UI.

See also

▶ Refer to the *Binding to a checkbox* recipe in this chapter for another example

Binding to an input text field or a text area

In this recipe, we will show you how to bind an input value from a text field or text area to a variable; so in effect, we now perform data binding from the UI to the code, and we have two-way data binding. You can find the code in the project `pol_text`.

How to do it...

1. The script starts with `web\index.html`, where a component with the name `pol-text` is imported through the following line:

    ```
    <link rel="import"href="pol_text.html">
    ```

    From this, we know that the component is defined in `pol_text.html`, and the code behind it is in a file named `pol_text.dart`. For a discussion of the other tags, see the first recipe.

2. The code for `pol-text` is defined in `pol_text.dart`:

    ```
    import'package:polymer/polymer.dart';

    @CustomTag('pol-text')
    classPoltext extends PolymerElement {
      @observable String comps;

      Poltext.created() : super.created() {  }
    }
    ```

3. The structure of the component is outlined in `pol_text.html`:

    ```
    <link rel="import"href="packages/polymer/polymer.html">
    <polymer-element name="pol-text">
    <template>
    <div>
    Which company do you want to work for?
    <input type="text" value="{{comps}}">
    <p> or type a few companies:
    <textarea value="{{comps}}"></textarea>
    </p>
    </div>
    <div>
    These are your favorite companies: {{comps}}
    ```

```
    </div>
    </template>
    <script type="application/dart" src="pol_text.dart"></script>
    </polymer-element>
```

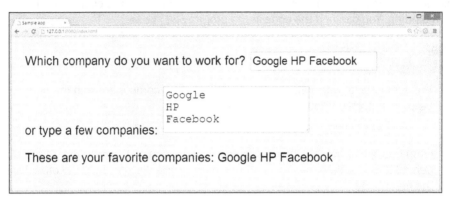

Two-way binding to text fields

How it works...

The input (content) from the simple text field or text area is bounded by the expression `value = {{variable}}` to `variable`. It shows up in the simple `{{variable}}` expression on the page, but also immediately reflects in the other input field, which proves that we have two-way data binding.

Binding to a checkbox

In this recipe, we will show you how to bind an input value from a checkbox to a variable; so in effect, we now perform data binding from the UI to the code and have two-way data binding. You can find the code in the project `pol_check`.

How to do it...

1. The script starts with `web\index.html`, where a component with the name `pol-check` is imported through the following line:

    ```
    <link rel="import"href="pol_check.html">
    ```

    From this, we know that the component is defined in `pol_check.html`, and the code behind it is in a file named `pol_check.dart`. For a discussion of the other tags, refer to the first recipe.

2. The code for `pol-check` is defined in `pol_check.dart`:

```
import 'package:polymer/polymer.dart';
@CustomTag('pol-check')
classPolcheck extends PolymerElement {
  @observable bool receive = false;

  Polcheck.created() : super.created();
}
```

3. The structure of the component is outlined in `pol_check.html`:

```
<link rel="import"href="packages/polymer/polymer.html">
<polymer-element name="pol-check">
<template>
<div>
Do you want to receive our jobs newsletter?
<input type="checkbox" checked="{{receive}}">
</div>
<div>
You will receive the newsletter: {{receive}}
<p>Confirmed:</p>
<template if={{receive}}>You will receive the newsletter</
template>
<template if={{!receive}}>You will not receive the newsletter</
template>
</div>
</template>
<script type="application/dart" src="pol_check.dart"></script>
</polymer-element>
```

The following screenshot is what you see when you run the app:

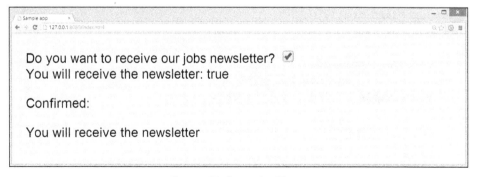

Two-way binding to checkboxes

How it works...

In step 3, the value from the `checked` attribute of the checkbox is bound by the expression `checked="{{receive}}"` to the variable `receive`. Through step 2, the value shows up in the simple `{{receive}}` expression on the page, but it is also used in template conditionals here.

See also

▶   Refer to the *Using custom attributes and template conditionals* recipe in this chapter for more information on template conditionals

Binding to radio buttons

In this recipe, we will show you how to bind an input value from a radio button to a variable; so in effect, we now perform data binding from the UI to the code and have two-way data binding. You can find the code in the project `pol_radio`.

How to do it...

1. The script starts with `web\index.html`, where a component with the name `pol-radio` is imported through the following line:

    ```
    <link rel="import"href="pol_radio.html">
    ```

    From this, we know that the component is defined in `pol_radio.html`, and the code behind it is in a file named `pol_radio.dart`. For a discussion of the other tags, refer to the first recipe.

2. The code for `pol-radio` is defined in `pol_radio.dart`:

    ```
    import'dart:html';
    import'package:polymer/polymer.dart';

    @CustomTag('pol-radio')
    classPolradio extends PolymerElement {
      @observable String favoriteJob = '';

      Polradio.created() : super.created();

      voidgetFavoriteJob(Event e, var detail, Node target) {
        favoriteJob = (e.target as InputElement).value;
      }
    }
    ```

3. The structure of the component is outlined in `pol_radio.html`:

```html
<link rel="import"href="packages/polymer/polymer.html">
<polymer-element name="pol-radio">
<template>
<div on-change="{{getFavoriteJob}}">
What is your favorite job?
<div>
<label for="sd">Software developer <input name="job" type="radio"
id="sd" value="Software developer"></label>
</div>
<div>
<label for="wd">Web Developer <input name="job" type="radio"
id="wd" value="Web developer"></label>
</div>
<div>
<label for="tt">Tester<input name="job" type="radio" id="tt"
value="Tester"></label>
</div>
</div>
<div>
You selected: {{favoriteJob}}
</div>
</template>
<script type="application/dart" src="pol_radio.dart"></script>
</polymer-element>
```

The following screenshot is what you see when you run the app:

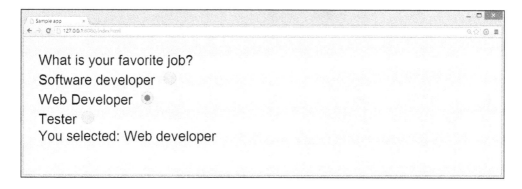

How it works...

On the web page (step 3), we see that the three radio buttons are grouped together by giving them the same value for the `name` attribute, which is `name="job"`. Their values are literal strings, which they can deliver to code. This connection is made because the radio buttons are encapsulated in a `<div>` tag, which has a change event-handler defined in it:

```
<div on-change="{{getFavoriteJob}}">
```

The method `getFavoriteJob` in step 2 will extract the selected radio button's value, and assign it to the variable `favoriteJob`:

```
favoriteJob = (e.target as InputElement).value;
```

This variable is defined as `@observable`, so it shows up on the page with `{{favoriteJob}}`.

Binding to a selected field

In this recipe, we will show you how to bind a selected value from a `<select>` tag to a variable; so in effect, we now perform data binding from the UI to the code and have two-way data binding. We show a list of companies. You can find the code in the project `pol_select`.

How to do it...

1. The script starts with `web\index.html`, where a component with the name `pol-select` is imported through the following line:

   ```
   <link rel="import"href="pol_select.html">
   ```

   From this, we know that the component is defined in `pol_select.html`, and the code behind it is in a file named `pol_select.dart`. For a discussion of the other tags, see the first recipe.

2. The code for `pol-select` is defined in `pol_select.dart`:

   ```
   import'package:polymer/polymer.dart';

   @CustomTag('pol-select')
   classPolselect extends PolymerElement {
       final List companies = toObservable(['Google', 'Apple',
       'Mozilla', 'Facebook']);
       @observable int selected = 2; // Make sure this is not null;
       // set it to the default selection index.
   ```

```
@observable String value = 'Mozilla';

    Polselect.created() : super.created();
}
```

3. The structure of the component is outlined in `pol_select.html`:

```
<link rel="import"href="packages/polymer/polymer.html">
<polymer-element name="pol-select">
<template>
<select selectedIndex="{{selected}}" value="{{value}}">
<option template repeat="{{comp in companies}}"> {{comp}} </
option>
</select>
<div>
You selected company {{selected}} <br/>
or from index:    {{companies[selected]}} <br/>
or from binding: {{value}}
</div>
</template>
<script type="application/dart" src="pol_select.dart"></script>
</polymer-element>
```

The following screenshot is what you see when you run the app:

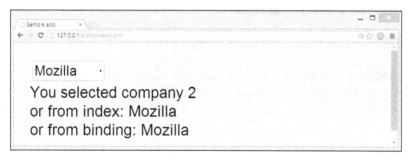

Binding with a select field

How it works...

Step 2 defines the list of companies to be shown. It also declares an index to be selected in `List` and `value` as a variable. Step 3 shows that to populate a `<select>` tag, the repeating template from the *Binding and repeating over a list* recipe in this chapter can be used. It also shows that the `selectedIndex` attribute is set from the code. When another company is selected, this also changes the values of `selected` and `value`.

Event handling

In this recipe, we will show you how to handle events in a Polymer component. You can find the code in the project `event_handling`.

How to do it...

1. The script starts with `web\index.html`, where a component with the name `pol-select` is imported through the following line:

   ```
   <link rel="import"href="pol_events.html">
   ```

   From this, we know that the component is defined in `pol_events.html`, and the code behind it is in a file named `pol_events.dart`. For a discussion of the other tags, refer to the first recipe.

2. The code for `pol-events` is defined in `pol_events.dart`:

   ```dart
   import 'package:polymer/polymer.dart';

   @CustomTag('pol-events')
   classPolevents extends PolymerElement {
   @observable String which_event = "no event";
   @observable String thing = "";
   @observable String message = "";

   Polevents.created() : super.created();

   enter(KeyboardEvent  e, var detail, Node target) {
     if (e.keyCode == KeyCode.ENTER) {
     which_event = "you pressed the ENTER key";
     }
   }

   btnclick(MouseEvent  e, var detail, Node target) {
     message = (target as Element).attributes['data-msg'];
     which_event = "you clicked the button";
   }

   txtChange(Event e, var detail, Node target) {
     varinp = (target as InputElement).value;
     which_event = "you entered $inp in the text field";
   }

   cbClick(Event e, var detail, Node target) {
   ```

```
        which_event = "you changed the checkbox";
      }

      selChange(Event e, var detail, Node target) {
        which_event = "you selected another option";
        }
      }
```

3. The structure of the component is outlined in `pol_events.html`:

```
<link rel="import"href="packages/polymer/polymer.html">
<polymer-element name="pol-events">
<template>
<div class="auto-style1" on-keypress="{{enter}}">
<input type="text" on-change="{{txtChange}}" value="{{thing}}">
<input type="checkbox" on-click="{{cbClick}}">
<select on-click="{{selChange}}">
<option>option 1</option>
<option>option 2</option>
<option>option 3</option>
</select>
<button on-click="{{btnclick}}" data-msg="Message from
button">Invoke button click</button>
</div>
<div> This event occurred: {{which_event}} </div>
<p>{{ message }}</p>
</template>
<script type="application/dart" src="pol_events.dart"></script>
</polymer-element>
```

Experiment with the different events. Each time you will see some text displaying which event was invoked, for example, when selecting from the drop-down list, you will see what's shown in the following screenshot:

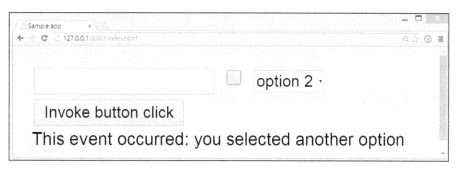

Handling events

How it works...

In step 3, we see a number of event-handlers defined in different HTML elements. They all have the same form, which is `on-event={{nameOfHandler}}`.

In Dart Editor and most plugins, you can find out which events are possible to handle in which tag by pressing *Ctrl + Space bar* within the HTML tag. Remember to put the dash between `on` and the event name; `onevent` throws a `ReferenceError` error in runtime.

In step 2, we see a number of different handlers; they all have the same signature:

```
nameOfHandler(Event e, var detail, Node target) {
  // code to be executed when event occurs
}
```

The `target` node is the HTLM node upon which the event occurred. If this was `InputElement`, you can get the input value with `varinp = (target as InputElement).value;;` notice how the `data-msg` attribute from the button is read out with `message = (target as Element).attributes['data-msg'];`.

Polymer elements with JavaScript interop

In this recipe, we will show you how to work with a JavaScript object in a Polymer component. You can find the code in the project `pol_js`.

How to do it...

1. The script starts with `web\index.html`, where a component with the name `pol-js` is imported through `<link rel="import"href="pol_js.html">` and instantiated through `<pol-js></pol-js>`.

    From this, we know that the component is defined in `pol_js.html`, and its code is in a file named `pol_js.dart`. For a discussion of the other tags, refer to the first recipe.

2. The `index.html` file also includes a JavaScript `person.js` object:

```
function Person(name, gender) {
this.name = name;
this.gender = gender;
  this.greeting = function(otherPerson) {
  alert('I greet you ' + otherPerson.name);
  };
}

Person.prototype.sayHello = function(times) {
```

```
    return times + ' x: hello, I am ' + this.name;
    };
```

3. The structure of the component is outlined in `pol_js.html`:

```
<link rel="import"href="packages/polymer/polymer.html">
<polymer-element name="pol-js">
<template>
<p>From JS interop: {{result}} </p>
<p>
<button on-click="{{btnClick}}">Click me</button>
</p>
</template><script type="application/dart"
src="pol_js.dart"></script>
</polymer-element>
```

4. The code for `pol-js` is defined in `pol_js.dart`:

```
import'dart:html';
import'dart:js';
import'package:polymer/polymer.dart';

@CustomTag('pol-js')
classPolJs extends PolymerElement {
  @observable String result;

  PolJs.created() : super.created();

  btnClick(Event e, var detail, Node target) {
  var pers1 = new JsObject(context['Person'], ['An', 'female']);
  result = pers1.callMethod('sayHello', [10]);
}
}
```

You will get what is shown in the following screenshot after you click on the **Click me** button:

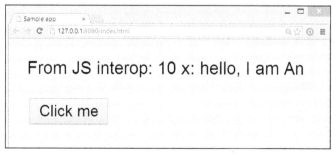

Polymer interop with JavaScript

How it works...

In the JavaScript from step 2 (which is known to the web page), a class `Person` with a method `sayHello` is defined. The parameter `times` says how many times the greeting is to be repeated. In step 3, a variable `result` is bound to be displayed, and an event `btnClick` is defined in the button. Step 4 shows us the code that does this; an object `pers1` is created, and the method `sayHello` is called upon it and assigned to `result`. Notice that we had to import `'dart:js';` to make Dart–JavaScript interaction possible.

See also

▶ To learn more about the Dart and JavaScript interaction, refer to the *Talking with JavaScript* recipe in *Chapter 5, Handling Web Applications*

Extending DOM elements

Instead of making a new Polymer component from scratch, as we did in the previous recipes, you can also start from a native HTML element and build upon that. This is made possible because our component is backed up by a class that can inherit the properties and behavior of an existing HTML element class. For our example, we will extend a `Div` element. You can find the code in the project `dom_extend`.

How to do it...

1. The script starts with `web\index.html`, where a component with the name `dom-extend` is imported through the following line:

    ```
    <link rel="import"href="dom_extend.html">
    ```

    From this, we know that the component is defined in `dom_extend.html`, and the code behind it is in a file named `dom_extend.dart`. For a discussion of the other tags, refer to the first recipe. Because we make a specialized `<div>` tag, we have to indicate this with an `is` attribute, as follows:

    ```
    <body>
    <div is="dom-extend">Initial div content </div>
    </body>
    ```

2. The code for `dom-extend` is defined in `dom_extend.dart`:

    ```
    import'dart:html';
    import'package:polymer/polymer.dart';

    @CustomTag('dom-extend')
    classDomextend extends DivElement with Polymer, Observable {
    ```

```
    Domextend.created() : super.created() {
      polymerCreated();
      text = "I am not an ordinary div!";
    }
}
```

3. The structure of the component is outlined in `dom_extend.html`:

```
<link rel="import"href="packages/polymer/polymer.html">
<polymer-element name="dom-extend" extends="div">
<template>
<style>
:host {
  background: lime;
  color: red;
  font-size: 12px;
  font-weight: bold, italic;
  border: 1px solid #ccc;
}
</style>
<content>Initial dom-extend content</content>
</template>
<script type="application/dart" src="dom_extend.dart"></script>
</polymer-element>
```

We will get the following output after running this app:

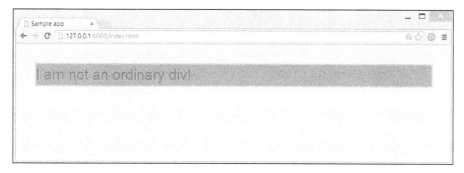

Extending a DOM element

How it works...

In step 1, you could read the `is="dom-extend"` attribute meaning, this is `<div>`, but it inherits the style, structure, and behavior of the `dom-extend` Polymer component. Step 2 shows us that class `Domextend` extends `DivElement` with Polymer, observable that `Domextend` itself inherits from class `DivElement` and mixes with the `Polymer` and `Observable` classes. Compare this with what we have for a normal Polymer component (from the *Binding and repeating over a list* recipe in this chapter), which only inherits from the `PolymerElement` class; class `Pollist` extends `PolymerElement`.

The `polymer` class is the mixing class for Polymer elements; it provides utility features on top of the custom web elements standard. If it is used in this way, you must call `polymerCreated()` from within the constructor. The constructor also changes the text in the `<div>` tag.

In step 3, we have a second but necessary statement, `<polymer-element name="dom-extend"extends="div">` with `extends="div"`, which `Domextend` inherits from `DivElement` in full.

We have also used the `host` selector in order to style the shadow DOM `<style>:host { ... } </style>`. This style can be overridden by the embedding web page. If this is not what you want, just use the normal style selectors, such as class, ID, and so on. The `<content></content>` area is used for content insertion; when a component has children, those children go where the `<content>` tags are. Here, the initial text is overwritten by the Polymer component `dom-extend`.

Working with custom elements

Instead of making a new Polymer component from scratch or starting with an existing HTML element and building upon that as we did in the previous recipe, you can also simply use custom-made Polymer elements.

This recipe will implement some of the core and paper elements of the Polymer project (`http://www.polymer-project.org/docs/elements/`). The `paper_elements` project is the Polymer implementation of Google's Material Design UI widgets (for more information, refer to `http://www.polymer-project.org/docs/elements/material.html`). There will be more and more of these, either written in JavaScript with a custom Dart wrapper to use them, or purely in Dart, and you can also combine them with your own Polymer components. You can find the code in the project `pol_custom`.

How to do it...

1. In our `pubspec.yaml` file, we add the following dependencies:

```
dependencies:
polymer: '>=0.11.0 <0.12.0'
core_elements: '>=0.0.6 <0.1.0'
paper_elements: '>=0.0.1 <0.1.0'
```

2. The script starts with `web\index.html`, where our core and paper components are imported through the following lines:

```
<link rel="import"href="packages/core_elements/core_icon.html">
<link rel="import"href="packages/core_elements/core_icons.html">
<link rel="import"href="packages/core_elements/core_menu.html">
<link rel="import"href="packages/core_elements/core_item.html">
<link rel="import"href="packages/paper_elements/paper_input.html">
<link rel="import"href="packages/paper_elements/paper_radio_group.
html">
<link rel="import"href="packages/core_elements/core_splitter.
html">
```

We randomly chose some components from the several dozen available.

The components are instantiated in the `<body>` tag:

```
<body unresolved>
<core-menu selected="0">
<core-item icon="settings" label="Settings"></core-item>
<core-item icon="dialog" label="Dialog"></core-item>
<core-item icon="search" label="Search"></core-item>
</core-menu>
<paper-input label="Waiting for input..."></paper-input>
<paper-radio-group selected="small">
<paper-radio-button name="small" label="Small"></paper- radio-
button>
<paper-radio-button name="medium" label="Medium"></paper-radio-
button>
<paper-radio-button name="large" label="Large"></paper-radio-
button>
</paper-radio-group>
<div horizontal layout>
<div>left <br/><br/><br/></div>
<core-splitter direction="left"></core-splitter>
<div flex>right</div>
</div>
</body>
```

Running this app will give you the following output:

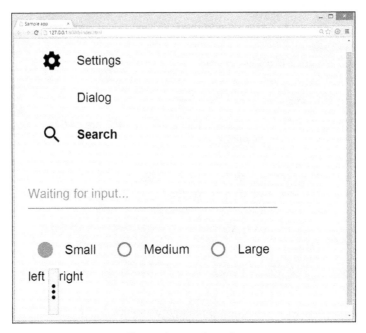

Core and paper elements

How it works...

The `core_elements` and `paper_elements` pub packages are wrappers and ports for Polymer's element collections with the same name. They package the elements into single pub packages to be able to add them as a `pubspec` dependency. Most core elements are wrapped with Dart proxy classes to make them easier to interact with Dart scripts.

In step 2, a random selection of these elements is imported and instantiated in the page. Most properties are changeable via attributes such as icons, labels, and so on. The `<body>` tag needs the `unresolved` attribute to ensure that no Polymer custom elements are displayed before Polymer is ready. Since these are custom elements, there are no steps 3 and 4 as in the previous recipes!

The `Index.html` file also shows how to use the core and paper icons; import them with the following code:

```
<link rel="import"href="packages/paper_elements/paper_icon_button.
html">
<link rel="import" href="packages/core_elements/src/core-icons/
iconsets/social-icons.html">
```

In the preceding code, you choose the name according to the set you want to load, for example, social icons. Then, use the icon by setting the `icon` attribute; the value consists of icons set, -ID, a colon followed by the icon name. This icon for example, shows a +1 value:

```
<paper-icon-button id="bookmark-button" icon="social:plus-one"
style="fill:steelblue;"></paper-icon-button>
```

Automatic node finding

Like jQuery with its $ function, Polymer also has a very handy way to locate nodes in the DOM of the page. This recipe shows you how to use it. You can find the code in the project `find_nodes`.

How to do it...

1. The script starts with `web\index.html`, where a component with the name `find-nodes` is imported through the following line:

```
<link rel="import"href="find_nodes.html">
```

From this, we know that the component is defined in `find_nodes.html`, and the code behind it is in a file named `find_nodes.dart`. For a discussion of the other tags, refer to the first recipe.

2. The code for `find-nodes` is defined in `find_nodes.dart`:

```
import'dart.html';
import'package:polymer/polymer.dart';

@CustomTag('find-nodes')
classFindnodes extends PolymerElement {
  Findnodes.created() : super.created();

  btnclick(MouseEvent  e, var detail, Node target) {
    // making the paragraph visible:
```

```
$['show'].style
..display = 'inline'
..color = 'red';
// changing the text inside the div:
Element insideDiv = $['findme'];
insideDiv.text = 'I was looked up by \$ and changed!';
  }
}
```

3. The structure of the component is outlined in `find_nodes.html`:

```
<link rel="import"href="packages/polymer/polymer.html">
<polymer-element name="find-nodes">
<template>
<div class="auto-style1">
<div id="findme">Hello from inside a div</div>
<button on-click="{{btnclick}}">Click to find</button>
</div>
<p id="show" style="display:none">==&gt; I was found by $ and
became visible! </p>
</template>
<script type="application/dart"
src="find_nodes.dart"></script>
</polymer-element>
```

The following screenshot shows you what you will see when you run the app:

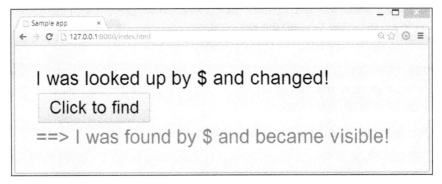

Binding with a select field

How it works...

In step 2, we see that the paragraph with ID `show` is shown when the button is clicked because of the line `$['show'].style.display = 'inline';` in the event handler. Likewise, an element reference to `<div>` with the ID `findme` is found with `$['findme']`. The code uses automatic node finding, a Polymer feature, to get a reference to each HTML element. Every node in a custom element (so inside the shadow DOM!) that is tagged with an `id` attribute can be referenced by its ID using the syntax `$['ID']`.

 This example requires Polymer dart 0.8.0 or higher.

Internationalizing a Polymer app

What if you want your web app to display information in several languages, depending on the language of the web client user? This recipe will show you how to accomplish this. You can find the code in the project `pol_intl`.

How to do it...

1. Add the `intl` package from the pub package to your app through `pubspec.yaml`.

2. The script starts with `web\pol_intl.html`, where a component with the name `localized_text` is imported through the following line:

```
<link rel="import"href="localized_text.html">
```

From this, we know that the component is defined in `localized_text.html`, and the code behind it is in a file named `localized_text.dart`. For a discussion of the other tags, see the first recipe.

3. The structure of the component is outlined in `localized_text.html`:

```
<link rel="import"href="packages/polymer/polymer.html">
<polymer-element name="localized-text">
<template>
<p>{{startMsg}}</p>

<select value="{{selectedLocale}}">
<option value="en_US">English</option>
<option value="fr">French</option>
<option value="nl_NL">Dutch</option>
<option value="de">German</option>
<option value="it">Italian</option>
```

```
<option value="jp">Japanese</option>
</select>

</template>
<script type="application/dart"
src="localized_text.dart"></script>
</polymer-element>
```

4. The code for `localized-text` is defined in `localized_text.dart`:

```
import 'package:polymer/polymer.dart';
import 'package:intl/intl.dart';
import 'messages_all.dart';

@CustomTag('localized-text')
classLocalizedText extends PolymerElement {
  @observable String selectedLocale;
  @observable String startMsg;

  LocalizedText.created() : super.created() {
  updateLocale(Intl.defaultLocale);
  }

  voidselectedLocaleChanged() {
  initializeMessages(selectedLocale).then(
  (succeeded) =>updateLocale(selectedLocale));
  }

  voidupdateLocale(localeName) {
  Intl.defaultLocale = selectedLocale;
  startMsg = start();
}

start() =>Intl.message("Please choose your language and then start
the tour.",
name: 'startMsg',
desc: "Starting the tour",
args: [], // needed if arguments.
examples: {"" : 0});
}
```

The following screenshot shows what you will see when you run the app:

あなたの言語を選択し、ツアーを開始してください。

Japanese ·

Using intl with Polymer

How it works...

The package `intl` is imported in step 1; it is maintained by the Dart team, which provides internationalization and localization facilities, for example, message translation, plurals and genders, date/number formatting and parsing, and bidirectional text. In step 3, a drop-down list of languages is offered to choose a language from. The value of the chosen option is bound to the variable `selectLocale`. The purpose of the rest of the code is to translate the content of `startMsg` to this language.

In step 4, the method `selectedLocaleChanged()` is triggered when a language is chosen. This calls the `updateLocale` method with `selectedLocale`, which sets the value as `defaultLocale` and sets `startMsg` to the result of the `start()` function. This executes `Intl.message` for the message we want to translate, returning that message in the chosen language. All messages to be localized are written as functions that return the result of an `Intl.message` call.

Internally, `intl` works as follows:

▶ The messages to be translated are stored in a file named `intl_messages.json`, with their names and the message in the default language. They are extracted from the program source, either manually or by running `dart extract_json.dartlocalized_text.dart`, which produces the JSON file.

▶ From this file, the different `translation_locale.json` files are produced; one for each language to be used. These files contain a map with the locale, and its name and translation for each message. For example, here is the Italian version `translation_it.json`:

```
{"_locale" : "it",
  "startMsg" : "Scegliere la lingua e poi iniziareil tour."}
```

Now, run `dart generate_from_json.dartlocalized_text.darttranslation_fr.jsontranslation_nl.json`. This will generate `messages_all.dart`, `messages_fr.dart`, `messages_nl.dart`, and so on.

► Now import `messages_all.dart` in the main Dart script, and the mechanism is in place. If the number of messages is small, you could work with the `messages_` files themselves, without having to generate them from JSON files.

There's more...

For more detailed information on `intl`, see its documentation at `http://www.dartdocs.org/documentation/intl/0.11.3/index.html#intl`.

If instead of letting your user choose the language, you want to derive it from the information the browser gives you, then use the following code:

```
import"package:intl/intl_browser.dart";
...
findSystemLocale().then(runTheRestOfTheProgram);
```

11
Working with Angular Dart

This chapter contains the following recipes:

- ▶ Setting up an angular app
- ▶ Using a controller
- ▶ Using a component
- ▶ Using formatters as filters
- ▶ Creating a view
- ▶ Using a service
- ▶ Deploying your app

Introduction

In this chapter, we are going to use Angular Dart to build client web applications. Angular Dart (`https://github.com/angular/angular.dart`) is the porting of AngularJS to Dart. AngularJS, or Angular for short (refer to `www.angularjs.org`), is a popular open source JavaScript framework, maintained by Google, to develop single-page dynamic web applications. Its goal is to create web-based apps with **Model-View-Controller** (**MVC**) or **Model-View-ViewModel** (**MVVM**) capabilities in an effort to make both development and testing easier.

It accomplishes this using declarative programming to build UI and wire software components so that you can concentrate on your application's logic and not on DOM manipulation. It uses a templating system with a number of so-called directives (starting with `ng-`) to specify customizable and reusable HTML tags and expressions that control the behavior of certain elements: in effect, you extend HTML with custom elements and attributes. Google uses Angular Dart to build internal applications. Each recipe explored in this chapter exposes a major component of Angular. The most up-to-date documents can be found at `https://docs.angulardart.org/`.

Setting up an Angular app

This recipe is a preliminary step necessary for every other recipe in this chapter. It shows you how to make the Angular Dart functionality available to your app.

How to do it...

1. There is no `angular` template yet in Dart Editor, so start your app from a web application (mobile friendly), and call it, for example, `angular_setup`. Clear the sample code from the `html` and `dart` files.

2. Add `angular` to the dependencies in `pubspec.yaml`. Saving will start the `pub get` procedure.

3. Also add `js` and `shadow_dom` to `pubspec.yaml`.

4. Add the shadow DOM script to the `html` file:
   ```
   <script
     src="packages/shadow_dom/shadow_dom.min.js"></script>
   ```

5. Also, include the Angular transformer:
   ```
   transformers:
   - angular
   ```

6. Provide the `ng-app` attribute in the `<html>` element.

7. Add the following statement to the top of your main Dart script:
   ```
   import 'package:angular/angular.dart';
   import 'package:angular/application_factory.dart';
   ```

8. In `main()`, insert the code `applicationFactory().run();`.

9. Provide the `ng-cloak` attribute in the `<body>` element.

10. Add the following section to your CSS file:
    ```
    [ng-cloak], .ng-cloak {
        display: none !important;
    }
    ```

How it works...

Step 2 downloads the basic Angular Dart framework as well as the packages it depends on. Notice that it uses the `web_components` package. Steps 3 and 4 turn on the Shadow DOM for older browsers that do not yet implement this feature natively, in which case, the package `js` is needed for JavaScript interoperability.

Shadow DOM is the ability of the browser to include a sub-tree of DOM elements into the rendering of a tag, the so-called shadow root. For example, an `<input type="date">` element hides a whole HTML table to create a slick calendar that highlights the range of dates and that reacts to click events. It is on this basis that web components are built. For more detailed information, refer to `http://www.html5rocks.com/en/tutorials/webcomponents/shadowdom/`.

Step 5 is necessary to deploy your app when you convert your app to JavaScript (refer to the *Deploying your app* recipe). The `ng-app` directive in Step 6 tells Angular which element is the root element of the application: everything inside of it is part of the page template managed by Angular. In most cases, this is the outermost `<html>` tag; anything inside of this element is part of the page template managed by Angular. After the page is loaded, Angular looks for the `ng-app` directive. Upon finding it, it bootstraps the application, with the root of the application DOM being the element on which the `ng-app` directive was defined.

Step 7 makes Angular available to your code, and step 8 starts Angular's event-loop to handle every browser event. If anything in the model changes in this event handling, all corresponding bindings in the view are updated.

Steps 8 and 9 are necessary to avoid the display of {{...}} before the correct values from the model are inserted. This happens because there is a little time gap between the time when you load HTML and the time when Angular is ready with bootstrapping, compiling the DOM, and substituting in the real values for the data binding expressions.

There's more...

If you need the mirrors library, `dart:mirrors`, to use Dart's reflection capabilities, provide a temporary fix using the mirrors annotation:

```
@MirrorsUsed(override:'*')
import 'dart:mirrors';
```

The processes of minifying and tree-shaking your app performed by the dart2js compiler will generally not detect reflected code so that the use of reflection at runtime might fail, resulting in `noSuchMethod()` errors. To prevent this from happening, use the mirrors annotation, which helps the dart2js compiler to generate smaller code.

For more information on mirrors, see the *Using reflection* recipe in *Chapter 4, Object Orientation*, and also `https://www.dartlang.org/articles/reflection-with-mirrors/`.

Using a controller

The web page is our view in the MVC pattern. The controller object is responsible for showing data from the model (binding them to DOM elements in the view) and in response to events, possibly changing model data and displaying these changes in the view. All public fields of the controller can be shown, and all public methods can be invoked from within the view. Data binding is done through the same syntax as in Polymer using double curly braces { { ... } }. A controller should contain only the business logic needed for a single app or view; it should not manipulate the DOM.

In this recipe, we'll show you how to work with an Angular controller step by step. You can follow along with the code in the project `angular_controller`.

How to do it...

Our app will show job type data in a list, and when a job is selected, its details are shown, as shown in the following screenshot:

The controller in action

Its working is explained as follows:

- ▶ The `Job` class, which is the model, is defined in `angular_controller.dart` as follows:

```dart
class Job {
  String type;
  int salary;
  String company;
  DateTime posted; // date of publication of job
  bool open = true; // is job still vacant?
  List<String> skills;
  String info;
  Job(this.type, this.salary, this.company, this.posted, this.
skills, this.info);
}
```

- ▶ The `controller` is a separate class, `JobListingController`, in the same file:

```dart
@Controller(
    selector: '[job-listing]',
    publishAs: 'ctrl')
class JobListingController {
  Job selectedJob;
  List<Job> jobs;

  JobListingController() {
    jobs = _loadData();
  }

  void selectJob(Job job) {
    selectedJob = job;
  }

  // model data:
  List<Job> _loadData() {
    return [
      new Job('Web Developer',7500, 'Google', DateTime.
parse('2014-07-03'),
    ["HTML5", "CSS", "Dart"], "on-site job Palo Alto, California"),
    // other job data
      ];
  }
}
```

▶ In the web page, everything happens in `<div>` marked with `job-listing`:

```
<div job-listing>
    <h3>Job List</h3>
    <ul>
      <li class="pointer"
          ng-repeat="job in ctrl.jobs"
          ng-click="ctrl.selectJob(job)">
        {{job.type}}
      </li>
    </ul>
    <h3>Job Details</h3>
    <div><strong>Type: </strong>{{ctrl.selectedJob.type}}</div>
    <div><strong>Company: </strong>{{ctrl.selectedJob.company}}</div>
    <div><strong>Salary: </strong>{{ctrl.selectedJob.salary}}</div>
    <div><strong>Posted: </strong>{{ctrl.selectedJob.posted}}</div>
      <div><strong>Skills: </strong>
      <ul>
        <li ng-repeat="skill in ctrl.selectedJob.skills">
          {{skill}}
        </li>
      </ul>
    </div>
    <div><strong>More info: </strong>{{ctrl.selectedJob.info}}</div>
</div>
```

▶ To start up the Angular machinery, something more has to be done now as shown in the following code:

```
void main() {
  applicationFactory()
        .addModule(new AppModule())
        .run();
}

class AppModule extends Module {
  AppModule() {
    bind(JobListingController);
  }
}
```

How it works...

The controller in step 2 contains the list of jobs to be shown; it loads them in through _ loadData() in its constructor. It also holds the selected job, if any. This controller is marked with the @ annotation. Have a look at the following code:

```
@Controller(
    selector: '[job-listing]',
    publishAs: 'ctrl')
```

The string after selector, between brackets, is the name of a CSS selector (here, job-listing) in the page. In step 3, we see that there is a <div> element that has this name as selector. This <div> element defines a scope in which the controller is active and known. When Angular sees this <div> element, it instantiates the controller class, making its content available. The publishAs code gives the name (here, ctrl) that the controller is known by in the <div> scope in the view: that's why we see that name appear throughout the HTML code.

In <ul>, all the jobs from the list in the controller known as ctrl are shown through the directive ng-repeat="job in ctrl.jobs"; this iterates over the model (the job property in JobListingController) and the clone <li> in the compiled DOM for each job in the list. More specifically, only type is shown because the <li> tag contains {{job.type}}.

The same tag also contains an ng-click directive, which registers an event-handler for a click event on the list item ng-click="ctrl.selectJob(job)". This can be attached to any HTML element, and here it calls the method selectJob in the controller, passing the job that was clicked. In step 2, we see that this method passes this job to selectedJob. Because this variable now gets a value, the view updates, and all {{ctrl. selectJob. } expressions are evaluated and shown, including the list of skills, where an ng-repeat="skill in ctrl.selectedJob.skills" directive is used.

To make this work in Angular, we need to wrap our controller in the class AppModule, which inherits from Module. To instantiate this new module, it has to be added to the Angular engine via the method addModule(), a dependency injection technique that is used for other Angular items too as we will see in the next recipes; in general, an Angular app will have a list of modules with which it works.

There's more...

A control in the view can be disabled when a certain condition is met if you add the following HTML attribute: ng-disabled="ctrl.condition", where condition is a Boolean property or function in the controller. To make the control visible or not, use ng-show or ng-hide.

Using a component

In this recipe, we'll show you how to work with an Angular component step by step. Components are lightweight, reusable, and self-contained UI widgets that have a single specific purpose. We'll use a component that shows a graphical representation of the job's salary. You can follow along with the code in the project `angular_component`.

How to do it...

Our app shows job type data in a list, together with a number of stars, to indicate the salary. This is also shown when selecting a job to show its details, as shown in the following screenshot:

A component showing the salary

Its working is explained as follows:

▶ The following is the startup script `angular_component.dart`:

```
import 'package:angular/angular.dart';
import 'package:angular/application_factory.dart';
import 'package:angular_component/salary/salary_component.dart';
import 'package:angular_component/job_listing.dart';

void main() {
  applicationFactory()
       .addModule(new AppModule())
       .run();
}

class AppModule extends Module {
  AppModule() {
    bind(JobListingController);
    bind(SalaryComponent);
  }
}
```

▶ In the web page, we see a new HTML element `<x-salary>` for our component, as follows:

```
<x-salary max-sal="10" salary="job.rate_salary"></x-salary>
```

This is also found in the job details section, which is now surrounded by the following code:

```
<div ng-if="ctrl.selectedJob != null">
   ...
<x-salary max-sal="10" salary="ctrl.selectedJob.rate_salary"></x-salary>
   ...
</div>
```

The component is defined in the folder `lib\salary`, with an HTML file `angular_component.html` that defines its structure, a Dart file that describes its behavior, and a CSS file to style it.

▶ The following is the Dart code:

```
import 'package:angular/angular.dart';

@Component(
    selector: 'x-salary',
```

```
      templateUrl: 'packages/angular_component/salary/salary_
component.html',
      cssUrl: 'packages/angular_component/salary/salary_component.
css',
      publishAs: 'cmp')
class SalaryComponent {
  static const String _STAR_ON_CHAR = "\u2605";
  static const String _STAR_OFF_CHAR = "\u2606";
  static const String _STAR_ON_CLASS = "star-on";
  static const String _STAR_OFF_CLASS = "star-off";

  static final int DEFAULT_MAX = 5;

  List<int> stars = [];

  @NgOneWay('salary')
  int salary;

  @NgAttr('max-sal')
  void set maxSal(String value) {
    var count = (value == null)
        ? DEFAULT_MAX
        : int.parse(value, onError: (_) => DEFAULT_MAX);
    stars = new List.generate(count, (i) => i + 1);
  }

  String starClass(int star) =>
      star > salary ? _STAR_OFF_CLASS : _STAR_ON_CLASS;

  String starChar(int star) => star > salary ? _STAR_OFF_CHAR :
_STAR_ON_CHAR;
}
```

► The following is the HTML code for the component:

```
<span class="stars"
      ng-repeat="star in cmp.stars"
      ng-class="cmp.starClass(star)">
          {{cmp.starChar(star)}}
</span>
```

How it works...

In step 1, you can see that we refactored the code of `JobListingController` into its own library in `lib\job_listing.dart`. A component called `SalaryComponent` is now also bound to `AppModule`. Step 2 demonstrates how the component is used in HTML as a new kind of tag `<x-salary>`, with properties `max-sal` and `salary`. Why `x-`? In order to be W3C compliant, custom components should have a dash (-) in their names.

Additionally, we see how we control the inclusion of HTML sections in Angular with `ng-if="condition"`. If the condition is false, then that `<div>` section is removed from the DOM.

In step 3, we see how the definition of the class `SalaryComponent` is preceded by the `@Component` annotation. Its `selector` part states the HTML element that will instantiate the component, which also defines its scope. Note that `templateUrl` and `cssUrl` refer to the definition of the component, and `publishAs` is the name for the component in its scope, which is used in step 4. How does the component depict the salary? The star character comes from the Unicode `"\u2605"`, shown through `{{cmp.starChar(star)}}`. When the component is instantiated, its properties get set, in particular, `salary="job.rate_salary"`. `rate_salary` is a getter in the class `Job`: the properties are set as `int get rate_salary => salary~/1000`. Thus, the salary in the component is the number of thousands in the job's salary. Note that `salary` is annotated by `@NgOneWay`, which means that it is a one-way property and its value flows from the object to the UI, but the UI cannot change it in the code. Note that `max-sal`, being an attribute, is annotated by `@NgAttr`. The NgAttr annotation on a field maps this to a DOM attribute. The `stars` list gets set to a list of `max-sal` numbers by `List.generate()`: `[1,2,3,4,5,6,7,8,9,10]`. The `ng-class` directive sets the CSS class on the component dynamically; its expression is the name of the class to be added to it, which amounts to `"star-on"` or `"star-off"`. The star is pictured yellow when `star` is still smaller than or equal to `salary`. Thus, for every thousand dollars in `salary`, a yellow star is shown by `ng-repeat`, while `max-sal` determines the number of uncolored stars.

There's more...

If a user needs to be able to change a property through the web page (for example, changing the salary), they will have to declare it as `@TwoWay` in the code. In our example, this can be done by defining an `ng-click="event-handler"` for our component.

See also

▸ For another example of a component, see the *Creating a view* recipe in this chapter

Using formatters as filters

Formatters are helper tools to view your data differently from how they are stored in the model. Angular has built-in formatters, for example, `Date` to format date-times, `Currency` to format money data, and `LimitTo` to limit the view to a certain number of results. The `Filter` class displays items based on whether they satisfy the criteria set up in the filter. Sorting works through an `orderBy` attribute in `ng-repeat`. In this recipe, we will show you how to use filters to make different views on your data possible. You can follow along with the code in the project `angular_formatter`.

How to do it...

The job listing is now preceded by an input field; when you start typing the job type, the list of only those jobs that start with these letters are shown. The checkboxes allow you to filter on company, and the type of job is shown in uppercase in the job details section, as shown in the following screenshot:

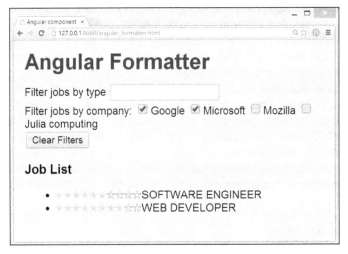

Using formatters to limit the view

Perform the following steps to use formatters as filters:

1. We've added two filters: the first on the job type, the second on the company. They are expressed through HTML in `angular_formatter.html`. Have a look at the following code:

   ```
   <div id="filters">
   <div>
   <label for="type-filter">Filter jobs by type</label>
   <input id="type-filter" type="text"
   ```

```
        ng-model="ctrl.typeFilterString">
  </div>
  <div> Filter jobs by company:
    <span ng-repeat="company in ctrl.companies">
      <label>
      <input type="checkbox"
     ng-model="ctrl.companyFilterMap[company]">{{company}}
      </label>
    </span>
  </div>
  <input type="button" value="Clear Filters" ng-click="ctrl.
clearFilters()">
</div>
```

2. The actual filtering takes place in the same file; instead of a simple `ng-repeat = "job in ctrl.jobs"`, we now have the following:

```
ng-repeat="job in ctrl.jobs
 orderBy:'type'
   filter:{type:ctrl.typeFilterString}
   companyfilter:ctrl.companyFilterMap"
```

We have shown here the different filter parts on consecutive lines for readability, but in HTML, they must be on one line.

In the controller code (`lib\job_listing.dart`), we now have two lists:

```
List<Job> jobs;
List companies = [];
```

The `_loadData()` option now returns jobs, and in the constructor companies is filled through as follows:

```
for (job in jobs) {
      companies.add(job.company);
}
```

The filters need the following code:

```
final companyFilterMap = <String, bool>{};
String typeFilterString = "";

void clearFilters() {
    companyFilterMap.clear();
    typeFilterString = "";
}
```

Furthermore, we have refactored the model code (class `Job`) in its own file `lib\model\job.dart`.

The company filter is a custom formatter that has to be coded. We find it in `lib\formatter\company_filter.dart` as follows:

```dart
library company_filter;

import 'package:angular/angular.dart';

@Formatter(name: 'companyfilter')
class CompanyFilter {
  List call(JobList, filterMap) {
    if (JobList is Iterable && filterMap is Map) {
      // If there is nothing checked, treat it as "everything is
checked"
      bool nothingChecked = filterMap.values.every((isChecked) =>
!isChecked);
    return nothingChecked
      ? JobList.toList()
      : JobList.where((i) => filterMap[i.company] == true).toList();
    }
return const [];
  }
}
```

3. In `<div job-listing>` in `angular_formatter.html`, we now format the job type as `{{job.type | uppercase}}`.

4. In `lib\formatter`, we code this uppercase formatter as follows:

```dart
import 'package:angular/angular.dart';

@Formatter(name: 'uppercase')
class UppercaseFormatter {
  call(String name) {
    if (name == null || name.isEmpty) return '';
    return name.toUpperCase();
  }
}
```

5. The `angular_formatter.dart` script has two additional import statements and two bind statements for the formatters, as follows:

```dart
import 'package:angular_formatter/formatter/company_filter.dart';
import 'package:angular_formatter/formatter/uppercase_formatter.dart';

class AppModule extends Module {
  AppModule() {
```

```
        bind(JobListingController);
        bind(SalaryComponent);
        bind(CompanyFilter);
      bind(UppercaseFormatter);
    }
```

How it works...

In step 1, we see the two filters. The filter on type is done with an input text field that has a special attribute, `ng-model="ctrl.typeFilterString"`. This tells us that the `JobListingController` must have a property `typeFilterString`, which is bound to this input field by `ng-model`. The same goes for the checkboxes, which are bound to a controller property, `companyFilterMap`:

```
    ng-model="ctrl.companyFilterMap[company]"
```

Indeed, we see these properties declared in the additional controller code in step 3. Note that `companyFilterMap` is a map built from the company names and the Boolean values of the checkboxes. Step 2 shows us the filtering declaration: first the jobs are ordered by type, then the type filter is applied (if any), and then the company filters (if any). The results are piped (or chained) with a | operator from one filter to the other.

Step 4 shows the code for the company filter: it has to be a separate class, `CompanyFilter`, that is annotated with `@Formatter(name: 'companyfilter')`, where the name is used in the `ng-repeat` attribute. This class must have a `call` method, as first argument the model object to be formatted (here, `JobList`), the second argument `filterMap` is the filter to be applied. So the return value of `call` is the filtered (formatted) job list. The `filterMap` parameter is the data that comes from the checkbox inputs. Steps 5 and 6 show how to add a simple uppercase formatter. In step 7, we add our custom filters and formatters to our `AppModule`.

See also

▶ The `Angular.dart` framework here makes use of the special method `call`, which is explained in the *Using the call method* recipe in *Chapter 4, Object Orientation*

Creating a view

In this recipe, we isolate the code for the filters from previous recipe in its own component: `search_job` in the folder `lib\component\`. You can follow along with the code in the project `angular_view`.

How to do it...

The change we make in this recipe is transparent to the user; the web page stays the same, but the project code is refactored.

1. In our main web page `angular-view.html`, the `<div id="filters">` section is now replaced by the HTML code for the component. Have a look at the following code:

    ```
    <search-job
          type-filter="ctrl.typeFilter"
          company-filter-map="ctrl.companyFilterMap">
    </search-job>
    ```

2. In the constructor of `JobListingController`, the following code is added:

    ```
    for (var company in companies) {
          companyFilterMap[company] = false;
    }
    ```

3. The behavior of the component is coded in `search_job_component.dart` as follows:

    ```
    import 'package:angular/angular.dart';

    @Component(
        selector: 'search-job',
        templateUrl: 'packages/angular_view/component/search_job_
    component.html',
        publishAs: 'cmp')
    class SearchJobComponent {
      Map<String, bool> _companyFilterMap;
      List<String> _companies;

      @NgTwoWay('type-filter')
      String typeFilter = "";

      @NgTwoWay('company-filter-map')
      Map<String, bool> get companyFilterMap => _companyFilterMap;
      void set companyFilterMap(values) {
        _companyFilterMap = values;
        _companies = companyFilterMap.keys.toList();
      }

      List<String> get companies => _companies;

      void clearFilters() {
    ```

```
    _companyFilterMap.keys.forEach((f) => _companyFilterMap[f] =
false);
    typeFilter = "";
  }
}
```

4. The structure of the filter component is now coded in `search_job_component. html` as follows:

```html
<div id="filters">
    <div>
     <label for="type-filter">Filter jobs by type</label>
<input id="type-filter" type="text"                              ng-
model="cmp.typeFilter" value=" ">
    </div>
    <div>
      Filter jobs by company: <span
ng-repeat="company in cmp.companies"> <label> <input type="checkb
ox"                                     ng-model="cmp.comp
anyFilterMap[company]">{{company}}
     </label>
     </span>
    </div>
    <input type="button" value="Clear Filters"
     ng-click="cmp.clearFilters()">
</div>
```

How it works...

In step 1, we see that the main web page is now greatly simplified; instead of containing all of the markup to set up the search and filter views, it now just contains the reference to the component `search_job`. This component has two attributes, whose values must be set by `ctrl`, our `JobListingController`. Step 2 shows the code to set `companyFilterMap`. The two filter attributes are declared in step 3 as `@NgTwoWay`. Indeed the user must be able to set them, and we want to be able to clear them in code in `clearFilters()`. The component template code in step 4 is not changed.

Using a service

The following step is to read the data from a JSON file, which we will use in this recipe. Angular has a built-in core functionality called the HTTP Service to make HTTP requests to a server. In our example, the job data has been serialized to the JSON format in the file `jobs.json`, and we will make an HTTP request to the web server to get this data. You can follow along with the code in the project `angular_service`.

How to do it...

The change we make in this recipe is nearly transparent to the user; the web page stays the same, but because making an HTTP request is asynchronous, we will work with a Future and must provide a message, such as `"Loading data..."`, as long as the request is being executed.

1. In our `JobListingController` controller class, `lib\job_listing.dart`, we define a new variable of the type `Http:   final Http _http;`. The constructor now becomes the following:

```
JobListingController(this._http) {
    _loadData();
}
```

The bulk of the change takes place in its `_loadData()` method, as shown in the following code:

```
static const String LOADING_MESSAGE = "Loading jobs listing...";
static const String ERROR_MESSAGE = "Sorry! The jobs database
cannot be reached.";
String message = LOADING_MESSAGE;

void _loadData() {
    jobsLoaded = false;
    _http.get('jobs.json')
        .then((HttpResponse response) {
jobs = response.data.map((d) => new Job.fromJson(d)).toList();
            jobsLoaded = true;
            for (var job in jobs) { // extract companies:
                companies.add(job.company);
            }
        })
        .catchError((e) {
            print(e);
            message = ERROR_MESSAGE;
        });
}
```

In the class `Job` we have a new named constructor, as follows:

```
Job.fromJson(Map<String, dynamic> json) : this(json['type'],
json['salary'], json['company'], DateTime.parse(json['posted']),
json['skills'], json['info']);
```

How it works...

In step 1, we see that Angular uses dependency injection when instantiating the controller to supply it with an `Http` object. Step 2 shows how the `get` method from the `Http` service is used to make a `GET` request and to fetch data from the server (here the data is local, but it could be fetched from a remote site). This method returns a Future `<HttpResponse>` when the request is fulfilled. That's why we have to use a `.then` construct to register a callback function and a `.catchError` to handle exceptions. In the callback function, we have the data in `response.data`. With `map`, we call for each job as a JSON string. The named constructor `fromJson` in the class `Job` from step 3 to transform it into a `Job` object. Finally, a list is made with all job data, which is bound to the view in the same way as in the previous recipes.

See also

▸ For more information about Futures, refer to *Chapter 8, Working with Futures, Tasks, and Isolates*

▸ For more details about JSON HTTP requests, refer to the *Downloading a file* recipe in *Chapter 6, Working with Files and Streams*

Deploying your app

To run in any modern browser, your Angular app has to be compiled to minimal JavaScript. Minimal means tree-shaken (so that unused code is left out) and minified (shortening of names and minimum use of spaces).

But first, test your app in other browsers by performing the following steps:

1. First, test in your default browser by right-clicking on the startup web page and selecting **Run as JavaScript**. This will compile to JavaScript and execute the app in the browser, but the compiled code will be kept in memory and not written to disk.

2. To change browsers, go to the menu-item and navigate to **Tools | Preferences | Run | Debug**, uncheck **Use system default browser**, and select the other browser. You can also just start that browser and copy the URL from the app in your default browser.

How to do it...

1. Include the Angular transformer into the app's `pubspec.yaml` file:

   ```
   transformers:
   - angular
   ```

2. Also, add the `js` and `shadow_dom` packages to your `pubspec.yaml` file.

3. Add the shadow DOM script to the startup HTML file, as follows:

```
<script src="packages/shadow_dom/shadow_dom.min.js"></script>
```

4. Use `pub build` either from the command line or from Dart Editor.

How it works...

Step 2 will make sure that Angular can work with Shadow DOM in all browsers (for more information on Shadow DOM, refer to the *How it works* section in the *Setting up an angular app* recipe in this chapter).

 Instead of `shadow_dom.min.js`, you can use `shadow_dom.debug.js` while debugging.

Step 3 will generate all deployable files in your app's directory in a subfolder named `build/web`. For example, if we apply this to the `angular_view` app, we get a JavaScript file, `angular_view.dart.js`, of about 1.7 MB to start up together with `angular_view.html`. The following screenshot gives us an overview of the `angular_view` project:

Overview of the project layout

See also

▸ You can learn more about transformers at `https://www.dartlang.org/tools/pub/assets-and-transformers.html`. For more information about compiling to JavaScript, see the *Compiling your app to JavaScript* recipe in *Chapter 1, Working with Dart Tools* and the *Publishing and deploying your app* recipe in *Chapter 2, Structuring, Testing, and Deploying an Application*.

Index

Y

Z

Thank you for buying
Dart Cookbook

About Packt Publishing

Packt, pronounced 'packed', published its first book "*Mastering phpMyAdmin for Effective MySQL Management*" in April 2004 and subsequently continued to specialize in publishing highly focused books on specific technologies and solutions.

Our books and publications share the experiences of your fellow IT professionals in adapting and customizing today's systems, applications, and frameworks. Our solution based books give you the knowledge and power to customize the software and technologies you're using to get the job done. Packt books are more specific and less general than the IT books you have seen in the past. Our unique business model allows us to bring you more focused information, giving you more of what you need to know, and less of what you don't.

Packt is a modern, yet unique publishing company, which focuses on producing quality, cutting-edge books for communities of developers, administrators, and newbies alike. For more information, please visit our website: www.packtpub.com.

About Packt Open Source

In 2010, Packt launched two new brands, Packt Open Source and Packt Enterprise, in order to continue its focus on specialization. This book is part of the Packt Open Source brand, home to books published on software built around Open Source licenses, and offering information to anybody from advanced developers to budding web designers. The Open Source brand also runs Packt's Open Source Royalty Scheme, by which Packt gives a royalty to each Open Source project about whose software a book is sold.

Writing for Packt

We welcome all inquiries from people who are interested in authoring. Book proposals should be sent to author@packtpub.com. If your book idea is still at an early stage and you would like to discuss it first before writing a formal book proposal, contact us; one of our commissioning editors will get in touch with you.

We're not just looking for published authors; if you have strong technical skills but no writing experience, our experienced editors can help you develop a writing career, or simply get some additional reward for your expertise.

Object-Oriented JavaScript
Second Edition

ISBN: 978-1-84969-312-7   Paperback: 382 pages

Learn everything you need to know about OOJS in this comprehensive guide

1. Think in JavaScript.

2. Make object-oriented programming accessible and understandable to web developers.

3. Apply design patterns to solve JavaScript coding problems.

4. Learn coding patterns that unleash the unique power of the language.

Building Web and Mobile ArcGIS Server Applications with JavaScript

ISBN: 978-1-84969-796-5   Paperback: 274 pages

Master the ArcGIS API for JavaScript, and build exciting, custom web and mobile GIS applications with the ArcGIS Server

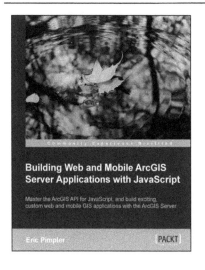

1. Develop ArcGIS Server applications with JavaScript, both for traditional web browsers as well as the mobile platform.

2. Acquire in-demand GIS skills sought by many employers.

Please check **www.PacktPub.com** for information on our titles

www.ingramcontent.com/pod-product-compliance
Lightning Source LLC
Chambersburg PA
CBHW062056050326
40690CB00016B/3115